IT'S ALL ABOUT THE NUMBERS

IT'S ALL ABOUT THE NUMBERS

The Legends and Lore of Jersey Numbers in Sports

The Culture, Superstition, and Stories Behind the Digits

Rob Lorton

IT'S ALL ABOUT THE NUMBERS

The Legends and Lore of Jersey Numbers in Sports

ISBN: 979-8-9949-4520-9 (paperback, independently published)

ISBN: 979-8-9949-4521-6 (hardcover, independently published)

Library of Congress Control Number: 2025927924

This book represents the author's independent research and perspective on sports history and jersey number traditions. It is not affiliated with, endorsed by, or representative of any professional sports team, league, or organization. The views and interpretations expressed are solely those of the author.

This book contains brief excerpts from published sources and publicly available information used under Fair Use for purposes of commentary, criticism, and education. All trademarks and names are property of their respective owners.

Printed in the United States of America

To my wife, Diane.

I've always said you were #1 in my book,
and well, now it's official.
This is my book about numbers, and you're #1!

#1 teammate, #1 coach, #1 cheerleader,
#1 supporter, #1 believer, #1 inspiration,
#1 mentor, #1 advocate, #1 partner,
#1 friend, #1 fan, #1 love of my life,
and my #1 in every season of the game.

TABLE OF CONTENTS

It's Just a Number ... Right?

Michael Jordan's #23 is perhaps the most recognized number in sports history. Air Jordan. His Airness. The GOAT wearing twenty-three.

Yet Jordan didn't choose #23 to be legendary. He chose it because of his older brother.

Larry Jordan was the star of the family, the one everyone watched, the athlete Michael looked up to. Larry wore #45—which was also Michael's favorite number. But when young Michael entered high school, he didn't want to just copy his brother. He wanted to honor him while carving his own path.

So Michael did some math: half of 45, rounded up, equals 23.

That simple calculation—born from respect, sibling rivalry, and a desire to stand on his own—changed sports history forever.[1]

Numbers aren't just numbers.

They're tributes to fallen heroes. They're superstitions that control careers. They're brands worth hundreds of millions of dollars. They're the source of lawsuits, million-dollar negotiations, and locker room confrontations. They're chosen for love, revenge, faith, and sometimes just for really good puns.

This book tells the stories behind the numbers—the ones chosen with purpose, the ones assigned by accident, and the ones that became worth fighting for.

You'll meet athletes who paid $250,000 for two digits, who gave away Porsches to claim a number, who turned down legends' jerseys out of respect, and who built their entire identity on a girlfriend's miscount.

You'll discover why Tom Brady settled for #12,[2] how your brain processes athletes differently depending on whether they wear #7 or #87, and why some players have worn fractions, engaged in arm-wrestling matches, and signed contracts with ice cream cone clauses— all for the right number.

Numbers can be currency—sold, traded, and negotiated for cash, luxury watches, or cars. They can be sacred—retired to honor icons whose impact transcends the game. They spark drama between rookies and veterans, stars and role players. And they define identity—stitched into jerseys, painted on helmets, tattooed on skin, hung in rafters.

By the time you finish this book, you'll never look at a jersey number the same way again. Behind every number, you'll see the negotiations, the tributes, the sacrifices, the science, and the legends.

So no, it's not "just a number."

It's identity. It's legacy. It's psychology, neuroscience, marketing, and mysticism—all rolled into one or two digits on the back of a jersey.

Welcome to *It's All About the Numbers*.

A Note on Sources

This project draws on nearly 400 sources—work stemming from thousands of hours of research, player interviews, team records, contemporary news reports, and sports databases. I'm deeply grateful for the journalists, historians, statisticians, archivists, dedicated bloggers, and storytellers whose reporting and scholarship make a book like this possible. Their work forms the backbone of this compilation, and I take full responsibility for any errors or inconsistencies.

Where stories are well-documented, they're presented as fact and cited in the endnotes under standard principles of fair use. Where they exist as persistent sports legends without solid confirmation—like the infamous arm-wrestling hoax or certain Rolex exchanges—I've noted that clearly. Sometimes the legend tells us as much about the significance of numbers as the facts do.

Every verifiable claim includes an endnote. While every effort has been made to confirm information, any errors or omissions will be remedied in future editions. When sources conflict or details remain uncertain, I've acknowledged that openly. Sports history is wonderfully messy, and I've tried to honor both its facts and its folklore.

How to Use This Book: Two indices at the back help you navigate: the Player Index shows every athlete featured by chapter, while the Story Index organizes the narratives thematically. Feel free to read straight through or jump to whatever catches your eye.

CHAPTER 1

Where Did All These Numbers Come From?

Every jersey number in this book has a story behind it. But before athletes selected digits to honor their parents, their faith, or their fallen heroes, someone had to invent the system itself.

And like most great inventions, jersey numbers started with a simple question: How do we tell these guys apart?

Baseball: When Babe Ruth Batted Third

Organized baseball dates back to the 1840s, but numbers on jerseys? That didn't really take off until 1929. Sure, a few teams experimented earlier—the Cincinnati Reds in 1888, Cleveland Indians in 1916, and St. Louis Cardinals in 1924 all tried numbers on sleeves for single seasons. But none of it stuck—until the New York Yankees stepped up to the plate with something different.[3]

In 1929, the Yankees started wearing numbers on the backs of their jerseys with a specific system: each player's number matched their place in the batting order.

This explains why Babe Ruth wore #3 and Lou Gehrig wore #4. Here's how the 1929 Yankees lineup looked:

> #1: Earl Combs, center field
> #2: Mark Koenig, third base
> #3: Babe Ruth, right field
> #4: Lou Gehrig, first base

#5: Bob Meusel, left field

#6: Tony Lazzeri, second base

#7: Leo Durocher, shortstop

#8: Johnny Grabowski, catcher

Number 9 was reserved for the backup catcher, pitchers wore 10 through 19, and everyone else got numbers in the 20s or higher.

The trend caught on immediately. By the next season, nearly every team in baseball had followed suit—because when the Yankees led, everyone else followed.

Football: Numbers Based on Position

In American football, numbering isn't just tradition—it's regulated. Both the NFL and NCAA assign number ranges to positions, helping referees, coaches, and fans quickly identify who does what.[4]

By 1973, the NFL's guidelines looked like this:

#1–19: Quarterbacks, kickers, punters

#20–49: Running backs, defensive backs

#50–59: Linebackers, centers

#60–79: Offensive (non-centers) and defensive linemen

#80–89: Wide receivers, tight ends

Under those rules, numbers 0, 00, and 90–99 could no longer be issued—though players already wearing them were grandfathered in. The system has evolved over time, but its purpose remains the same: to help officials manage eligibility and substitutions during fast-paced play. And every so often, those rules end up creating moments fans never forget.

William "The Refrigerator" Perry: #72—Reported As Eligible

According to NFL rules, players wearing numbers 50–79 are ineligible to handle the ball unless they report as eligible receivers before the play.

So when William "The Refrigerator" Perry—a 335-pound defensive tackle wearing #72—lined up in the backfield for the Chicago Bears during their remarkable 1985 season, fans knew something special was happening. Perry's number fit his primary position, but each goal-line appearance required the Bears to report him as eligible.

The result? Perry's appearances in the backfield—including his famous Super Bowl XX touchdown—were completely legal, and watching a defensive lineman score touchdowns became one of the most memorable moments in NFL history.[5]

Keyshawn Johnson: #19—A Number That Started a Movement

When Keyshawn Johnson entered the NFL as the overall number one pick in 1996, he wanted to stand out. A wide receiver out of USC, Johnson originally hoped to wear #3, his college number. But the NFL said no—league rules at the time required wide receivers to wear numbers in the 80s.

However, the league had a little-known exception: if a team ran out of numbers in the 80s, a receiver could wear a number between 10 and 19. Johnson waited until the New York Jets had assigned all available 80s numbers during training camp, then claimed #19. The NFL allowed it, and Johnson kept it for his entire career.

"When you saw No. 19, you automatically knew what that stood for," he said. "It was all about looking cool and different, and being someone that people could identify with."

His bold move helped pave the way for a rule change in 2004, allowing all receivers to wear numbers from 10 to 19.[6]

More Flexibility in Modern Numbering

Johnson's challenge to the system foreshadowed bigger changes. Beginning in 2021, the NFL loosened the rules even more, expanding numbering options for several positions. This change has led to some high-profile number switches:[7]

> **Jalen Ramsey:** switched from #20 to #5 with the Dolphins
> **Budda Baker:** changed from #32 to #3 with the Cardinals
> **Jaylon Smith:** moved from #54 to #9 with the Cowboys
> **Darius Slay:** transitioned from #24 to #2 with the Eagles
> **Tee Higgins:** switched from #85 to #5 with the Bengals

While football uses numbers to identify positions and enforce substitution rules, basketball's system emerged from an entirely different practicality: referee hand signals.

Basketball: The "1–5 Digits Rule" You Never Knew About

Basketball approached numbering differently: it began with simplicity and later evolved into player choice. By the mid-20th century, players began choosing numbers that had personal meaning or just looked cool. The NBA allows most numbers today, though some have been retired by individual teams—and in one case, league-wide for Bill Russell's #6.

But here's something surprising: in high school and, up until recently, college basketball, jersey numbers can only use the digits 0 through 5.

Why such a strange rule? It's all about the referees.

When signaling fouls, referees use their hands to communicate numbers to scorers and fans. By restricting digits to 0–5, refs can easily show any number with a single hand. A player wearing #24 gets signaled with two fingers for "2" and four fingers for "4." Simple.

But a player wearing #6? That would require more complicated hand signals, so those numbers were avoided.

That's why in high school basketball, you rarely see numbers like 6, 7, 8, or 9. Most jerseys feature combinations of 0–5: think 10, 12, 15, 23, 35, and so on.[8]

The NBA doesn't have this restriction, which is why legends like LeBron James (#6), Kobe Bryant (#8), and Dennis Rodman (#91) could choose whatever number they wanted. Beginning in the 2023–24 season, the NCAA also did away with this restriction.

The Olympics add another wrinkle. International basketball followed similar logic to high school and college rules, but with an even narrower range. FIBA, the governing body for international basketball, historically limited jersey numbers to 4 through 15 to simplify officials' hand signals during games. Though FIBA eliminated this restriction in 2014, USA Basketball continues to honor the tradition for both men's and women's Olympic teams.

NBA and WNBA stars often wear completely different numbers when representing their country. Michael Jordan, forever linked to #23 for the Chicago Bulls, wore #9 at the 1984 and 1992 Olympics. At the 2024 Paris Olympics, only two players on the U.S. men's team— Anthony Edwards (#5) and Bam Adebayo (#13)—wore their NBA numbers, while not a single player on the women's team kept their

WNBA jersey number. The tradition persists as a nod to basketball's international roots, even as the rules have evolved to allow greater flexibility.[9]

Hockey: Why Goalies Wore #1— And Why Most Don't Anymore

In ice hockey, #1 has long been associated with goaltenders. Dating back to the early days of the NHL, the number became tradition to mark a goalie's primary role. Legendary netminders like Jacques Plante, Glenn Hall, Terry Sawchuk, and Turk Broda proudly wore it, and as of October 2025, eight NHL teams have retired the #1 jersey in honor of their goalies.[10]

But where did this tradition come from?

According to hockey lore, it dates back to the 1930s when teams traveled overnight by train.

The sleeping quarters—railroad car berths—were cramped, with bunk beds stacked two high. Everyone wanted the lower bunks (better sleep, easier access), but there weren't enough to go around.

The solution? Lower-numbered players got first pick—#1 chose first, #2 second, and so on. This system also benefited veterans, whose seniority was demonstrated by their low numbers.

Playing goalie was—and still is—a brutal position. Goalies were often the most exhausted players after games, so teams agreed that goalies would wear #1, ensuring they always got the best sleeping accommodations.[11]

The game has changed significantly since then, and many modern goalies prefer higher numbers. Notable departures from the #1 tradition include:[10]

> **Ed Belfour:** briefly wore #1 and #31 early on, but spent most of his career wearing #20 and #30
>
> **Ilya Bryzgalov:** never wore #1, opting for #30 and #80
>
> **Kevin Weekes:** began and ended his career wearing #1, but primarily wore #35 and #80
>
> **Martin Biron:** wore #00 early in his career—the last NHL goalie to do so—before switching to #43
>
> **Sergei Bobrovsky:** initially wore #35 before adopting #72, which became his signature number

This flexibility reflects a shift happening across all sports—from rigid traditions toward personalization, where numbers become part of an athlete's identity and brand.

Soccer: Why All the Greats Wear #10

Soccer numbering has deep historical roots tied to position. The classic assignments in a starting eleven looked like this:

> #1: Goalkeeper
>
> #2–5: Defenders
>
> #6–8: Midfielders
>
> #9–11: Forwards

Though modern squads allow greater flexibility, with numbers often extending into the 30s and 40s, many players still honor this traditional position-based system.[12]

If you follow soccer (or football, depending on where you're from), you've probably noticed that many of the world's biggest stars wear

#10: Lionel Messi, Francesco Totti, Wayne Rooney, Landon Donovan, and Pelé all had that honor.

Why do all the greats seem to wear the same number?

The answer lies in soccer's positional history. Traditionally, #9 and #10 were the main attacking positions—the most prolific scorers and the most recognized players on the field.

But while #9 remained associated with the pure striker—the goal scorer—#10 evolved into something more. Over time, it became representative of the playmaker, the creative genius, the player who makes magic happen. Not just the player who scores, but the player who orchestrates everything.[13]

Pelé wore it as a teenager in 1958, unaware of its significance, and transformed it into soccer's most coveted number. Every playmaker since—from Maradona to Messi—has inherited that legacy. It's not just a positional marker; it's soccer's most prestigious number.

From batting order assignments to position-based restrictions, jersey numbers evolved from practical tools into symbols of identity. What began as simple identification became something far more meaningful—the foundation for every story in this book.

CHAPTER 2

The Birth of a Number

Numbers in sports are never just numbers. They carry weight, emotion, and identity. But behind every number is a story—sometimes chosen with care, sometimes born from tribute, and sometimes reflecting a mood or a moment in time.

So why do athletes choose certain jersey numbers? Sometimes it's destiny—like Sidney Crosby wearing #87 because he was born on 8/7/87. Sometimes it's homage—like David Beckham choosing Michael Jordan's #23. Sometimes it's gamesmanship—like Mario Lemieux picking #66 as an upside-down version of Wayne Gretzky's #99. And occasionally, it's just a really good pun—like Heinz 57 steak sauce inspiring players named Heinze and Heins to wear #57.[14]

Numbers That Moved with the Mood

Ron Artest: Seven Numbers in 17 Years

Throughout his NBA career, Ron Artest—later known as Metta World Peace and, most recently, Metta Sandiford-Artest—wore a dizzying array of jersey numbers. From #15 to #37, and even #93 and #96, each choice told a different story, reflected a different emotion, or paid tribute to something meaningful in his life.

He wore #15 with the Chicago Bulls, his college number from St. John's, returning to it years later with the Lakers. With the Indiana Pacers, he switched to #23 to honor Michael Jordan, then to #91 as a tribute to Dennis Rodman's rebellious spirit.

His time with the Sacramento Kings and Houston Rockets brought #93 and #96—numbers chosen to represent Queensbridge, his childhood neighborhood in Queens, New York. Artest explained that the 9 resembled a Q, the 3 a capital B, and the 6 a lowercase b—a creative interpretation requiring considerable imagination.

Perhaps his most notable choice was #37 with the Los Angeles Lakers, worn to honor Michael Jackson. Why 37? Jackson's *Thriller* album spent 37 weeks at the top of the Billboard charts.

He wore #51 briefly with the New York Knicks, a nod to his father's high school number. Following Kobe's retirement, he hinted at wearing #60 to honor Bryant's 60-point farewell. He also considered switching to #70 to honor Martin Luther King Jr.—the first two digits of King's Birmingham jail ID number, 7089.

For Artest, jersey numbers expressed mood, memory, and meaning—each change marking a new chapter of intensity, reinvention, and cultural connection.[15]

Ish Smith: The Jersey Number Journeyman

While Artest changed jersey numbers frequently and for some of the most entertaining reasons, he certainly doesn't hold the record for the most numbers worn throughout a career.

That distinction rests with NBA journeyman Ish Smith, who wore ten different numbers throughout his 14-year career spanning tours with thirteen teams.

Across his many stops—which often meant taking whatever number the equipment room had available—Smith recalled how the numbering assignments usually went: "When they was trading me, as soon as I would get into an arena, it was, 'Ish, this is the number we got, bro. You don't have a choice.'"

Smith did have a couple of numbers that carried meaning to him: wearing #3 in Phoenix in honor of Allen Iverson and wearing #5 with Philadelphia to reflect the number he wore in high school. But for the most part, he played the role of the perfect journeyman—willing to play wherever needed and to wear whatever was available.[16]

Edwin Jackson: Baseball's Nomad

Basketball isn't the only sport where players can change numbers frequently. Pitcher Edwin Jackson's career is remembered for its breadth: 14 Major League teams over 17 seasons, a record he shares with Rich Hill. Along the way he wore a variety of nine jersey numbers, usually dictated strictly by what was available whenever he joined a new club.

Jackson did gravitate to one number throughout his career: the first he was issued in the Major Leagues in 2003. Dan Evans, the Dodgers' General Manager at the time, assigned Jackson #36 in honor of Don Newcombe, the Dodgers' first star African-American pitcher. Jackson even has the number tattooed on his left forearm, showing a pair of dice with a three and a six.

That image became his connection to the number 36, which he wore for six different ballclubs. Unlike most of his digits, which reflected availability and circumstance, when given a choice, #36 tied directly to his own identity. Whenever possible, it was a rare moment of continuity in a career defined by constant change.[17]

Switching Numbers, Switching Identity

While some athletes change numbers frequently, either by choice or by circumstance, other athletes make a single, defining switch midcareer—marking a transformation in how they see themselves or want to be seen.

Kobe Bryant: #8 to #24—A New Chapter

Kobe Bryant's career is unique for many reasons, and one is that he became a legend in two different numbers.

He started with #8, a number from his youth in Italy derived from his Adidas camp number 143 (1 + 4 + 3 = 8). For ten years, #8 represented young Kobe—the high-flyer, the showman, the player who wanted to prove everything.

Then, in 2006, he switched to #24—the number he'd worn as a high school freshman. The change was intentional and symbolic. It was Kobe declaring a new chapter, moving beyond his past identity into something greater. He wanted to shed the controversies and drama of his early years and focus purely on winning and excellence.

By switching numbers, Kobe created two distinct legacies. Both #8 and #24 now hang in the rafters at Crypto.com Arena (formerly Staples Center)—a rare honor that reflects the two sides of one extraordinary career.[18]

Carlton Fisk: #27 to #72—Changing Sox

Hall of Fame catcher Carlton Fisk wore #27 during his beloved days with the Boston Red Sox. But when he joined the Chicago White Sox, he wanted to leave Fenway Park behind—both literally and symbolically.

So he switched to #72.

For Fisk, #72 represented a turnaround in his career. Same digits, reversed order, new beginning. It was perfect.[19]

Curiously, #72 has become a number associated with memorable nicknames across sports—Carlton "Pudge" Fisk in baseball, and in football: William "The Refrigerator" Perry, Ed "Too Tall" Jones, and John "Tooz" Matuszak.

Lionel Messi: #10 to #30—A Return to His Roots

When Lionel Messi joined Paris Saint-Germain in 2021, fans expected him to wear his traditional #10 jersey—the number he prominently wore at Barcelona. But #10 was already taken by his close friend and former teammate Neymar.

Neymar offered to give it up, but Messi declined. Instead, he chose #30.

Why? It was the first number Messi ever wore when he debuted for Barcelona's senior team in 2004. As a 17-year-old, he came off the bench wearing #30 and made his mark. He kept it for his first two seasons before moving to #19 and eventually to #10 after Ronaldinho's departure.

By choosing #30 at PSG, Messi wasn't just picking a number—he was reconnecting with the beginning of his journey. It was a return to his roots, a reminder of where it all started, even as he began a new chapter far from home.[20]

Numbers as Personal Symbols

Russell Westbrook: #0—Starting Fresh

Russell Westbrook chose #0 when he arrived at UCLA in 2006, and the number became inseparable from his identity. Westbrook saw #0 as a fresh start—a chance to prove himself and rise above expectations. It aligned perfectly with his personal mantra: "Why

Not?"—a mindset rooted in confidence, resilience, and belief in limitless possibility.[21]

He carried #0 into the NBA, wearing it with the Oklahoma City Thunder, Houston Rockets, Los Angeles Lakers, and LA Clippers. Those digits became emblematic of his explosive style, relentless energy, and record-setting triple-doubles.

When #0 wasn't available—as during his stints with the Washington Wizards and Denver Nuggets—Westbrook wore #4, his high school number. But #0 remains the number most closely tied to his legacy— the symbol he unmistakably made his own.

Wilfried Bony: #2—A Second Chance

When Wilfried Bony returned to Swansea City in 2017 after stints with Manchester City and Stoke City, fans expected him to reclaim #10. But Tammy Abraham already wore it.

Instead, Bony made an unconventional choice: #2, a number traditionally worn by defenders.

His reasoning was both personal and symbolic: "It's a special number for me. It's the second time I am at the club, hence I wanted to wear number two, and I want to achieve more for the team."[22]

The decision raised eyebrows—a striker wearing a defender's number?—but for Bony, it marked a fresh start and a second chapter with the club where he'd once been a fan favorite.

Digits From the Draft:
Those Who Wore Their Draft Position

For some athletes, their jersey number isn't just a number—it's a timestamp. A reminder of where they were ranked, how they were valued, and what they've done since to redefine that number. Whether chosen out of pride, motivation, or quiet symbolism, these digits reflect the moment their professional journey began.

First and Proud: #1—The Top Picks

Being drafted first overall comes with massive expectations. In the NFL, Cam Newton embraced that pressure by wearing #1.[23] In the NBA, Derrick Rose, Greg Oden, Markelle Fultz, and Anthony Edwards did the same—turning their draft position into a symbol of expectation, leadership, and spotlight.[24]

But each had different reasons for wearing it. Newton wore #1 only because his preferred #2 was unavailable (Chapter 16).[25] Rose embraced #1 not just as a draft badge, but as a persona—an alter ego he stepped into every time he hit the court (Chapter 6).[26] Edwards initially wore #1 because his preferred #5 wasn't available, later switching back to the number rooted in family and personal meaning (Chapter 3).[27]

Andre Iguodala: #9—Ninth Pick, Ninth Jersey

The Philadelphia 76ers selected Iguodala 9th overall in 2004. He wore #9 to match—a straightforward choice that became his identity throughout his 19-year career, from Philadelphia to Golden State, where he became a Finals MVP and defensive anchor for a dynasty. His jersey represented both where his journey began and the chip-on-his-shoulder mentality that came with being passed over eight times.[28]

Klay Thompson: #11—Picked Perfect

Drafted 11th overall in 2011, Thompson chose #11 to match. But the number ran deeper: his childhood home was #11 on 11th Lane, "K" is the 11th letter of the alphabet, and he famously scored 60 points using just 11 dribbles. For Thompson, #11 symbolized precision and balance.[29]

Jahan Dotson: #1—First in Franchise History

Though Dotson was the 16th player chosen in the 2022 NFL Draft, he wore #1 for a different reason: he was the first player ever drafted by the franchise under its new name, the Washington Commanders.[30]

Rudy Gobert: #27—From Late Pick to Defensive Force

Gobert was selected 27th overall in the 2013 NBA Draft. He embraced the number, turning it into a badge of resilience. From a late first-round pick to a multiple-time Defensive Player of the Year, #27 became a symbol of his rise—and his rebuttal to being overlooked.[31]

The Slugger's Number: #44

Unlike draft-based numbers tied to a single moment in time, in baseball, #44 became something bigger—a badge of power and prestige. It symbolizes not just one player's story, but a tradition carried by legends across generations.

Hank Aaron: #44—Hammerin' Hank

Hank Aaron originally wore #5 in the Negro Leagues, but when he joined the Milwaukee Braves in 1954, he took the available #44. His reasoning? He liked double numbers—simple as that.

The choice proved prophetic. He hit 44 home runs in four different seasons and broke Babe Ruth's all-time home run record while wearing the number. In a fitting coincidence, Al Downing—the pitcher who gave up Aaron's record-breaking 715th home run—also wore #44.[32]

Willie McCovey: #44—Stretching the Limits

Aaron made #44 famous, but he wasn't alone. Though McCovey never explained why he chose #44, another slugger giving the number new life felt poetic. McCovey blasted 521 career home runs. The San Francisco Giants retired his #44, and he was elected to the Baseball Hall of Fame in 1986.[33]

Reggie Jackson: #44—Mr. October

Reggie Jackson originally wore #9 with the Oakland Athletics, but when he joined the Yankees in 1977, third baseman Craig Nettles already claimed it.

Jackson chose #44 to honor Aaron and McCovey, claiming his place among slugging legends.[34] As it turned out, he was in good company. His explosive performance in the 1977 World Series—including three home runs in Game 6—revived the mystique of #44. They called him "Mr. October," and #44 became symbolic of clutch postseason heroics.[35]

Eric Davis: #44—Passing the Torch

The torch would be passed again in Cincinnati. When Eric Davis arrived with the Reds, equipment manager Bernie Stowe handed him #44. "I didn't ask for 44; he gave it to me," Davis recalled. "He saw something in me that would match that number ... with Hank Aaron, Willie McCovey, Reggie Jackson and some of the great people that wore that number. That's why Bernie gave it to me. I was just trying to live up to that."

Davis did more than live up to it. He became a two-time All-Star and one of the most electrifying players of the 1980s, hitting 37 home runs and stealing 50 bases in 1987—blending power and speed in ways reminiscent of Aaron himself.[36]

Elly De La Cruz: #44—Cincinnati's Next Chapter

In 2023, when 21-year-old phenom Elly De La Cruz was called up to the Reds, clubhouse manager Rick Stowe—Bernie Stowe's son—assigned him #44, continuing the family's quiet tradition of recognizing greatness. The youngster's explosive combination of power and speed reminded him of Eric Davis.

Davis endorsed the choice: "It's not the number, it's the player. Now my number is being moved on and hopefully he takes it and runs with it the way I took it and ran with it."

The number had come full circle in Cincinnati—from Bernie Stowe recognizing greatness in Davis, to Rick seeing that same spark in De La Cruz, to Davis blessing the next generation.[36]

Justyn-Henry Malloy: #44—A Name, A Number, A Legacy

Justyn-Henry Malloy was named after his father Henry, who was named after Hank Aaron. When he made his MLB debut with the Detroit Tigers in June 2024, there was only one number he wanted: #44.

But there was a problem: first-base coach Gary Jones was wearing #44. Malloy debuted wearing #36. Behind the scenes, negotiations began. Malloy made his case to Jones—the family history, the cultural significance of a young Black player wearing Aaron's number, everything it meant.

When the team returned home for their next series, Malloy found a surprise waiting in his locker: a #44 jersey with his name on it. Jones had switched to #86 in honor of his eldest daughter's birth year.

"It's not only a nod to history," Malloy explained, "it's also a bit of an early Father's Day present." For Malloy, wearing #44 honors both

Hammerin' Hank and his father Henry—three generations connected through one number.[37]

Baseball's Tribute to #44

When Hank Aaron passed away in January 2021 at age 86, MLB honored him during that year's All-Star festivities in Denver by having every player in the Home Run Derby wear #44. Players even wore their usual team uniforms with #44 replacing their regular numbers during workouts and team photos.

Four years later, in 2025, MLB paid tribute again when the All-Star Game returned to Atlanta. National League participants in the Home Run Derby wore Aaron's #44 while American League players wore Babe Ruth's #3. The events were scheduled for July 14 and 15—dates whose numerical format (7/14, 7/15) echoed Aaron's historic 715th home run.[38]

The Tradition Continues

Throughout baseball's modern era, #44 continued to be worn by power hitters who carried forward the slugger's legacy—names like Adam Dunn, Anthony Rizzo, and Paul Goldschmidt. Mike Cameron wore #44 across seven seasons with three different teams. Decades later, when Mariners center fielder Julio Rodríguez chose the same number, Cameron tweeted: "I transfer the universal power number 44 to the young phenom—can't wait to see him do his thing."[39]

Some wore it by assignment, others by choice, still others to honor the legends who came before. Whether inherited or claimed, #44 remained what Aaron, McCovey, and Jackson had made it: a number synonymous with power, excellence, and the drive to be great.

These numbers aren't random. They're chosen with purpose. Whether born from circumstance like Messi's #30, transformed through reinvention like Kobe's shift from #8 to #24, or worn as a badge of resilience like Gobert's #27, each digit tells a story. Some mark new beginnings. Others honor the past. A few become mirrors of identity—changing as the athlete changes, reflecting mood, memory, and meaning.

A jersey number is never just a number. It's an assertion of where you've been, who you are, and what you're determined to prove.

CHAPTER 3

All in the Family

Some numbers are chosen not for glory, but for memory. In every sport, athletes wear their numbers not to define themselves, but to honor someone else—a parent, a sibling, a child, or a mentor who shaped their path. These digits become living tributes, stitched into jerseys and carried into competition with quiet reverence.

The Curry Legacy: #30

Steph Curry: #30—Honoring His Father

Steph Curry didn't just pick #30 because it was available. He chose it for the man who gave him his love of the game: his father, Dell Curry, who wore #30 across his NBA career.

From high school to college to the professional stage, #30 has been part of Steph's identity. For him, it wasn't just a number—it was a lineage, a way to honor the person who taught him everything about basketball.

"I wear number 30 to pay homage to my dad," Curry explained. "It was the number he wore from high school to college to the pros."[40]

Every time fans chant "30" at Chase Center, it's not just a tribute to Steph's skills—it's a nod to his roots, to family, and to the story that made him who he is.

Seth Curry: #30—Respecting the Legacy

Seth Curry, following in the family footsteps, also wore #30 throughout much of his NBA career—another tribute to their father Dell.

But when Seth signed with the Golden State Warriors for the 2025–26 season, he faced a unique situation: #30 was already celebrated there, worn by his older brother Steph. In a lighthearted moment, Seth joked about the dilemma: "I tried to buy it from him. He said he didn't need the money," Seth recalled with a laugh.[41]

Ultimately, Seth chose #31—a respectful nod to the family tradition while allowing Steph to keep the number that has become a defining symbol of his Hall of Fame career.

When Your Hero Is Your Brother

Michael Jordan: #23—Half of 45, Rounded Up

Jordan's choice of #23—a mathematical tribute to his brother Larry introduced earlier[1]—reveals something profound about identity formation when your hero lives in your house.

Larry wasn't just wearing #45; he was the better player. At least at first. Michael openly admitted his older brother could beat him one-on-one during those early years.

But Jordan didn't reject his brother's number or pick something completely different to prove independence. Instead, he found a way to carry Larry with him while forging his own identity. Half of 45, rounded up—a mathematical declaration that said, "I see you, I honor you, but I'm building something that's mine."

That calculated compromise between homage and independence became the starting point for one of basketball's most accomplished careers. Jordan wanted to be good enough that Larry would be proud. And eventually, good enough that #23 would mean something all on its own.

Larry Bird: #33—Following His Brother Mark

Larry Bird wore #33 throughout his Hall of Fame career with the Boston Celtics. Many fans assumed it was a tribute to Kareem Abdul-Jabbar, the dominant center who wore the same number and whom Bird faced in multiple Finals matchups.

The real story was simpler—and more personal.

Bird chose #33 because his older brother Mark wore it. Mark was Larry's hero growing up in French Lick, Indiana, and when Larry started playing basketball, he wanted to follow in his brother's footsteps—right down to the number on his back.

Mark had chosen #33 to honor Rick Mount, a renowned Indiana high school shooter who became the first high school player ever featured on the cover of *Sports Illustrated* in 1966. Mount wore #33 at Lebanon High School, starred at Purdue, and played in the ABA. In Indiana, Mount was basketball royalty.[42]

Thanasis Antetokounmpo: #43—Reversing His Brother's Digits

While Giannis Antetokounmpo chose #34 to honor his parents' birth years (see the next section "Honoring the Parents Who Sacrificed Everything"), his older brother Thanasis took a different approach when he joined the NBA.

Thanasis chose #43—simply reversing Giannis's digits. It was both a tribute to their parents and a way to honor his younger brother, who had already made #34 dominant in Milwaukee.[43]

The reversed number became Thanasis's response—not an imitation but an echo, carrying the same legacy forward in his own voice.

For brothers playing together on the Milwaukee Bucks, #34 and #43 became a visible symbol of family unity—two numbers that resonate with each other, just like the brothers themselves.

Tim Duncan: #21—For the Brother-in-Law Who Became His Guide

When Tim Duncan arrived at Wake Forest, he chose #21 as a tribute. His jersey honored his brother-in-law, Ricky Lowery, who had taught him to play basketball and had worn the same number in college.

Lowery had married Duncan's older sister and became a mentor and guide after Duncan's mother, Ione, died of breast cancer when Tim was just 14. During those difficult years, Lowery was there—teaching him post moves, taking him to the gym, showing him that basketball could be both an escape and a purpose.

Duncan wore #21 throughout his college career at Wake Forest and carried it into the NBA, where it became a hallmark of fundamental excellence, five championships, and quiet greatness. The San Antonio Spurs retired the number in 2016, but its origin remained personal: a tribute to the brother-in-law who stepped up when Duncan needed him most.[44]

Peyton Manning: #18—For the Brother Who Never Got to Play

Peyton Manning wore #18 throughout his Hall of Fame NFL career, but the number wasn't about him—it was about his older brother Cooper, who never got the chance to play professionally.

Cooper had been a promising wide receiver at Ole Miss, the same school where their father, Archie Manning, had worn #18 as a star quarterback and campus legend. But Cooper's football dreams ended when he was diagnosed with spinal stenosis as a freshman, forcing him to give up the sport he loved.

Peyton wore #18 in honor of Cooper—the brother who never got his chance. It was a tribute to the career that should have been, carried onto NFL fields for nearly two decades.[45]

Honoring the Parents Who Sacrificed Everything

Angel Reese: #10 and #5—Family Legacy Meets New Beginnings

When Angel Reese arrived at LSU, there was never any question about which number she'd wear. Number 10 wasn't just a number—it was her family's identity.

Her mother, Nikki Reese, wore #10 during her college basketball career at UMBC. Her younger brother Julian wears it too. For the Reese family, the number represents continuity, legacy, and shared identity across generations.

"Number 10 is just our number, really," Angel explained. "When you see number 10, you see the Reese family."[46]

Angel made #10 stand out at LSU, leading the Tigers to the 2023 NCAA championship while becoming one of the most dominant and charismatic players in women's college basketball. Her signature "you can't see me" celebration and her unapologetic confidence made #10 impossible to ignore.

When she entered the WNBA in 2024, #10 wasn't available—her fellow Chicago Sky rookie Kamilla Cardoso had also worn it in college and kept it. Angel switched to #5, a number she'd worn earlier at Maryland, calling it "new era, new beginnings."[47]

Number 10 will always be the Reese family number. But #5 became Angel's way of showing that honoring your family doesn't mean you can't forge your own path.

Giannis Antetokounmpo: #34—For Mom and Dad

When Giannis Antetokounmpo entered the NBA, he chose #34—not to honor a basketball legend, but to pay tribute to his parents.

His mother, Veronica, was born in 1963, and his father, Charles, in 1964. Giannis combined the final digits from their birth years—3 and 4—to create #34, a personal symbol of gratitude for the sacrifices they made as immigrants raising a family in Greece.

Many fans assumed #34 was a tribute to fellow Nigerian-born NBA great Hakeem Olajuwon, who also wore the number. But Giannis set the record straight: "A lot of people think I wear it because of Hakeem. No—I wear it because of my parents."[43]

As mentioned above, his brother Thanasis followed suit, choosing #43—reversing the digits to honor their parents in his own way.

Shaquille O'Neal: #34—"This One's for You, Sarge"

When Shaquille O'Neal joined the Los Angeles Lakers in 1996, he couldn't wear his previous numbers—#33 from LSU and #32 from the Orlando Magic—because both were already retired by the Lakers for Kareem Abdul-Jabbar and Magic Johnson.

Instead, Shaq chose #34 as a tribute to his stepfather, Phillip Harrison, a U.S. Army sergeant who played a major role in shaping his life and keeping him out of trouble as a kid. Harrison had worn #34 when playing basketball during his military service, and Shaq honored him by adopting the number with the Lakers.

"If you're watching, this one's for you, Sarge," Shaq said at the time.[48]

Shaq defined the number during his time in Los Angeles, winning three consecutive NBA championships and an MVP award. In 2013, the Lakers retired his #34 jersey, forever linking the number to both his dominance on the court and the man who helped raise him.

Pascal Siakam: #43—A Family Portrait in Two Digits

When Pascal Siakam chose #43, he wasn't honoring one person—he was honoring his entire family in a single number.

The math is beautiful in its simplicity: The 4 represents the four men in his family—his father and his three brothers. The 3 represents the three women—his mother and his two sisters.

"It's for my family," Siakam explained. "Four plus three—my brothers, my dad, my sisters, my mom."

For Siakam, who came from Cameroon to pursue basketball in North America, #43 became a way to carry his entire family with him onto every court. Every rebound, every defensive stop, each of his three All-Star selections, and his 2019 championship with the Toronto

Raptors—all of it done while wearing a number that represented the seven people who made him who he is.[49]

Domantas Sabonis: #11—Following in His Father's Footsteps

Domantas Sabonis switched to #11 to honor his father, Arvydas Sabonis, a Lithuanian basketball legend who wore the same number during his time with the Portland Trail Blazers.

"The number 11 holds a special place in mine and my family's lives, having worn it throughout my career in honor of my father," Domantas said in a statement.

What makes this story remarkable is that no one on the Sacramento Kings had worn #11 since it was retired to honor Hall of Famer Bob "Harrisburg Houdini" Davies. Domantas needed permission from the Davies family to wear it—and they graciously agreed.[50]

Now #11 represents two generations of Sabonis excellence.

Natasha Cloud: #9—Her Father's Dream

WNBA guard Natasha Cloud has worn #9 throughout her professional career, but the number wasn't her choice—it was her father's vision. Growing up, he told his kids to wear #9 whenever possible, a family rule that stuck. "Clearly, my daddy was a marketing genius even back in the day," Cloud recalled with a laugh.

For Cloud, the number has become more than a uniform detail. "When it comes down to it, my dad is such an important piece to my life, and it's a huge way of respecting the man that stepped up for me big in my lifetime," she said. "So I'm very proud to wear his name, but especially that I can wear that number that he always wanted, too."[51]

He passed his passion—and his number—down to his children. Cloud has carried it onto professional courts, wearing #9 with the Washington Mystics—where she won a WNBA championship in 2019—and later with the New York Liberty.

It's a reminder that some numbers aren't picked by the athlete at all. Sometimes they're chosen by the people who believed first, who drove them to practice, who dreamed alongside them. For Cloud, #9 is both a family legacy and a personal brand—her own version of "Cloud nine."

Maya Le Tissier: #4—A Number Written in Her Past

When Maya Le Tissier joined Manchester United Women, she had a clear choice for her jersey number: #4.

"When I was younger ... I always used to wear number four," Le Tissier explained. "And for Guernsey as well. So, I thought it would be really nice to have the #4 shirt."

But there was more to the story. Le Tissier's father had also worn #4 during his playing days, creating a thread that connected her youth career, her father's legacy, and her professional identity.

"I'm pretty sure my dad used to wear that as well when he was playing," she added—a family connection that, while not entirely certain in her memory, felt right.

That digit became part of her identity as a central defender for Manchester United—a position that demands leadership, composure, and strength. All qualities her father passed down, along with the number itself.

For Le Tissier, #4 represents continuity—a number she's worn since childhood, a number her father wore before her, a number that connects past and present in a single digit.[52]

Numbers That Keep Loved Ones Close

Aaron Gordon: #32—For His Brother Drew

Aaron Gordon wore #00 in Orlando and #50 with the Denver Nuggets. But prior to the 2024–25 season, he made a change that meant far more than a fresh start.

He switched to #32 to honor his late older brother, Drew Gordon, who wore #32 during his professional career. Drew died in a car accident in May 2024, and choosing #32 became Aaron's way of keeping him close—every practice, every arena, every night.

Now every game he plays is a tribute to Drew—a number that carries his brother's memory.[53]

Anthony Edwards: #5—For Mom and Grandma

Anthony Edwards has worn #5 since high school to honor his mother Yvette and his grandmother Shirley—both of whom died on the 5th day of the month. Edwards lost them both to cancer in the same year, when he was just 14 years old.[27]

When the Minnesota Timberwolves drafted him, Edwards wanted #5, but a teammate already had it, so he wore #1 initially. When the opportunity came in 2023, he switched to #5.

Now every time he steps on the court, he carries their memory with him—a number that represents love, loss, and the strength they gave him to keep going.

Rasheed Wallace: #36—When Grief Became a Jersey

Rasheed Wallace wore #30 when he helped the Detroit Pistons win the 2004 NBA championship. But the following season, he made a change that had nothing to do with basketball—and everything to do with loss.

In 2004, Wallace's brother died at age 36. To honor him, Rasheed switched from #30 to #36, transforming his jersey into a memorial.

He wore #36 with Detroit through four more trips to the Eastern Conference Finals, including the 2005 NBA Finals. Wallace also wore #36 during brief stints with the Atlanta Hawks and New York Knicks, keeping his brother's memory alive each time he stepped onto the court.

For Wallace, one of the NBA's most intense and passionate competitors, #36 wasn't about statistics or legacy. It was about carrying his brother with him, game after game, year after year.[54]

Mike Muscala: #57—Born in '57, Honored Forever

When Mike Muscala joined the Boston Celtics in 2019, he chose #57—an unusual number that immediately raised questions.

"That was the year my mom was born," Muscala explained to reporters. "She passed right before the season. I thought it would be a nice way to remember her while I'm here."

It's a reminder that some numbers aren't chosen for their history or their symmetry—they're chosen because 1957 was the year your mother was born, and you want to make sure she's with you for every tip-off.[55]

DeAndre Bembry: #95—Days Before the Dream

DeAndre Bembry was selected 21st overall in the 2016 NBA Draft by the Atlanta Hawks. It should have been one of the happiest moments of his life.

But just 12 days before the draft, his brother Adrian Potts was killed while trying to break up a fight. When Bembry entered the NBA, he chose #95—the year his brother was born.

"That was like my best friend. I just loved that guy and I'm definitely going to put more effort out there just for him," Bembry said.

For Bembry, #95 became more than a number—it became a promise that his brother's memory would live on every time he stepped onto an NBA court.[56]

DeAndre Hopkins: #10—Ten Years Gone

When DeAndre Hopkins chose to wear #10 throughout his NFL career, he initially said that it was in honor of soccer legend Lionel Messi. The truth, however, was far more personal.

In June 2020, Hopkins revealed the real reason behind his choice on Twitter: "My big cousin from South Carolina did 10 years in jail for $600 worth of drugs, Let that sink in. That's the real reason I wear number 10."[57]

Hopkins had hidden the truth behind a more comfortable story about a soccer legend. But the real tribute was to family—to a cousin whose decade in prison for a minor offense became a reminder Hopkins carried onto every field.

The Numbers That Connect Generations

Ed and Shawn Hochuli: #85 and #83—Like Father, Like Son

For nearly three decades, Ed Hochuli was one of the NFL's most recognizable referees—the muscular, articulate official in black and white stripes with #85 on his back. Fans knew him for his booming explanations, his steady control of chaos, and his knack for making sense of the most tangled plays.

When Ed's son Shawn followed him into officiating, many wondered if he'd inherit more than his father's confident presence on the field—perhaps even his number. As Ed later shared, there was no story behind #85 at all: it was simply the number the league assigned when he was hired. But when Shawn joined the NFL, the league began allowing new officials to select from unassigned numbers.

Shawn chose #83—the closest he could get to his father's #85. He even considered switching to #85 after Ed retired, but Ed quickly talked him out of it. "He needs to be his own guy—not Ed's son," he explained. "He already gets too many comparisons to me."[58]

In time, Shawn has done just that. Today, when you see #83 on the field, you're not thinking of Ed's son—you're watching a referee who's earned his own respect, in his own right.

Ken Griffey Jr.: #24 and #30—Following His Father's Path

Just as much as the smile, the backward cap, and the sweet swing, #24 became synonymous with Ken Griffey Jr. He chose it after hitting 24 home runs in a single season split between his high school and summer baseball teams, and he wore it throughout his 13 seasons with the Seattle Mariners. "Baseball is all about numbers," Griffey once explained. "Some of the greatest players to play in sports wore 24. It wasn't planned, but when I signed my first contract, one of the things I asked for was to be able to wear 24. It's extremely important. My first apartment in Seattle was 1124. My house number was 24606. There are a lot of things that have to do with 24."

But numbers also tied him directly to family. His father, Ken Griffey Sr., wore #30 during much of his own career—including his time with the Cincinnati Reds, where he won back-to-back World Series titles in the 1970s. When Junior was traded to Cincinnati in 2000, he finally stepped into that same number. The switch was partly practical—his beloved #24 was retired there for Tony Pérez—but it was also symbolic, a chance to wear the exact digits his father had carried on those same Reds uniforms.

For the Griffeys, baseball wasn't just a career. It was a family business, passed down through swings, smiles, and numbers. Griffey's #24 became a defining symbol in Seattle, but his time in Cincinnati showed how even legends sometimes follow in their father's footsteps—by slipping on the same jersey number his dad had worn before him.[59]

Kyrie Irving: #11—A Number Written in His DNA

Kyrie Irving began his NBA career wearing #2 with the Cleveland Cavaliers because #11 was unavailable—the team was planning to retire it for Zydrunas Ilgauskas.

When he was traded to the Boston Celtics in 2017, he finally had the chance to wear #11, and he wore it through stints with the Brooklyn Nets and most recently with the Dallas Mavericks.

The number is deeply personal and almost mystical. His father, Drederick Irving, wore #11 while scoring 1,931 points at Boston University. Kyrie wore #11 in high school at St. Patrick in New Jersey. He was born at 1:11 AM. His full name (Kyrie Irving) has 11 letters. The letter K is the 11th letter of the alphabet. He played 11 games at Duke. He was drafted pick 1, round 1 in 2011. He scored his 11,000th career point on March 11.[60] The coincidences are so numerous they feel destined rather than chosen.

When Irving joined the Mavericks in 2023, Tim Hardaway Jr. was wearing #11, so Kyrie temporarily wore #2. But after Hardaway switched to #10 to honor his own father, Irving reclaimed #11—completing another full-circle moment.

Chris Paul: #3—CP1, CP2, CP3

Chris Paul has worn #3 throughout his entire NBA career, a number deeply tied to both his identity and his nickname, "CP3."

The choice was personal and symbolic: Paul, his father, and his brother all share the same initials—CP—and their birth order inspired the numbers. "Me, my brother, and my dad, we all got the same initials," Paul explained. "My dad is CP1. My brother is CP2, he's second, and I'm CP3."[61]

Beyond family ties, Paul has also pointed to Allen Iverson—who made #3 his signature—as one of his childhood idols. For him, the number became a blend of personal meaning and basketball inspiration.

Numbers Chosen for Their Children

Maurice Richard: #9—For His Daughter

Maurice "The Rocket" Richard is one of hockey's foundational legends, and his #9 became the first number ever retired by the Montreal Canadiens. But the number's origin was surprisingly personal.

Richard wore #15 during his first two seasons with the Canadiens. Before the 1943–44 season, his first daughter Huguette was born weighing nine pounds. To honor her birth, Richard switched to #9.

That quiet tribute became one of the most recognizable numbers in hockey history. Richard went on to become the first player to score 50 goals in 50 games, won eight Stanley Cups, and became a cultural icon in Quebec.

When the Canadiens retired his #9 in 1960, they weren't just honoring a hockey legend—they were honoring a number chosen for a nine-pound baby girl.[62]

Joe Beimel: #97—For His Son

Joe Beimel's jersey carried a meaning far deeper than baseball tradition. When he joined the Tampa Bay Devil Rays in 2005, he chose #97—the highest number ever worn by a Devil Ray at the time. The reason was simple and personal: it was the birth year of his first child.[63]

That choice turned an unusual number into a family tribute. For Beimel, #97 wasn't about standing out or superstition—it was about carrying his son's birth year with him every time he stepped onto the mound.

The number followed him across the majors and was on display for six different teams over his 13-year career. Fans may have remembered him for his beard or his role as a reliable lefty reliever, but for Beimel, the number carried his family into every appearance.

LeBron James: #6—Two Sons, One Number

LeBron James has worn different numbers throughout his storied career—#23 with the Cavaliers and Lakers, #6 with the Heat and briefly with the Lakers. But when he chose #6, the decision was deeply personal.

"Twenty-three is one of my favorite numbers, so two times three is six," James explained. But there was more to it than math. His first son, Bronny, was born in October—the sixth day of October. His second son, Bryce, was born in June—the sixth month of the year.

"Six has always been with me ever since I was a kid for some reason, especially when it relates to my family," James said.[64]

For one of basketball's all-time greats, #6 wasn't about legacy or brand—it was about carrying his sons' birthdays with him onto the court, a reminder that family comes before championships.

Carmelo Anthony: #7—For Kiyan

When Carmelo Anthony joined the New York Knicks in 2011, he couldn't wear his signature #15—it had been retired for Earl Monroe and Dick McGuire. So Anthony chose #7, and the reason was simple and personal.

His son Kiyan's birthday is March 7th.

Anthony later explained there was also a mathematical element: his high school number was 22, his college and Denver number was 15, and 22 minus 15 equals 7. But at its core, #7 was about his son—a number that kept Kiyan close every time Melo stepped onto the floor at Madison Square Garden.[65]

Family numbers remind us that greatness isn't built alone. Behind every jersey is someone who sacrificed, inspired, or gave meaning to the digits. These numbers don't just honor the past—they carry it forward, woven into every game, every season, every generation.

CHAPTER 4

When Dates Become Digits

Jersey numbers are supposed to be simple—just digits on a uniform. But for some athletes, they're anything but. These numbers carry memories, commemorate milestones, and whisper stories of birth, loss, rebellion, and redemption. They mark birthdays, anniversaries, political upheavals, and personal turning points—dates that became digits, moments that became permanent.

When History Meets the Heart

Jaromir Jagr: #68—Never Forget

Future Hockey Hall of Famer Jaromir Jagr chose #68 to remember the Prague Spring and the Soviet invasion of 1968—a pivotal year in Czech history when tanks rolled into Czechoslovakia to crush a movement for freedom and reform.

The number honors both of his grandfathers, who were imprisoned during the Soviet crackdown; one died later that year. Jagr's grandmother ensured he never forgot what happened. The invasion shaped his family's lives and the fate of his nation.

At a time when few players wore uncommon numbers in the high 60s, #68 became inseparably tied to Jagr. More than a jersey number, it was a political statement, a family memorial, and a permanent reminder of a nation's turning point.[66]

It's the Year I Was Born

Sidney Crosby: #87—Written in the Stars

Sidney Crosby's jersey number is more than just digits—it's autobiographical. He wears #87 to match his birthdate: August 7, 1987 (8/7/87).

The symmetry between his number and birthday became part of his identity—a quiet symbol of destiny. From his rookie season to his multiple Stanley Cups and Olympic gold medals, #87 has been Crosby's signature, stitched into every highlight and etched into hockey history.

Even his contract became part of the legend: in 2012, he signed a deal that would give him an $8.7 million cap hit, further cementing the connection to his number.[67]

Connor McDavid: #97—Following the Blueprint

Similar to Crosby, Connor McDavid has worn #97 since childhood, a number he picked long before he became the face of modern hockey.

"I chose to wear number 97 when I was seven years old because that's the year I was born," McDavid explained simply.[68]

Following Crosby's lead, McDavid transformed his birth year into hockey royalty—winning five scoring titles, three MVP awards, and a Conn Smythe Trophy, making #97 the perfect complement to #87.

The Birth Year Club

Crosby's choice inspired a trend across the league. Soon, birth years became badges of identity: Patrick Kane's #88, Vladimir Tarasenko's #91, Gabriel Landeskog's #92. Each number told a story—not of stats, but of origin. A generation of players turned their birth years into identities.[69]

Here are just a few notable examples:[70]

> **Patrick Kane: #88**—The Blackhawks legend turned his 1988 birth year into a symbol of American hockey excellence, winning three Stanley Cups and the Conn Smythe Trophy.
>
> **Sam Gagner: #89**—Wearing #89 for six teams across 17 seasons, Gagner made history in 2012 with an eight-point game, one of the most remarkable single-game performances in NHL history.
>
> **Marcus Johansson: #90**—The Swedish forward wore #90 in over 1,000 NHL games, with six different teams over his 16-year career.
>
> **Vladimir Tarasenko: #91**—Known as the Russian Sniper, made #91 a signature of precision, helping the Blues capture their first Stanley Cup in 2019.
>
> **Gabriel Landeskog: #92**—The Avalanche captain wore his birth year while leading Colorado to the 2022 Stanley Cup.
>
> **Ryan Nugent-Hopkins: #93**—Drafted first overall in 2011, Nugent-Hopkins has worn #93 his entire 15-year career with the Edmonton Oilers.

The trend crossed into international soccer as well, evidenced by the 2008 roster of AC Milan which included:[71]

> **Andriy Shevchenko: #76**—After wearing #7 during his first tour with AC Milan, in 2008 he opted to wear #76 reflecting his birth year of 1976.
>
> **Ronaldinho: #80**—Typically known for wearing the prestigious #10 which was unavailable at AC Milan, Ronaldinho opted to wear #80 to represent the year he was born.

Mathieu Flamini: #84—Perhaps following the lead of Shevchenko and Ronaldinho, Flamini chose to wear #84 to coincide with his birth year of 1984.

Gianluigi Donnarumma: #99—The Boy Wonder

When Gianluigi Donnarumma burst onto the scene with AC Milan at just 16 years old, he chose a jersey number that stood out: #99. Unusual for a goalkeeper, #99 carried deep personal meaning—Donnarumma was born in 1999.

Those digits became a symbol of his rapid rise and youthful promise. As one of the youngest starting goalkeepers in Serie A history, wearing #99 felt like destiny—a number as bold and unconventional as his teenage breakthrough.

For Donnarumma, #99 wasn't just a number. It was a statement: a reminder of where he came from, how young he started, and the legacy he was building.[72]

When Practicality Becomes Prophecy

Rick Tocchet: #92—The Year Everything Aligned

When Rick Tocchet arrived in Pittsburgh in 1992, his preferred #22 was already taken. So he made a simple choice: he wore the year itself.

It was practical, not prophetic. But sometimes fate has other plans.

That spring, everything clicked. Tocchet posted career-best playoff numbers, meshed perfectly with Mario Lemieux, and helped the Penguins capture their second straight Stanley Cup—the only championship of his career. Wearing #92 in 1992 while winning it all? That's the kind of uncanny alignment that makes numbers feel magical.

Tocchet didn't choose #92 to predict greatness. But he wore the year, won the Cup, and gave #92 a legacy no one saw coming. Sometimes the number you settle for becomes the number you're remembered by.[73]

Numbers from the Calendar

Caitlin Clark: #22—Written in January

Caitlin Clark has been wearing #22 for as long as she can remember, and the reason is beautifully simple: it's the day she was born.

"Honestly, I'm not a very creative person," she explained. "I was born on January 22, so it's what I went with when I was about five years old."[74]

What started as a childhood choice became one of the most celebrated numbers in women's college basketball. At the University of Iowa, Clark's #22 became instantly linked to deep three-pointers, no-look passes, and a competitive fire that made her one of the most captivating players in the sport's history.

Clark didn't choose #22 for luck, legacy, or superstition. She chose it because it was the day she was born—and somehow, that simple connection made it feel right.

As Clark shattered scoring records and led Iowa to back-to-back national championship appearances, #22 became more than just her birthday. It became her brand, her signature, her legacy.

When she entered the WNBA in 2024 as the #1 overall pick by the Indiana Fever, there was never any question: she'd wear #22, just as she had since she was a kindergartner shooting hoops on the playground.

Evina Westbrook: #22—A Date That Connects Generations

For Evina Westbrook, #22 isn't just a number—it's a family constellation of dates that all align on the 22nd.

"My grandfather from my dad's side, his birthday's on the 22nd. His wife's birthday is on the 22nd and their anniversary is on the 22nd," Westbrook explained during her time at UConn.[75]

Three milestones, three 22s, all falling on the same date. It's the kind of numerical serendipity that feels like destiny—a number that was meant to be hers.

Every time Westbrook stepped on the court wearing #22, she carried that love with her. Three 22s, one number, and a reminder that some dates are so significant they deserve to be worn on your back.

Matisse Thybulle: #22—February 2nd

For Matisse Thybulle, #22 is more than a number—it's a memory. He wears it to honor his mother, Elizabeth, who passed away from cancer when he was 17 years old. In college, Thybulle had worn #4, her favorite number. But when he arrived in Philadelphia, that number was already retired. His solution was simple but symbolic: $2 + 2 = 4$. By choosing #22, he carried her favorite number forward in a new form.[76]

Only later would the full weight of that choice reveal itself. Elizabeth had passed away on February 2—2/2. What began as a mathematical tribute had become something deeper: the date of her passing was written into the very number on his back.

Every time Thybulle pulls on his jersey, #22 honors his mother's love, strength, and legacy—a number that carries both her favorite four and the date that shaped his life.

Dwight Howard: #8—The Eighth One Who Lived

Dwight Howard wore #12 for most of his career—the reverse of his idol Kevin Garnett's #21—but when he signed with his hometown Atlanta Hawks in 2016, he made a deeply personal change to #8, a number tied to both celebration and survival.

"My birthday is December 8th," Howard explained, "and I was supposed to be dead. My mom lost seven kids and I was supposed to be the eighth one and I ended up being the eighth one that lived out of all the ones that passed away."[77]

Howard's mother, Sheryl, had endured seven miscarriages before Dwight was born—her eighth pregnancy. The number represented not just his birthday, but his very existence against the odds. As Howard put it, #8 symbolized "new beginning and new life."

For Howard, switching to #8 marked a homecoming to Atlanta, carrying the weight of his mother's perseverance and the gift of life itself.

Prince Fielder: #84—A Fresh Start

Prince Fielder wore #28 throughout his career with Milwaukee and Detroit—1,322 games spanning nearly a decade. But when he was traded to the Texas Rangers in November 2013, he decided it was time for a change.

"Fresh start," Fielder explained at his introductory press conference. "That's the year I was born. That's as deep as I'm going to go into that."[78]

Born May 9, 1984, Fielder chose #84 to mark a new chapter—a symbolic break from his past and a fresh beginning in Texas. Those digits represented both his birth year and his hope for reinvention after a disappointing playoff run in Detroit.

For Fielder, #84 became more than a birth year—it was a declaration that sometimes you need to start over, shed the old identity, and embrace something new.

Carlos May: #17—The Only One

Carlos May holds a distinction no other professional athlete can claim: he's the only player in Major League Baseball history to wear his actual birthday on his jersey.

Born on May 17, 1948, May was assigned #17 by the Chicago White Sox equipment manager when he was called up in 1968. "They picked my number for me," May recalled. "So, when I came to spring training, at first, they gave me No. 29. But when I came up to the big club, they gave me No. 17. I was just glad to be there. They could have given me 100—I was in the big league and that's what I wanted."[79]

The White Sox jerseys at the time displayed both the player's last name and number on the back. For May, that meant his jersey read "MAY 17"—his birthday spelled out for everyone to see.

What started as pure coincidence became part of baseball lore. May went on to become a two-time All-Star, but he's best remembered as the only player whose uniform literally displayed his birthday.

Cosmic Coincidences—Unconfirmed Birthday Representations

While many athletes have confirmed they wear their birthday digits, others have been less outspoken about it, but thanks to some great historical databases, like Basketball-Reference.com, we can identify birthdays and the number worn by any NBA player. These are just some of the honorable mentions across the Association. Sometimes, obvious is just obvious.

Coincidence?: While not publicly confirmed, Clyde Drexler wore #22 his entire career. Perhaps just a neat coincidence, he was born on June 22.[80]

Double Coincidence?: When Shaquille O'Neal joined the Boston Celtics late in his career in 2010, he chose #36—and was born on March 6 (3/6). Three years later, when the Celtics drafted Marcus Smart in 2014, he also wore #36 and carried it with him to the Grizzlies, Wizards, and Lakers. Smart was also born on March 6.[81]

A Whole Lot of Coincidence?: Our Birth Year Club listed earlier in this chapter featured players who openly stated their jersey numbers were intentionally chosen to represent the year they were born. The following is just a sampling of NBA players that wore their birth year, even if the choice wasn't intentional or widely discussed:[82]

> **Semih Erden**: #86 in Boston, born in 1986
> **Danilo Gallinari**: #88 in Washington, born in 1988
> **Nicolas Batum**: #88 in Portland, born in 1988
> **Brodric Thomas**: #97 in Boston, born in 1997
> **Eugene Omoruyi**: #97 for three teams, born in 1997
> **Tyrese Haliburton**: #0 for Sacramento and Indiana, born in 2000

Numbers From the Year They Broke Free

Alexander Mogilny: #89—The Defector

In 1989, Alexander Mogilny didn't just cross an ocean—he crossed a line few dared to approach. At just 20 years old, he became the first Soviet hockey player to defect to the NHL, slipping away from his national team during the World Championships in Sweden and flying to North America to join the Buffalo Sabres.[83]

The Sabres had drafted him 89th overall, and when Mogilny arrived, he chose to wear #89. It wasn't just a number—it was a declaration of freedom, a marker of the year he broke free from the Iron Curtain and began a career that would span over 16 seasons.[84]

Petr Klíma: #85—A New Beginning

Petr Klíma, a talented forward for the Detroit Red Wings, wore #85 to mark a life-changing moment: the year he defected from Czechoslovakia to the United States in 1985.[85]

The number wasn't about stats—it was a tribute to freedom, opportunity, and a new life in the NHL. Like Mogilny, Klíma's number told a story that went far beyond hockey—it was about choosing a different life and never looking back.

Pavel Bure: #96—When the Date Doesn't Deliver

Not every significant number delivers what you hope for.

When Pavel Bure arrived in North America on September 6, 1991 (9/6), he wanted to wear #96 to mark the moment he began his NHL career. But the Vancouver Canucks assigned him #10, citing a team policy against high numbers. Bure made #10 famous, becoming one of the league's most electrifying scorers.

In 1995, after teammate Alexander Mogilny joined the team wearing #89—his own defection year—Bure was finally allowed to switch to #96, the number he'd longed to wear since arriving.

The switch didn't bring the spark he hoped for. Bure played just 15 games that season before suffering a torn ACL. The following season was marred by injuries and inconsistency. In 1997–98, Bure switched back to #10—and promptly scored 51 goals, reclaiming his dominance.[86]

Unlike Mogilny and Klíma, whose defection numbers became symbols of freedom and fresh starts, Bure's story offers a different truth: sometimes the number you earn matters more than the number you choose. His arrival date held meaning, but #10 held magic.

Jersey numbers may seem like random digits stitched onto fabric, but for these athletes, they're coded memories—birthdays, revolutions, defections, and sometimes, unexpected prophecies. These numbers don't just mark who they are on the ice or court; they mark where they came from, what they survived, and what they hoped to become. When dates become digits, the game becomes personal.

CHAPTER 5

Honoring Those Who Came Before Us

In sports, jersey numbers aren't just identifiers—they're tributes. For many athletes, the digits on their back honor mentors, heroes, and legacies that shaped their journey. These numbers carry memory, meaning, and respect.

Honoring Fallen Mentors and Teammates

Kevin Garnett: #21 and #2—Honoring a Teammate

Kevin Garnett chose #21 when he entered the NBA in 1995, the same number worn by two players he idolized: Dominique Wilkins and Malik Sealy. When Sealy joined the Minnesota Timberwolves in 1998, the two became teammates and close friends. Since Garnett already wore #21, Sealy chose a new number: #2.

After Sealy's tragic death in a car accident in 2000, Garnett continued wearing #21 in Minnesota as a tribute. Years later, when he joined the Brooklyn Nets, he switched to #2—honoring Sealy once again.[87]

When Garnett was traded to the Boston Celtics in 2007, he chose #5. His longtime #21 was already retired in honor of Bill Sharman, and #2 was retired for coach Red Auerbach, so Garnett embraced a fresh start. He later acknowledged a connection to Bill Walton, who had worn #5 in Boston. The choice marked a new chapter—culminating in an NBA championship in 2008.

Kevin Durant: #35—Honoring a Coach

For the majority of his career, Kevin Durant wore his jersey number to honor someone taken too soon. His first basketball coach, Charles Craig—affectionately known as "Big Chucky"—was shot and killed in 2005. Craig was like a father to Durant when he was just eight years old, taking him to the movies, giving him money when he needed it, and helping take care of his mom.

Craig was only 35 years old when he died.

Durant chose #35 as a constant reminder—not just of his mentor, but of how fragile life can be. Every time Durant stepped on the court wearing #35, he carried his mentor's memory with him—a tribute stitched into every shot, every game, every championship.[88]

Eric Lindros: #88—Honoring a Mentor

Before playing in the NHL, Eric Lindros chose #88 to honor the memory of John McCauley, a family friend and mentor. McCauley was an NHL referee who wore #8 and later became the director of NHL officiating in the 1980s before passing away in 1989.

Doubling McCauley's #8, Lindros turned a quiet tribute into one of hockey's most memorable numbers. He wore #88 throughout his entire career—from junior hockey with the Oshawa Generals to the NHL with Philadelphia, New York, Toronto, and Dallas.

The legacy continues today through John McCauley's son, Wes McCauley, who has become one of the most respected referees in NHL history—carrying on his father's tradition just as Lindros honored it every time he stepped on the ice.[89]

Mike Ricci: #40—Honoring a Hero

In 2004, NHL veteran Mike Ricci made a quiet but powerful gesture. He changed his jersey to #40 to honor Pat Tillman, the former NFL safety who left behind a multimillion-dollar contract to enlist in the U.S. Army Rangers. Tillman was killed in action in Afghanistan that same year.

Ricci, deeply moved by Tillman's sacrifice, chose to wear #40 as a tribute—not just to a fallen athlete, but to a man who lived by principle.[90]

The Roberto Clemente Legacy: #21

For many players, a jersey number is just a number. But for a growing group of Major League stars, #21 means something more—a tribute to a man whose impact stretched far beyond the diamond.

Roberto Clemente was a Puerto Rican icon who dazzled with his bat, his arm, and his heart. A Hall of Famer and humanitarian, Clemente died tragically in 1972 while delivering aid to earthquake victims in Nicaragua. No number is more revered in Puerto Rican sports than Roberto Clemente's #21, a symbol of both baseball greatness and humanitarian legacy.

The Players Who Wore #21

Sammy Sosa, born in the Dominican Republic, wore it as a quiet homage stitched into every swing, while Carlos Delgado and Rubén Sierra carried it through much of their careers as well—Delgado respected the number so much that during the 2006 World Baseball Classic he suggested Puerto Rico retire it, a conviction strong enough that he chose to wear #25 instead.

Yankees outfielder Paul O'Neill honored Clemente by wearing #21 throughout his career, and Nick Markakis kept the number alive during his long tenure in the majors. This is only a small sampling of the players who ensured Clemente's legacy continued to inspire across generations and cultures.[91]

Michael Lorenzen's connection to Clemente's number came in 2016, during a trip to Puerto Rico. Over dinner at the Clemente family's home, Lorenzen asked Clemente's widow, Vera, for permission to wear #21 in honor of Roberto. "I remember sitting around the table saying, 'If I get the chance, do you mind if I wear the number in honor of Roberto?'" Lorenzen recalled. "She loved it. She loved the idea." Deeply moved by her blessing, Lorenzen returned to spring training and permanently switched his jersey to #21, making the gesture both personal and enduring.[92]

Roberto Clemente Day: A Field of #21s

Every September 15th, Major League Baseball celebrates Roberto Clemente Day—and the field transforms into a living memorial. Puerto Rican stars like Francisco Lindor, Carlos Correa, Javier Báez, and Yadier Molina all don #21 for one game, turning the ballpark into a tribute. Only a handful of players wear #21 full-time to honor Clemente, but on this day, dozens more temporarily adopt the number.

As part of the league-wide recognition, all players, managers, coaches, and umpires wear a white "21" patch on the upper left chest. In addition, players of Puerto Rican heritage, past Clemente Award recipients, and each team's annual nominee have the option to wear #21 as their uniform number during the games. Together, these gestures ensure Clemente's legacy is honored not just by a few, but by the entire sport.[93]

Francisco Lindor's Daily Tribute

Francisco Lindor wears #21 on Roberto Clemente Day, but his everyday #12 carries deeper meaning.

Growing up in Puerto Rico, his father wore #21 in local leagues; his brother chose #12 for Roberto Alomar, who revered Clemente.

When Lindor reached the majors, he embraced #12—the reverse of his father's #21 and a subtle echo of Clemente's influence—a symbolic blend of family, heritage, and admiration.[94]

The Kareem Abdul-Jabbar Tree: #33

Where It Started: Kareem Abdul-Jabbar

Kareem chose #33 in high school to honor his favorite football player, New York Giants fullback Mel Triplett. As an aside, #33 is rather fitting for somebody named Triplett.[95]

Those digits became a hallmark of Kareem's skyhook and championship excellence. But its legacy didn't stop there—it inspired a generation.

Patrick Ewing: #33—Following the Footsteps

Patrick Ewing wore #33 in college at Georgetown, inspired by Kareem. When he arrived in New York, the number was available, and Ewing kept it. His relentless play made #33 the number of New York basketball through the 1980s and '90s.[96]

Bill Walton: #32 and #5—One Number Less

When Bill Walton played for UCLA in the early 1970s, he wore #32. Why? Because Lew Alcindor (later Kareem Abdul-Jabbar) had worn

#33 just before him. Walton didn't feel he was quite equal to Alcindor, so he took one number less out of respect.

He continued wearing #32 in the pros with the Portland Trail Blazers, leading them to a championship. But when he signed with the Boston Celtics in 1985, #32 belonged to Kevin McHale.

So Walton looked at who he was following: Hall of Fame Celtics center Bill Russell, who wore #6. Once again showing respect and humility, Walton took one number less—#5.[97]

The pattern was complete—each number a gesture of humility and respect for those who came before.

Childhood Heroes and Lifelong Tributes

Rickey Henderson: #24—For Willie Mays

Rickey Henderson wore #24 because his idol Willie Mays wore it. Rickey would go on to break Mays' records and make the number his own as baseball's premier leadoff hitter and base stealer.[98]

The student honored the teacher, then surpassed him.

David Robinson: #50—Honoring Ralph Sampson

David Robinson is widely considered the best basketball player in Naval Academy history, and he chose jersey number 50 after his idol Ralph Sampson.

In the early 1980s, Ralph Sampson was one of the NBA's emerging superstars—a 7'4" center who combined size with agility. After being selected first overall by the Houston Rockets in 1983, Sampson formed the original "Twin Towers" alongside Hakeem Olajuwon.

For young David Robinson at the Naval Academy, Sampson represented everything a dominant center could be. Inspired by his hero, Robinson wore #50 both as a Navy Midshipman and throughout his entire NBA career with the San Antonio Spurs.

The parallel is striking: both were dominant college centers, both were first overall picks, and both formed dominant "Twin Towers" partnerships—Sampson with Olajuwon, Robinson with Tim Duncan.

But while injuries derailed Sampson's career, Robinson exceeded his hero's achievements, winning two NBA championships, an MVP award, and earning Hall of Fame induction.[99]

Walt Weiss: #22—For Mercury Morris

As a boy, Rockies manager Walt Weiss was a huge fan of Miami Dolphins running back Mercury Morris. His first youth football team was even named the Dolphins. Morris wore #22 throughout his career, and Weiss adopted that number for himself—wearing it during his playing days and later as the Rockies' manager.[100]

Luka Dončić: #77—Doubling Down on His Idol

Dallas Mavericks star Luka Dončić revealed that Greek professional basketball player Vassilis Spanoulis was his idol since he was little, and watching Spanoulis inspired his jersey number choice.

Spanoulis, a EuroLeague legend who wore #7 throughout his career, was the player young Luka studied and admired. When Dončić played for Real Madrid, he proudly wore #7 to honor his hero.

But when Dončić joined the Slovenian national team, #7 was already taken by veteran Klemen Prepelič. Rather than making a fuss, Dončić simply doubled the digit and embraced #77.

The same situation repeated when the Dallas Mavericks drafted him—#7 belonged to Dwight Powell. Once again, Dončić chose #77, maintaining the nod across both international and NBA play.

The #77 jersey has become a defining emblem of Dončić's excellence, one of the NBA's best-selling jerseys despite being one of its most unusual numbers. What started as a creative solution became a defining symbol of respect.[101]

Xander Bogaerts: #2—For Derek Jeter

Boston Red Sox shortstop Xander Bogaerts grew up idolizing Derek Jeter. "Derek Jeter is one of the prime examples of how you want any kid growing up to be, just to take the good habits that he had. He has been a huge role model," Bogaerts said. When Jacoby Ellsbury left Boston for the Yankees, Bogaerts asked if he could take over #2, the number Jeter embodied.

For Bogaerts, wearing #2 wasn't about copying Jeter—it was about carrying forward the standard of professionalism and clutch performance that Jeter represented. During Jeter's farewell season, Bogaerts recalled their brief interaction at Fenway Park—the words were simple, but coming from Jeter they landed with weight: "He told me, 'Keep working hard. You are a good player.'"[102]

Chris Mullin: #17—For John Havlicek

As a young player in New York, Chris Mullin studied the games of Knicks stars Walt Frazier and Earl Monroe and admired Celtics great Larry Bird, but he wore #17 in honor of Boston Celtics legend John Havlicek.

Mullin wasn't blessed with blazing speed or elite athleticism. What he had was an unmatched work ethic and an unshakable commitment to excellence—qualities he saw in Havlicek, who was known for his relentless movement and conditioning.

The ultimate gym rat, Mullin wore #17 in honor of his boyhood hero and, like Havlicek, rarely stopped moving on the court. He honed his craft through countless hours in the gym, developing a sweet left-handed jumper that carried him through a 16-year NBA career.

Mullin wore #17 from St. John's University, where he won the Wooden Award, to the Golden State Warriors, where he became a five-time All-Star and member of the legendary 1992 Dream Team.

In 2012, the Warriors retired his #17 jersey. The number he chose to honor his childhood hero had become his own legacy.[103]

Brad Daugherty: #43—Being Richard Petty

Brad Daugherty grew up in the mountains of North Carolina, where racing wasn't just a sport—it was a way of life. His family loved racing, and young Brad's hero was Richard Petty, NASCAR's "King" whose STP #43 became one of the most recognizable cars in motorsports history.

Daugherty wore #43 in high school to honor Petty. When he arrived at the University of North Carolina, he tried to claim it again, but teammate Curtis Hunter wanted the same number. Coach Dean Smith settled the dispute with a coin toss. Daugherty lost, so Hunter got #43 and Daugherty settled for #42—Kyle Petty's car number.

When the Cleveland Cavaliers drafted Daugherty first overall in 1986, he had one condition: his jersey number would be #43. "I always thought of myself as being Richard Petty one day," Daugherty later explained. He didn't just admire Petty from afar—he wanted to *be* him.

Daugherty went on to become a five-time NBA All-Star while wearing #43. But his connection to racing never faded. After retiring from basketball, he became a NASCAR team co-owner, staying connected to the sport that first captured his imagination as a boy in the Carolina mountains.

In 2023, when his team won the Daytona 500—NASCAR's most prestigious race—Daugherty called it "the pinnacle of my sports career." The kid who wore #43 to honor his hero had come full circle, achieving success in both the sport he played and the sport he loved.[104]

George Springer: #4—For Torii Hunter ... Kind Of

Houston Astros outfielder George Springer's story is a bit more lighthearted. His favorite player as a kid was Torii Hunter, who wore #48, so Springer always gravitated toward multiples of 4.

But here's how he ended up with #4:

"When I was at Connecticut, we were at a fall practice and I was screwing around, and my coach, Jim Penders, said, 'What, are you 4 years old?' When it was time to pick our jerseys, that was the smallest one. I weighed like 170 pounds at the time, and I needed it to fit. I was like, 'I need the smallest jersey, and coach says I act like I'm 4. So I'll be 4.'"[105]

Sometimes the most memorable tributes come from unexpected moments—even when honoring your heroes.

Tracy McGrady: #1—The Home Visit That Changed Everything

Growing up in Auburndale, Florida, Tracy McGrady didn't dream of being like Michael Jordan—he dreamed of being like Penny Hardaway. When the Orlando Magic acquired Hardaway, McGrady saw himself in that uniform and identified with Penny's versatile game.

As a teenager, McGrady attended a playoff game where Hardaway scored 42 points against Miami. What happened next changed his life. At just 17 years old, McGrady was invited to Penny Hardaway's home, and the experience opened doors for him, giving him a glimpse of what was possible.

McGrady recalled how meeting Penny had the same effect on him that Michael Jordan had on others—Penny was glowing, and McGrady knew he was in the presence of greatness.

When McGrady signed with the Orlando Magic in 2000, he immediately chose to wear #1—the same number Penny had worn—to honor his childhood hero. He didn't disappoint. In four years with Orlando, McGrady became one of the NBA's elite scorers, winning back-to-back scoring titles in 2003 and 2004 while wearing #1.[106]

The student didn't just honor his teacher—he became a legend in his own right.

Skip Schumaker: #55—The Kindness of a Stranger

Skip Schumaker was six years old when his parents took him to Dodger Stadium to meet his heroes. Clutching his baseball and pen, he waited nervously as players walked by. Several Dodgers brushed past him without stopping. The young boy started to cry.

Then a pitcher named Orel Hershiser noticed him.

"I play for the Dodgers, I'm not famous, but I would be happy to sign for you," Hershiser said.

That simple act of kindness changed Schumaker's life. He never forgot the player who stopped when others didn't, who made a heartbroken kid feel important.

Years later, when Schumaker made it to the major leagues, he chose #55—Hershiser's number. He wore it for most of his 11-year career, a tribute to the man who taught him that greatness isn't just about fame—it's about how you treat people when no one's watching.[107]

For Schumaker, #55 wasn't just a number. It was a reminder that one moment of compassion can inspire a lifetime.

Danny Granger: #33—For Scottie Pippen

Danny Granger, the smooth-scoring forward who carried the Indiana Pacers through the late 2000s, chose #33 because his childhood idol was Scottie Pippen. Growing up, Granger admired Pippen's versatility—a forward who could defend, distribute, and score while winning six championships alongside Michael Jordan.

Granger's own game reflected that influence. At his peak, he was an All-Star and one of the league's most complete forwards, capable of filling the box score in true Pippen fashion. Injuries cut short his prime, but his number choice told the story: he wanted to model himself after the ultimate do-everything wing.[108]

The Greatest of All Time: #23

Michael Jordan's Legacy

Michael Jordan wore #23 to honor his older brother Larry while carving out his own identity—choosing half of Larry's #45, rounded up. That choice became one of the most recognizable numbers in sports history.

But Jordan didn't just make #23 famous—he made it aspirational. For a generation of athletes who grew up watching him, wearing #23 became a way to carry his legacy, to channel his competitiveness, and to chase the standard he set.

While #23 is one of the most revered numbers in NBA history thanks to Michael Jordan, only a handful of players—including LeBron James—have publicly stated they wore it to honor him. Others may have worn it for personal reasons or by assignment.

According to Basketball-Reference.com, 268 players have worn #23 at some point. As Gatorade's popular 1991 commercial declared, everyone wanted to "Be Like Mike."[109]

That number would be even higher if teams could field multiple players with the same jersey. Take Blake Griffin: he wore #23 at Oklahoma, but when the Los Angeles Clippers drafted him first overall in 2009, the number was already claimed by veteran Marcus Camby. Griffin didn't push, negotiate, or even ask. Instead, he simply flipped the digits and made #32 his own.[110]

Those Who Followed #23
(To Name Just a Few)

From the NBA to the WNBA, and even crossing into soccer, #23 became more than a number. It was a lineage—passed from Jordan to his admirers, and then to their admirers in turn. Here are just a few of the athletes who carried #23 forward.

LeBron James: Following His Childhood Hero

James chose #23 because Jordan was his childhood hero. He admired Jordan's dominance and wanted to emulate his greatness. When he moved to Miami, he wore #6 to mark a new chapter. But upon returning to Cleveland, he reclaimed #23, signaling continuity with his original goals.[111]

Anthony Davis: Another Branch on the Jordan Tree

Anthony Davis grew up in Chicago and wears #23—which seems like an obvious Michael Jordan tribute. But there's a twist. While at Perspective Charter High School, Davis won a Black History Month trivia contest and received a $10 gift card. He used it to buy a book on his favorite player: LeBron James. From that moment on, Davis wore #23 not to honor Jordan, but to honor LeBron—the player who wore #23 to honor Jordan. It's a tribute to a tribute—a number that honors greatness honoring greatness.[110]

Ron Artest: Honoring His Favorite Player

Ron Artest (later Metta World Peace, and currently Metta Sandiford-Artest) wore #23 during his time with the Indiana Pacers specifically to honor Michael Jordan, whom he called his favorite player. Artest was a devoted Jordan fan who modeled his defensive game after MJ.[112]

Maya Moore: Crossing Leagues

Maya Moore also chose #23 to honor Jordan. In her WNBA career with the Minnesota Lynx, #23 became a statement of skill, leadership, and advocacy. Beyond basketball, her activism for criminal justice reform elevated #23 as a number representing courage and social impact.[113]

David Beckham: Crossing Sports

David Beckham chose #23 as homage to Michael Jordan early in his career when he couldn't get his preferred #7. Even in soccer, Jordan's influence reached across the globe.[114]

The Kobe Bryant Tributes

Just as Jordan's #23 inspired a generation, Kobe's numbers—#8, #24, and his Olympic #10—became badges the next wave of stars would honor. His sudden death in 2020 transformed those tributes from admiration into memorial.

Jayson Tatum: #10—Olympics

Jayson Tatum wore #10 for Team USA at the 2024 Paris Olympics—the same number Kobe Bryant donned in 2008 and 2012. Prior to the Games, while speaking at USA Basketball's training camp in Las Vegas, Tatum emphasized the significance of honoring his late idol: "Wearing No. 10 after Kobe is nothing short of an honor. It's definitely not something I take for granted or lightly."[115]

Paul George: #8—Coming Home

When Paul George signed with the Philadelphia 76ers in 2024, his usual #13 was unavailable—retired in honor of Wilt Chamberlain. Rather than choose a new number at random, George made a meaningful break from his PG13 identity and selected #8 to honor Kobe Bryant. George grew up in the Los Angeles area, where Kobe became a Lakers legend.

Now, George plays in Philadelphia, where Kobe was born and attended high school at Lower Merion—a beautiful cross-country tribute that connects Kobe's birthplace with the city where he built his legacy.[116]

Kobe Bryant's #24—All-Star Tribute

While Kobe's Olympic #10 and early-career #8 inspired specific tributes, his iconic #24 became so universally associated with excellence that countless players across multiple sports have worn it in his honor.

The number's influence was most visible at the 2020 NBA All-Star Game, held just weeks after Kobe's death, where Team Giannis wore #24 and Team LeBron wore #2 (for Kobe's daughter Gianna) in an emotional tribute that united the entire league in mourning.[117]

Los Angeles Dodgers: #8 and #24—A City in Mourning

The tributes extended beyond basketball. On August 23, 2020—what would have been Kobe's 42nd birthday—the Los Angeles Dodgers honored him in a pregame ceremony before their game against the San Francisco Giants.

Every player and coach lined up wearing gold Lakers jerseys with either #8 or #24, the two numbers Kobe wore during his Hall of Fame career. The team also painted "2" and "24" on the pitcher's mound to honor both Kobe and his daughter Gianna.[118]

It was a powerful reminder that Kobe's impact transcended basketball—he belonged to all of Los Angeles, a city still mourning one of its most beloved sports heroes.

Hockey's Greatest: #99 and #66

Wayne Gretzky: #99—Doubling Down on Howe

Wayne Gretzky originally wore #9 in junior hockey, idolizing Gordie Howe. When he joined the Indianapolis Racers, #9 was taken, so his coach suggested #99. Gretzky thought it was a bit "showy" but agreed to try it.

It stuck.

Those digits became so synonymous with Gretzky that the NHL retired them league-wide—the only time in league history they've done so. Gretzky doubled the number of his idol and became the greatest player in hockey history in the process.[119]

Mario Lemieux: #66—The Upside-Down Tribute

Mario Lemieux chose #66 as a subtle nod to Wayne Gretzky's famous #99—flipped upside down.[120] It wasn't about copying; it was a quiet way to acknowledge greatness while carving out his own path.

Over time, Lemieux made #66 unmistakably his own through his smooth style and overwhelming dominance.

Creative Tributes and Symbolic Choices

Dirk Nowitzki: #41—Flipping Barkley's Number

Dirk Nowitzki's signature #41 wasn't his first choice. Growing up in Germany, Dirk initially wore #11, his father's handball number. But everything changed in 1992 when he watched Charles Barkley dominate the Olympics wearing #14. Inspired by Barkley's passion and power, Dirk adopted #14 for his international career.

When Dirk entered the NBA in 1998 and joined the Dallas Mavericks, he hoped to continue wearing #14, but the number was unavailable (Chapter 16).

Rather than push the issue, Dirk made a simple yet symbolic decision: he flipped the digits, turning 14 into 41.[121]

That flip became more than a workaround—it became a legacy. Over 21 seasons, Dirk transformed #41 into a symbol of loyalty, humility, and excellence.

Bryce Harper: #3—For Roy Halladay

For the first seven years of his MLB career, Bryce Harper wore #34 with the Washington Nationals. The number was a tribute to Mickey Mantle—Harper was a Mantle fan, and since #7 was unavailable in the minors, he chose #34 because 3 + 4 = 7.

But when Harper signed a record-breaking 13-year deal with the Philadelphia Phillies in 2019, he made a surprising decision: he did not reclaim #34, even though it was available. Out of respect for the late Roy Halladay, who wore #34 in Philadelphia, Harper chose to leave the number untouched and took #3 instead.

"I thought Roy Halladay should be the last one to wear it [in Philadelphia]," Harper said. "He's somebody in this game that's greater than a lot of guys who ever played it."[122]

Charles Barkley: #32—For Magic Johnson

In November 1991, the basketball world was stunned when Magic Johnson announced his retirement after being diagnosed with HIV. While many players responded with silence or uncertainty, Charles Barkley chose a bold tribute: he switched his jersey from #34 to #32, Magic's number.

Barkley debuted the number on November 5, 1991, scoring 28 points against the Boston Celtics. He wore it for the remainder of the season, hoping to raise awareness about HIV/AIDS and to show solidarity with his friend.

The gesture sparked controversy in Philadelphia because #32 had been retired by the 76ers in honor of Hall of Famer Billy Cunningham. Though Cunningham gave Barkley his blessing, many fans were outraged.

Barkley, never one to back down, responded bluntly: "I really don't give a f**k what they say on the call-in shows... It's not about the fans, it's about a friend. I really don't give a flying f**k what they think."[123]

Karl Malone: #11—Respecting Magic's Legacy

Karl Malone spent nearly his entire Hall of Fame career wearing #32 with the Utah Jazz. But when he joined the Los Angeles Lakers in 2003, he made a surprising change: he wore #11.

Why? Because #32 was already retired for Magic Johnson. In a rare gesture, Magic offered to unretire his number so Malone could wear it. Malone was deeply honored, even holding up a #32 Lakers jersey at his introductory press conference.

But after reflecting, Malone declined Magic's offer. He didn't want to overshadow Johnson's legacy or take away from what #32 meant to Lakers fans. Instead, he opted for #11—the same number he wore representing the United States in the 1992 Barcelona Olympics as part of the Dream Team.[124]

Honoring Home: Regional Pride

The Hawaiian #50—Island Pride

It started with Sid Fernandez, a lefty from Honolulu who pitched for the New York Mets in the 1980s. He chose #50 as a tribute to Hawaii—the 50th state, admitted to the Union in 1959. It wasn't just a number—it was a statement: island-born athletes belonged on the biggest stages.[125]

Fernandez's choice sparked a quiet tradition:

> **Benny Agbayani** picked up the torch with the Mets[126]
> **Shane Victorino** wore #50 for Team USA in the 2013 World Baseball Classic[127]
> **Jordan Yamamoto** wore it with the Marlins[125]

Though not every Hawaiian athlete wears it, #50 has become a quiet badge of honor—a numeric nod to the islands.

Bill Voiselle: #96—Ninety Six Pride

When Bill Voiselle joined the Boston Braves in 1947, he asked Commissioner Happy Chandler for permission to wear #96—the highest number ever worn in Major League Baseball at the time.

The reason? Voiselle grew up in Ninety Six, South Carolina, a small town with one of the most unusual names in America. For Voiselle, wearing #96 was about putting his hometown on the map.

Chandler approved, and "Ol' Ninety-Six" became a legend. The number stood as baseball's highest for decades—a badge of small-town pride that proved you didn't need to be from a big city to make it big.[128]

Kenley Jansen: #74—The House That Baseball Saved

When Kenley Jansen arrived at spring training as a major-league hopeful, he was assigned #74. For most players, it would be just another high number. For Jansen, it was fate.

He grew up at Kaya Kokolishi 74 in Willemstad, Curaçao. His family struggled to make payments and nearly lost the house. When Jansen saw #74 on his spring training jersey, he knew it was a sign.

"Seventy-four means everything for Kenley, because that's where he was raised," his wife Gianni said. "They were about to lose their home, and when Kenley got his first paycheck, he told his mom he'd pay the house off so they wouldn't lose it."[129]

Jansen kept his word. He wore #74 to the majors and saved Kaya Kokolishi 74. Number 74 is the only number he's worn in his 16-year career spanning four different teams. Today, he's a four-time All-Star with 476 saves and #74 will always represent the home he saved and the promise he kept.

Evan Fournier: #94—Repping the 94

Evan Fournier was born in Saint-Maurice, a small suburb outside of Paris in the Val-de-Marne department—and Val-de-Marne's postcode number is 94.

When Fournier was drafted by the Denver Nuggets in 2012, his preferred #10 (honoring Mike Bibby) was unavailable. So the French rookie chose #94—a tribute to home that only fellow Parisians would immediately recognize. Fournier also wore #94 with the Celtics in 2021.[130]

Mesut Özil: #67—Zonguldak Pride

Mesut Özil, one of the most gifted playmakers of his generation, rose to global fame with Real Madrid and later Arsenal, where he became known for his vision and passing artistry. When he joined Turkish powerhouse Fenerbahçe in 2021, his #10 jersey was already claimed.

Özil chose #67—a nod to Zonguldak, his family's hometown on Turkey's Black Sea coast, whose postal code is 67000.[131] By wearing #67, Özil honored his heritage with one of soccer's rarest numbers, turning his jersey into a symbol of regional pride. For Turkish fans, it was a reminder that a world-class star could carry his hometown roots onto the pitch with him.

Damian Lillard: #0—Three O's, One Journey

Damian Lillard wears #0, which represents the letter 'O' and his journey in life: from Oakland (where he was born), to Ogden (where he played college basketball at Weber State), to Oregon (where he became a Trail Blazers legend).[132]

For Lillard, #0 isn't about dominance or dismissing competition—it's a personal tribute to the three places that shaped his life and career, all beginning with the letter O.

Jari Kurri: #17—Honoring Finland's Independence?

Jari Kurri wore #17 throughout his Hall of Fame hockey career, and many believe the number honors 1917—the year Finland gained independence. While Kurri never publicly confirmed the connection, the symbolism resonated deeply with Finnish fans, especially when commemorative jerseys appeared during Finland's centennial celebration in 2017.

Whether Kurri chose #17 for this reason or the meaning developed organically, the number became inseparable from Finnish pride on ice. His legacy was cemented when both the Edmonton Oilers and his home team Jokerit retired his #17 jersey, honoring his impact on the sport in North America and Finland alike.[133]

Honoring and Raising Awareness

Katie Startup: #40—A Number That Saves Lives

Manchester City goalkeeper Katie Startup chose #40 as a gesture of remembrance, but also for a more urgent reason: to save lives.

Startup, who had worn #31 for years, made a deliberate switch to #40 to raise awareness for mental health and suicide prevention. "I decided to make the change based on the statistic ... one person every 40 seconds lost their life due to suicide," Startup explained.[134]

For Startup, wearing #40 isn't about personal glory or statistical achievement—it's about using her platform to start conversations, to break stigma, and to remind people that mental health matters.

Every time she takes the field, every time fans see #40 on her jersey, it's a quiet but powerful message: if you're struggling, you're not alone. Help is available.

It's one of the most meaningful number choices in sports—a reminder that athletes can use their jerseys for more than identification. They can use them for advocacy, awareness, and change.

Startup's #40 doesn't just represent her position on the field. It represents 40 seconds—and the hope that those seconds can be used to reach someone who needs help.

Some numbers honor the past. Some carry family legacy. Some celebrate championships. Startup's #40 fights for the lives still ahead—40 seconds at a time.

Jason Collins: #98—A Silent Tribute That Became a Rallying Cry

For years, NBA center Jason Collins wore #98 as a quiet gesture of solidarity—a number only his closest friends and family understood. The number referenced 1998, the year when Matthew Shepard, a University of Wyoming student, was murdered in one of the most notorious anti-gay hate crimes in American history.

Collins wore #98 with the Boston Celtics and Washington Wizards during the 2012–13 season, but the meaning remained hidden. As he later explained, every time he put on that jersey, it was a silent acknowledgment to himself and his friends and family of being a proud gay Black man playing in the NBA.

When Collins came out publicly in April 2013, becoming the first openly gay active player in any of the four major North American professional sports leagues, the world finally understood his number choice. He continued to wear #98 in Brooklyn the following season and presented the Shepard family with an autographed Nets jersey bearing the same number. "One of those cool treats in life," he said.[135]

The #98 jersey became the top-selling jersey at the NBA Store following Collins' announcement, with proceeds going to GLSEN and the Matthew Shepard Foundation. Collins' jersey was later added to the Smithsonian's permanent collection.

For Collins, #98 wasn't just about remembering a victim—it was about fighting for a future where LGBTQ+ athletes could live authentically.

From Roberto Clemente's #21 to Jason Collins' #98, these numbers prove that jerseys honor more than athletic achievement. They commemorate sacrifice, raise awareness, and connect athletes to causes larger than themselves. Some numbers represent points and championships. Some numbers shine a spotlight on social issues.

CHAPTER 6

Superstitions, Rituals, and Obsessions

Some athletes choose numbers to honor others. Another group treats their digits as something else entirely—anchors in a world built on uncertainty. In a world where outcomes can hinge on the smallest details, these digits become part of a delicate balance of routine, belief, and control.

Numbers become talismans—woven into routines, tied to milestones, or chosen to steady the mind when everything else feels unpredictable.

Lucky Numbers and Sacred Routines

For some athletes, their number isn't just what they wear—it's part of an elaborate system of belief and ritual. These players don't just pick a number; they weave it into every aspect of their preparation. Change the number, and you might break the spell.

Larry Walker: #33—The King of Superstition

Larry Walker wasn't the greatest #33 ever—hello, Kareem and Larry Bird—but Walker was, without a doubt, the most superstitious athlete ever to wear the number.

Walker had a thing for threes:

- He routinely set his alarm for 8:03 in the morning.
- His parking stall in the players' lot was #3.
- He took three practice swings in the on-deck circle.
- He dug his foot into the ground three times.

- He took three check swings before heading to the plate.
- He wore #33 to derive twice as much luck from his favorite number.
- He got married on November 3rd at 3:33 p.m.

When asked about his obsession with threes, Walker said simply: "I'd wear 333 if they'd let me."[136]

To Walker, #33 wasn't a number at all—it was a lifestyle, a ritual, a belief system. And apparently, it worked—he ended up in Cooperstown.

Wade Boggs: #26—The Comfort in Chicken

Wade Boggs wore #26 for most of his career. Whether he chose it or it was assigned to him is unclear—but given his well-documented superstitious nature, the number presumably became a source of good fortune.

Number 26 was just one piece of Boggs' elaborate superstition machine:[137]

- He ate chicken before every game (seriously, every single game).
- He ran the same route to the ballpark.
- He took batting practice at exactly 5:17 p.m.
- He drew the Hebrew word "chai" (meaning "life") in the dirt before each at-bat.

For Boggs, #26 was assuredly a talisman—a lucky charm that anchored a carefully constructed routine designed to maintain success.

Jason Terry: #31—The Pajamas of Power

Jason Terry didn't just believe in superstition—he *slept* in it.

The night before every game, Terry wore the official shorts of the opposing team to bed. He acquired authentic NBA shorts from every franchise and matched them to his schedule, believing that sleeping in the enemy's colors gave him a psychological edge. It wasn't just quirky—it was sacred. A ritual of mental dominance before the ball was ever tipped.

Terry ate chicken before every game. His headband and high socks had to be just right. And if he missed consecutive shots in the first quarter, he changed shoes at the next intermission—no questions asked.[138]

When Terry reunited with #31—his college number from Arizona, where he'd won a national title—it became the final piece of his superstition puzzle. He wore it with four NBA teams, most memorably with Dallas, where he won a championship in 2011. Every three-pointer, every Jet-arm celebration, fed the ritual.

For Terry, superstition wasn't a quirk—it was a system, and #31 was the thread that held it all together.

Roger Clemens: #21—Keeping the Baseball Mojo

Roger Clemens proved that sometimes the magic isn't the number—it's what you do while wearing it. Early in his career, he wore #21. With the Yankees, #21 was taken, so he switched to #12, then #22.

Different numbers. Same dominance. Why? Because Clemens' true superstitions had nothing to do with digits on his back. His pregame rituals remained constant regardless of the number: stretching routines, glove adjustments, and—most memorably—touching Babe Ruth's head in Monument Park before every Yankee Stadium start.[139]

With seven Cy Young Awards across multiple numbers, Clemens proved that superstition lives in the mindset, not the digits.

Jason Giambi: #25—When the Ritual Beats the Number

Jason Giambi wore #25 consistently across five teams, but the number wasn't the magic. When he fell into hitting slumps, Giambi wore a gold thong under his uniform for good luck. His teammates started borrowing it. It became clubhouse legend.[140]

For Giambi, the number stayed the same; the ritual was what mattered. Sometimes the strangest rituals work. The numbers change; the thong remains.

Derrick Rose: #1—The Alter Ego Theory

Derrick Rose wore #1 as a kid playing basketball, switched to #25 in high school and #23 at the University of Memphis, but returned to #1 in the NBA.

This wasn't about being the #1 overall pick in 2008—it was about unlocking something psychological.

"When I played for my club, I was more aggressive—I was more dominant," Rose said. "But when I played for my high school, I was more passive, getting my teammates involved. When I made it to the league, I kind of wanted that alter ego to be who I wanted to be throughout the whole league."[26]

For Rose, #1 wasn't about being the best player. It was about becoming the best version of himself. In a sport where belief can be as powerful as talent, Rose found his alter ego in a single digit.

The #13 Superstition:
Fear, Policy, and Defiance

In many cultures, #13 is considered unlucky. Hotels skip the 13th floor. People avoid sitting in row 13 on airplanes. *Friday the 13th* is an entire horror franchise. In sports, this superstition has taken many forms—from organizational policy to personal defiance.

Mike Cammalleri: #13—Not Only Taboo, but Forbidden

Mike Cammalleri wore #13 throughout his NHL career with the Kings, Flames, and Canadiens. It was his number, his identity on the ice. But when he signed with the New Jersey Devils in 2014, he couldn't have it.

The Devils banned #13 from the franchise's inception. Owner John McMullen believed the number brought bad luck, and when he sold the team in 2000, GM Lou Lamoriello maintained the ban. For 33 years, no Devils player wore #13. It didn't matter what a player wanted—organizational superstition overruled personal preference.

So Cammalleri wore #23 instead. For a full season, he played without the number that had been part of his identity for years.

In 2015, Ray Shero replaced Lamoriello as GM. The ban was lifted.

Cammalleri immediately switched back to #13, becoming the first player in Devils franchise history to wear it. After decades of institutional fear, the curse was broken—not by tragedy, but by a simple change in management philosophy.[141]

While certain organizations feared #13, some athletes saw opportunity in the superstition.

Wilt Chamberlain: #13—Bad Luck for Opponents

Wilt Chamberlain chose #13 specifically because people considered it unlucky. He was superstitious in reverse—he figured if everyone thought it was bad luck, maybe that meant it would be good luck for him.

When asked if he believed his jersey number was unlucky, Chamberlain quipped: "Yeah, for my opponents."[142]

Case in point: he scored 100 points in a single game wearing it.

Alex Morgan: #13—Making Unlucky Lucky

Alex Morgan took the same approach when she joined the United States Women's National Soccer Team. She didn't just accept #13— she embraced it, turning superstition on its head and making the "unlucky" number a symbol of fearlessness and success.

"We always told ourselves that when we got old and rich we would have a hotel called *The Lucky 13*, with every floor numbered 13a, 13b, 13c," Morgan recalled. "It was something we joked about, the ridiculousness of people thinking a simple number was unlucky. So I thought, 'I'm going to take it!' I've never seen any unluckiness in this number, and it's done great things for me."[143]

Morgan wore #13 through World Cup victories, Olympic gold medals, and a career that made her one of the most recognizable athletes in the world. Like Wilt Chamberlain before her, Morgan proved that the best way to defeat a superstition is to wear it proudly and win anyway.

Those digits became her brand: bold, defiant, unapologetic. She didn't wear #13 despite the superstition—she wore it because of it.

The Devils banned it. Wilt and Morgan claimed it. The same digits organizations feared became, in the right hands, weapons of psychological warfare.

Cultural Superstitions Around the World

Superstitions about numbers aren't just Western phenomena. Across cultures, certain digits carry deep meaning that shapes how athletes choose—and avoid—their numbers.

Number 4 in Asia: The Death Number

In Japan, China, and Korea, the number 4 is considered deeply unlucky because it sounds similar to the word for "death" in several Asian languages.[144]

This belief has seeped into sports culture:

- Some Japanese baseball teams avoid assigning #4 to players.
- Stadium seating sometimes omits row or seat number 4.
- Athletes may request different numbers to avoid the cultural taboo.

The superstition runs so deep that in Japanese baseball, few star players willingly wear #4, and those who do are often seen as defying tradition. Cultural beliefs shape not just athlete choice but fan experience itself.

Number 7: The Universal Lucky Digit

Number 7 carries prestige and is considered lucky in many cultures worldwide. In sports, it's often given to standout players:[145]

- In soccer, #7 is revered, worn by stars like George Best, David Beckham, and Cristiano Ronaldo.

- In rugby, #7 denotes a dynamic, influential position.
- In Western sports generally, #7 is sought after for confidence and perceived luck.

The cultural weight of #7 makes it one of the most coveted numbers across sports.

Number 8 in Chinese Culture: The Wealth Number

In Chinese culture, the number 8 is considered highly auspicious due to its phonetic similarity to the word for wealth and prosperity.

Athletes in Chinese leagues have been known to pay substantial amounts to secure this number, viewing it as a symbol of good fortune. The 2008 Beijing Olympics opened on 08/08/08 at 8:08 PM—no accident.[146]

In sports—especially in China—#8 isn't just a number. It's a statement of ambition and success.

Mookie Betts and #50: The Anti-Superstition

While some athletes embrace #13 to defy superstition, Mookie Betts took a similar approach with #50. His reasoning was beautifully simple:

"That's why I keep No. 50: because no one wants it."[147]

Rather than picking a flashy or traditional number, Betts embraced a non-traditional choice and made it his own. He became one of baseball's biggest stars wearing a number few players select—not because it's unlucky, but because it's outside the usual range of star numbers.

Betts proved that it doesn't matter what number you wear. What matters is what you do while wearing it.

From Larry Walker's obsession with threes to Jason Terry sleeping in enemy shorts, from the Devils banning #13 for 33 years to Wilt Chamberlain scoring 100 points while wearing it, these rituals reveal something fundamental about competition: athletes claim control wherever they can find it.

They can't control everything—the randomness of a bounce, the judgment of a referee, or the outcome of every shot—but they can shape their routine, their ritual, and when possible, their number.

Whether it's superstition or psychology, luck or mindset, these numbers become anchors in the chaos—small pieces of certainty in an uncertain game.

CHAPTER 7

Guided by Faith

Superstition and faith share common ground—both involve belief in forces beyond what's visible. But where Larry Walker's threes were personal ritual, the numbers in this chapter represent something larger: testimony. These numbers reference scripture, honor the Trinity, mark spiritual milestones, or commemorate moments when faith became everything. They're worn not for luck or legacy, but as expressions of belief—alignment with something greater than the game itself.

The Trinity: #3

In Christian faith, the number 3 represents the Holy Trinity—the Father, the Son, and the Holy Spirit. For athletes of faith, wearing #3 is a way to carry that belief with them into every game.

Dwyane Wade: #3—A Daily Reminder

Dwyane Wade chose #3 throughout most of his Hall of Fame career because it represents the Holy Trinity. For Wade, a devout Christian, the number wasn't just about basketball—it was about who he played for and why.[148]

Every time he stepped on the court, #3 was a daily anchor that his gifts came from something greater than himself. It grounded him, humbled him, and gave him purpose beyond the scoreboard.

Over time, #3 wove itself through Wade's career in remarkable ways. He led Marquette to the Final Four in 2003, was drafted in 2003, and won his first championship and Finals MVP three seasons later. By the time he retired, he'd won three NBA championships—each one a testament that the number he chose had followed him through his defining moments.[110]

Russell Wilson: #3 and #16—John 3:16

Russell Wilson wore #16 at NC State in honor of John 3:16, one of the most well-known verses in the Bible: "For God so loved the world that he gave his one and only Son, that whoever believes in him shall not perish but have eternal life."

When Wilson joined the Seattle Seahawks, #16 was already taken. So he chose #3—keeping the reference to John 3:16 alive by wearing the chapter number instead of the verse number.[149]

For Wilson, #3 represents both the Trinity and the verse that defines his faith—a number that carries double meaning every time he takes the field.[150]

The Biblical Number of Completion: #7

In the Bible, 7 is considered the number of completeness and perfection. God created the world in seven days. In the book of Revelation, there are seven seals, seven trumpets, seven churches. The number appears throughout scripture as a symbol of divine wholeness.

For athletes of faith, wearing #7 is a way to acknowledge that perfection and to keep God close.

Jeremy Lin: #7 and #17—Keeping God Close

Jeremy Lin chose his number through faith. He often spoke of seven as biblically significant, seeing it as a way of keeping God close wherever he went.

Lin has worn both #7 and #17 throughout his career, weaving that symbolism into his identity. During "Linsanity"—his breakout stretch with the New York Knicks in 2012—Lin wore #17, and his faith was as visible as his game. He openly credited God for his success, kneeling in prayer after games and speaking about how basketball was just one part of his calling.

As Lin explained, "The number 1 was kind of to represent me and the number 7 was to represent God."[110] For him, the number was a constant reminder that basketball was only part of a larger purpose—and that his talent was a gift to be used for something greater.

Kevin Durant: #7—Live for Eternity

Kevin Durant chose #7 when he joined the Brooklyn Nets because it represents completion in the Bible—God rested on the seventh day after creating Heaven and Earth. For a player who had worn #35 his entire career, the switch carried profound significance.

"The Bible both pumps me up and balances me to play my best, but it also tells me more about the Lord and how I can live for Him and what all He has done for me," Durant explained.[151] The decision to switch numbers carried spiritual weight.

Durant even added a tattoo above his wrist that says "live for eternity," explaining that God says that's where we're all headed, and he wants to start living with that eternal perspective now.

Though his time in Brooklyn didn't unfold as planned, Durant continues wearing #7 with the Houston Rockets—perhaps lining up career completion with biblical completion, the divine perfection that comes when creation is finished and blessed.

Scripture as Identity

Some athletes don't just choose numbers inspired by faith—they choose numbers that are scripture. Specific verses that have shaped their lives, guided their decisions, or given them strength in difficult times.

Curtis Martin: #28—Deuteronomy 28

Hall of Fame running back Curtis Martin chose #28 because his pastor talked to him about Deuteronomy 28, which talks about blessings for obedience.

When Martin started his college career, he was given #29. When that number wasn't available in the NFL, he consulted with his pastor about the available options (26–28). His pastor pointed him to Deuteronomy 28.

"So I took the number," Martin said, "and Deuteronomy 28 became my only ritual before every game."[152]

For Martin, #28 wasn't just a number. It was a promise. A quiet signal that faithfulness leads to blessing, and that his success on the field was connected to his obedience off it.

Cameron Johnson: #23—Psalm 23

NBA forward Cameron Johnson's connection to #23 is deeply personal and multilayered. His middle name is Jordan, and he grew up watching Michael Jordan videos. But the number means far more than basketball.

"There is no number that has the tie to me as 23 does," Johnson explained, "because of Psalm 23, and because my middle name is Jordan and I watched Jordan videos growing up like none other."[153]

His grandmother—whom he describes as "a prayer warrior to the fullest extent"—told his father to recite Psalm 23 before important events. His father instilled it in him, and now, before every game when the national anthem is played, Johnson recites it.

For Johnson, #23 isn't about emulating Michael Jordan—though he admired him. It's about carrying his grandmother's prayers, his father's wisdom, and the comfort of scripture with him onto the court.

Nana Osafo-Mensah: #31—31 Chapters in Proverbs

Notre Dame linebacker Nana Osafo-Mensah wore #31 because there are 31 chapters in the Book of Proverbs. For a player of deep religious conviction, the number connected him to scripture's wisdom—daily guidance for living righteously.

Osafo-Mensah leaned heavily on his faith after losing his best friend Ty Jordan to a tragic accident. In those dark moments, Proverbs became more than ancient text—it became a lifeline, offering wisdom for grief, strength for perseverance, and hope for tomorrow.

"Faith is something that can get you out of dark places. People go through a lot of situations out of their control, but they can really stay strong in their faith," he explained.[154]

Every time he wore #31, he carried all 31 chapters with him—a complete book of wisdom reminding him that even in loss, faith lights the way forward. The number became ritual: before each game, he would kneel at the 31-yard line in prayer.

Biblical Significance

Beyond specific verses, some athletes find meaning in the broader stories of scripture—tales of unexpected heroes and divine appointments that reframe their own journeys.

Kirk Cousins: #8—The Eighth Son

As Kirk Cousins waited anxiously during the 2012 NFL Draft, watching quarterback after quarterback get selected ahead of him, his father, Pastor Don Cousins, offered him a different perspective.

Kirk slipped all the way to the fourth round as the eighth quarterback selected. It felt like a disappointment, a sign that NFL teams didn't believe in him.

But his father reminded him of the Old Testament story of David. When the prophet Samuel came to anoint a new king, Jesse presented his seven oldest sons, expecting one to be chosen.

But God rejected all seven. Finally, Jesse called in his youngest son, David—the one no one expected. And David was chosen to be king.

Don reminded Kirk that he was the eighth quarterback chosen—like David, the eighth son, overlooked by men but chosen by God to become Israel's most revered king. Cousins later made clear that this didn't mean he expected to be "king of the NFL"—only that the story helped him see his draft position through a lens of purpose rather than failure.[155]

Cousins wore #8 with Washington and Minnesota, proving that being overlooked didn't mean being forgotten. When he joined Atlanta where #8 was taken, he chose #18—still carrying an 8, still carrying David's story, the eighth son who became king.

Robbie Chosen: #12—The Chosen Twelve

After reading the book of Matthew and feeling a true calling, Robbie Anderson legally changed his name to Robbie Chosen. He then made another switch when he joined the Washington Commanders. He chose #12.

While Chosen hasn't publicly explained the choice, the symbolism resonates: "Chosen 12" on the back of a jersey evokes the 12 disciples—the original twelve chosen by Jesus to spread his message. For a player who has been reborn through Christ, the name-and-number combination became a visible statement of faith.[156]

When Faith Takes Control

Kurt Warner: #13—Faith Trumps Superstition

While some fear #13 and others accept it, Kurt Warner embraced it like a calling. Warner was one of just five players in the entire NFL wearing #13 in 2008, and he chose it deliberately.

Warner stated that his life is never dictated by superstitions and that his faith comes first: "If you believe that God is in control, there is no reason to believe in superstitions."[157]

With the Rams, Warner chose #13 to show his disdain for superstition and anything that didn't align with his faith. Every snap, every throw, every game became a walking testimony—proof that faith in God trumps fear of bad luck.

For Warner, who went from stocking grocery store shelves to Super Bowl MVP, #13 wasn't unlucky—it was liberating. It represented the freedom that comes from trusting that your life isn't governed by chance, but by providence. While others avoided the number out of fear, Warner wore it as armor—a visible reminder that when God is in control, no number can curse you.

Sandy León: #12—Twelve Minutes From Breath to Life

For catcher Sandy León, #12 doesn't represent a Bible verse or symbolic number. It represents the 12 longest minutes of his life—when faith was all he had left.

On August 18, 2020, León's 15-month-old daughter Nahomy fell into the family pool while he was away with the team. His wife, Liliana, discovered her unconscious and began CPR while praying for a miracle. León watched the scene unfold in horror via his home security camera.

Nahomy had been without oxygen for 12 minutes. Doctors prepared the family for the worst. Twelve minutes is an eternity for a brain without oxygen. Survival seemed impossible. Full recovery was unthinkable.

But León and his wife prayed. Against every medical expectation, Nahomy not only survived—she regained full body and brain function. Doctors still can't explain it.

In 2023, when León joined the Texas Rangers he chose to wear #12 as a daily reflection of those 12 minutes—when his daughter hovered between life and death, and faith became his only lifeline. Each time he buttons up that jersey, he says a prayer of thanks that those twelve minutes didn't take his daughter away.

"I feel blessed and grateful every time I go onto the field knowing that she's normal and nothing happened," he said. "She has no idea, but it's so special for me."[158]

For these athletes, jersey numbers aren't about luck or legacy—they're about alignment with something greater. Whether honoring the Trinity, marking scripture, or remembering twelve miraculous minutes, these numbers transform jerseys into testaments. They're worn not for glory, but for gratitude. Not for the crowd, but for the Creator.

CHAPTER 8

When the Number Chooses You

Not every celebrated number starts with intention. Sometimes there's no tribute, no superstition, no carefully crafted personal brand. Sometimes the equipment manager just hands you what's left, or you take what's available, or you end up with a number because the guy in front of you took the one before it.

And then you go out and make it matter.

When Fate Wore a Number

Some assignments feel accidental at first—until you look closer. These athletes received their numbers through random chance, but what happened next felt almost predestined. The symmetry between number and achievement became so perfect that fans wondered if the universe had a plan all along.

Pete Maravich: #44—Meant to Be

When Pete Maravich joined LSU's varsity basketball team in 1967, he was assigned jersey #44. At the time, it was just a number handed out by the equipment staff—nothing special, nothing planned.

But over the next three seasons, something almost mystical happened.

Maravich averaged an astonishing 44.2 points per game—still the highest career scoring average in NCAA history. The symmetry between his number and his stats felt prophetic, as if the number had chosen him from the start.

He carried #44 into the NBA with the Atlanta Hawks, where his dazzling ball-handling and scoring ability made him one of the league's most exciting players. The Hawks retired #44 in his honor, cementing its place in franchise history.[159]

When Maravich was traded to the New Orleans Jazz in 1974, he made a change—switching to #7. The move symbolized a fresh start in a city that had embraced him since his college days at LSU. He wore #7 for the remainder of his career, and that number was later retired by both the Jazz and the New Orleans Pelicans.

Today, both numbers—#44 and #7—are forever linked to Maravich's legacy. One represents the record-breaking college phenom; the other, the NBA icon who brought flair and artistry to the game. Together, they tell the story of greatness that couldn't be contained by a single number.

Red Grange: #77—The Galloping Ghost and "Ol' 77"

Red Grange, known as "The Galloping Ghost," ranks among football's earliest superstars. He rose to fame at the University of Illinois in the 1920s, dazzling crowds with his speed and agility. In one remarkable game against Michigan, he scored five touchdowns and became a national sensation overnight.

Grange wore #77 for the Fighting Illini and continued wearing the double-sevens when he turned pro with the Chicago Bears. The number became inseparably linked to his name—fans called him "Ol' 77," and the digits became part of football lore.

So how did one of the most recognizable numbers in early football history come to be?

Years later, when asked about his jersey number, Grange gave a beautifully simple answer: "The guy in front of me got number 76; the guy behind me got 78."[160]

That's it. No symbolism. No tribute. Just the luck of the lineup.

Red Grange didn't choose #77. But he made it immortal.

Cal Ripken Jr.: #8—The Ironman and the Infinity Symbol

Cal Ripken Jr. wore #8 from the day he broke into the major leagues with the Baltimore Orioles. It was the number he was given, and it became forever tied to his ironman streak—2,632 consecutive games played, a record that may never be broken.[161]

Ripken didn't seek the spotlight with his number choice. He took the field every single day, and #8 became a monument to consistency, durability, and quiet excellence.

A fitting coincidence: when the number 8 is turned on its side, it resembles the mathematical symbol for infinity (∞). The number wasn't assigned with any symbolic intent, but sometimes random assignments create their own poetry.

Ripken made #8 immortal by answering the call. Every. Single. Day.

The Reluctant Legends

Not every legendary number starts with enthusiasm. Some athletes received their digits with indifference, others with anxiety. They didn't ask for these numbers, didn't particularly want them, and certainly didn't imagine they'd become noteworthy wearing them. But they did anyway.

Joe Namath: #12—Broadway Joe

Joe Namath's #12 wasn't a carefully chosen talisman—it was simply handed to him as a rookie with the New York Jets in 1965. There was no deep meaning, no family connection, no tribute.

As "Broadway Joe" delivered a Super Bowl guarantee before Super Bowl III and then backed it up with an upset win over the Baltimore Colts, #12 became woven into New York sports lore.

Namath's #12 became synonymous with swagger, confidence, and the ability to talk the talk and walk the walk. It wasn't about the number— it was about the man wearing it.[162]

Cristiano Ronaldo: #7—The Reluctant Icon

Cristiano Ronaldo is one of soccer's most influential players, and his #7 has become a global brand. "CR7" appears on merchandise, social media handles, and marketing campaigns worldwide.

When Ronaldo joined Manchester United in 2003 as an 18-year-old, the #7 shirt was assigned to him. He was unsure if he was ready for such a responsibility.

The number carried enormous weight at United—legends like Bryan Robson, George Best, Eric Cantona, and David Beckham had all worn it before him. Taking over from Beckham, a local hero who had just left for Real Madrid, felt like a monumental task.

But Sir Alex Ferguson's confidence in him made the difference. Ronaldo accepted the storied number and made his debut wearing #7 against Bolton Wanderers in the 2003–04 Premier League opener at Old Trafford.

What began as an intimidating assignment soon became his identity. Over time, he didn't just wear #7—he transformed it into "CR7," one of the most recognizable brands in sports history.[163]

Pau Gasol: #16—The Rookie Number That Became a Legacy

When Pau Gasol first joined FC Barcelona's youth academy, he didn't choose his jersey number—it chose him. In Spain's youth system, established players wore numbers 4 through 15, while newcomers were assigned #16 or #17. As the new kid, Gasol was handed #16.

It was meant to be temporary, a rookie's number that he'd eventually trade for something more prestigious. But Gasol kept winning while wearing it. The number became his good luck charm, and he never wanted to change it.

He wore #16 at Barcelona, where he won Spanish championships. He wore it with Memphis, where he became the first non-American to be named NBA Rookie of the Year. He wore it with the Lakers, where he won two NBA championships alongside Kobe Bryant.

What began as a rookie assignment—a number that essentially meant "you're new here"—became one of the most respected numbers in basketball. When the Lakers retired #16 in 2023, they celebrated what happens when you take what you're given and make it unforgettable.[164]

Barry Sanders: #20—The Lions' Legacy

Barry Sanders' #20 with the Detroit Lions became a signature of highlight-reel runs, impossible cuts, and unmatched agility. He didn't pick #20 for superstition or tribute—it was the number suggested to him by coach Wayne Fontes, and he embraced it.

Fontes proposed the idea because #20 had previously been worn by Billy Sims, the Lions' star running back of the early 1980s. Sanders admired Sims from their shared connection at the University of Oklahoma and was excited to carry on the tradition. What began as an assignment quickly became a tribute, linking Sanders to Sims and to the legacy of Lions greats.

Sanders revitalized #20 through pure performance. Every juke, every spin move, every jaw-dropping touchdown added to its legend. Today, the Lions honor #20 three times over: Sanders, Sims, and Hall of Fame cornerback Lem Barney all wore it, tying generations of Detroit greats together. After Sanders retired, the Lions retired #20 for good—a lasting monument to excellence.[165]

Emmitt Smith: #22—The Cowboys' Inheritance

Emmitt Smith's #22 followed a similar path of accidental inheritance. He wore it at the University of Florida largely because it was available—no tribute, no deeper meaning.

When Smith arrived in Dallas and found #22 open, he claimed it—unknowingly stepping into the legacy of Bob Hayes, the Cowboys legend who had worn the same number and blazed a trail of speed and greatness years earlier.

Smith didn't choose #22 to honor Hayes. But over 15 seasons, he made it a benchmark for NFL rushing excellence, becoming the league's all-time leading rusher while wearing a number that connected two generations of Cowboys greatness.[166]

Like Sanders before him, Smith was handed a number with history—and turned it into legend.

Zeros to Heroes

Some athletes don't get a choice. They arrive at a team, and all the coveted numbers are taken. What's left is a number nobody else wanted—often zero. For most, it could have been a mark of insignificance. For a few, it became a blank canvas. They made it their own, turning assignment into identity and leaving a mark on history that no superstar number could overshadow.

Robert Parish: #00—From Last to Legendary

Robert Parish didn't set out to define #00. As a junior high player, jerseys were handed out based on talent: the best players picked first, and the leftovers went to the rest. Parish, then the weakest player, was left with #00.[167]

What began as a symbol of being last became his lifelong number. He wore it at Centenary College of Louisiana and carried it into the NBA, where he anchored the Boston Celtics dynasty of the 1980s.

Over time, the double zero came to symbolize his durability and consistency—fitting for the "Chief," who played more games than anyone in NBA history. Parish proved that greatness isn't always assigned; sometimes it's claimed.

Kevin Love: #0—Zero Comes Full Circle

Kevin Love didn't arrive in Cleveland with #0 in mind. He'd worn #42 since his UCLA days, a number tied to his basketball identity. But when he joined the Cavaliers in 2014, #42 was retired in honor of Nate Thurmond. Other numbers didn't feel right.

Then Love remembered a moment from childhood. "I remembered showing up to a game in Beaverton, Oregon, with a brand new team," he said. "I was the last guy to the gym for the tournament, and there was the zero for me."[110]

That childhood leftover became a choice, a reminder of origin and opportunity. Number 0 wasn't about ego or legacy—it was about starting fresh, owning what was left, and turning absence into presence. Cavaliers GM David Griffin later pointed out another layer: the "O" also stood for Ohio, where Love would win a championship alongside LeBron James and Kyrie Irving.

Jackie Robinson: #42
The Number That Changed Everything

When Jackie Robinson broke Major League Baseball's color barrier in 1947, he was assigned #42 by the Brooklyn Dodgers equipment manager. At the time, players rarely chose their numbers—you just took what was available.

Robinson transformed that random assignment into a worldwide symbol of courage, perseverance, and equality.

Robinson's impact extended beyond baseball. NBA Hall of Famer James Worthy and two-time All-Star Jerry Stackhouse both chose to wear #42 specifically to honor Robinson's legacy.

Worthy's father, a huge baseball fan, convinced him to wear the number with the Lakers, telling him it would be a tribute to Robinson's courage and groundbreaking achievements. After playing his entire 12-year career in Los Angeles, Worthy's #42 was retired by the Lakers in 1995.[168]

Like Worthy, Jerry Stackhouse also made #42 a career-long commitment.

Stackhouse, who grew up in North Carolina and understood the significance of breaking barriers, wore #42 throughout his 18-year career across eight different franchises. He symbolically ended his career in Brooklyn—where Robinson's journey began—still wearing #42.[169]

What began as a random equipment room assignment in Brooklyn became a number that athletes across sports deliberately sought out—proof that Robinson had transformed #42 from coincidence into conscious tribute.

In 1997, on the 50th anniversary of Robinson's debut, MLB retired #42 across all teams—the only number to receive such an honor. Every player who wore it before the retirement was allowed to keep it, and the last to wear it was Yankees closer Mariano Rivera, who carried it with pride until his retirement in 2013.

Now, every April 15th—Jackie Robinson Day—every player in Major League Baseball wears #42.[170]

A number that started as a simple equipment room assignment became a symbol that transcends sports.

The Assignment Hall of Fame

Here are some more notable athletes who made their numbers unforgettable, even though they didn't pick them:

Brett Favre: #4—Favre wore #10 in high school, but when he arrived at Southern Mississippi, the equipment manager told him, "To tell you the truth, the only number we have left for you is number four."

Favre's response? "Hell, I was just happy to have any jersey at all."[171]

The most recognizable #4 in football history was just what was left in the equipment room. Favre carried it into the NFL, where it became a symbol of fearless, gunslinger-style quarterback play.

Nolan Ryan: #34—Ryan wore several numbers early in his career, including #30 and #31. But when he arrived in Houston, both numbers were already taken.

"It was a new ballclub, and I didn't want to take somebody else's number," Ryan said. "I took whatever was available, and 34 was the closest."[172]

He immortalized #34, keeping it through his years with the Astros and Texas Rangers. Seven no-hitters later, #34 wasn't just a number—it was intimidation personified.

Oscar Robertson: #14—In high school, Robertson's #12 jersey was simply assigned. At the University of Cincinnati, #12 was taken, so he took #14, and it stuck. He wore it throughout his pro career with the Cincinnati Royals, turning #14 into a mark of complete basketball excellence—he's still the only player to average a triple-double for an entire season.[173]

Hakeem Olajuwon: #34—Olajuwon entered the University of Houston wanting to wear #33 in honor of Kareem Abdul-Jabbar. But #33 was already taken, so he chose the next available option: #34. He kept #34 when he entered the NBA and joined the Houston Rockets, where his footwork, post moves, and championships turned it into a number every big man respected.[172]

Earl Campbell: #34—Campbell wore #20 in college at the University of Texas, but when he entered the NFL and joined the Houston Oilers, #20 was taken. Campbell later recalled how he got #34:

"Bum Phillips and I were walking to the locker room, and we passed the basket where you would pull your uniform off for it to be washed the next day. We saw number 34, and Bum said, 'Hey, what about this one?' I said, 'That's fine. The jersey doesn't get you in the end zone.' Bum said, 'Atta boy.'"[172]

Campbell's #34 was retired by the Houston Oilers in 1987 and remains retired by the franchise, now the Tennessee Titans.

Pelé: #10—Here's the irony behind soccer's premiere number: Pelé didn't choose it. He didn't even ask for it.

At the 1958 World Cup, Brazil's federation submitted its roster to FIFA without identifying jersey numbers. Tournament officials randomly assigned them, and the 17-year-old Pelé was handed #10. At the time, the number carried no special meaning—Pelé himself later said, "Nobody thought that it was important to wear the No. 10 … it coincidentally dropped to me to wear at the World Cup."[174]

What followed was history: Pelé scored six goals, including a semifinal hat trick and two in the final, as Brazil won its first World Cup. From then on, he refused to wear any other number—donning #10 for Santos for the next 16 years, for Brazil in three World Cups, and even for the New York Cosmos.

What Pelé did in those few weeks transformed #10 from a random assignment into a global symbol. He didn't inherit a legacy—he created one. Every playmaker who's worn #10 since, from Maradona to Messi, is walking in the path that teenage Pelé carved out of sheer brilliance and accidental numbering.

Sometimes the most enduring legacies begin with randomness. Pelé wasn't interested in #10, but he ended up making it soccer's most iconic number.

Mike Trout: #27—Mike Trout was assigned #27 when he joined the Angels. When asked on social media if #27 was his choice, Trout responded simply: "No, but when I got here I wasn't trying to ask for a different number."[175]

Over time, the number became linked to his combination of athleticism, baseball IQ, and humility. His consistent MVP-caliber performance has made #27 a modern baseball symbol of all-around excellence.

Mariano Rivera: #42—Though #42 is retired league-wide for Jackie Robinson and Mariano Rivera was the last player to wear it in his honor, it wasn't initially planned that way.

When Rivera joined the Yankees in 1995, Yankees clubhouse manager Nick Priore initially gave him #58, though he never appeared in a game wearing it. Priore later switched Rivera to #42, which the pitcher wore in each of the 1,115 regular-season games—plus 96 postseason contests—of his Hall of Fame career. "I didn't ask for it," Rivera said. "It was given to me."[176]

Rivera transformed #42 into a symbol of calm dominance and postseason mastery. Every time he jogged in from the bullpen to the sound of *Enter Sandman*, #42 meant the game was over.

Bill Belichick's Rookie Number System: Earn Your Identity

For years, the New England Patriots had one of the most unusual traditions in professional sports: rookies didn't get to choose their jersey numbers. They didn't even get numbers that fit their positions.

Bill Belichick assigned them temporary numbers in the 50s and 60s—in order of when they were drafted.

The first pick wore #50. The second wore #51. And so on, marching through the 50s until preseason arrived and they "earned" the right to wear a real number.

It led to absurd sights: Mac Jones, the team's first-round quarterback in 2021, wore #50 at training camp—typically a linebacker's number. Running back Sony Michel wore #51, wide receiver N'Keal Harry wore #50, and cornerback Christian Gonzalez wore #50.

When asked about the system, Belichick was typically matter-of-fact: "I don't think the numbers are the most important thing we do right now. We're trying to learn how to play football."[177]

The tradition wasn't just about organization—it was psychological. Belichick wanted rookies uncomfortable, focused, hungry to prove themselves worthy of a real identity within the team.

The practice ended when Belichick left the Patriots after the 2023 season. New head coach Jerod Mayo assigned rookies their actual numbers from day one in 2024—quarterback Drake Maye got his #10, receivers got numbers in the teens and 20s, and the uncomfortable 50s and 60s disappeared.

Red Grange stood in line and got #77. Pelé was randomly assigned #10. Mariano Rivera was handed #42. None of them chose their numbers—but all of them proved that greatness isn't about the number you pick. It's about what you do while wearing it.

The most memorable numbers in sports history often exist because someone gave you whatever was left, you were too young to ask for something different, or you showed up last and took what nobody else wanted.

Players can't always choose the numbers they wear, but they can choose what they do while wearing them.

CHAPTER 9

Let the Bidding Begin!

Red Grange didn't choose #77. Pelé didn't choose #10. But both made those numbers immortal through performance. Others, however, fought harder for their digits—and paid dearly for them. When a player arrives at a team and the number they want is already taken, it can spark negotiation, persuasion, or even an outright standoff.

Some exchanges are quiet. Others become part of sports lore. Some cost a case of beer. Others get wildly creative.

And some? Some never happened at all.

Charlie Whitehurst and Brett Kern: #6 The Arm-Wrestling Hoax

When Charlie Whitehurst joined the Tennessee Titans in 2014, he hoped to keep wearing #6, the number he'd worn since his rookie year in 2006. But punter Brett Kern already had it.

The two players offered a story that was too good to be true: they settled the number dispute with an arm-wrestling match, and Kern won. Whitehurst, nicknamed "Clipboard Jesus," reportedly lost both the number and his dignity in a locker-room showdown.

The tale gained traction quickly. Sports blogs ran with it. Fans quoted *Over the Top*. It was weird, wonderful, and just believable enough.

But it wasn't real.

Whitehurst and Kern had fabricated the story as a prank. There was no arm-wrestling match. No dramatic loss. Just two teammates having fun with the media.[178]

The hoax was harmless, but it highlighted something deeper: players have done far stranger things for jersey numbers—and those stories are real.

The Humble Approach: Patience and Respect

Not every negotiation involves money or drama. Sometimes the best strategy is simply to wait your turn and earn respect through performance.

Jalen Brunson: #11—From Circumstance to Choice

When Jalen Brunson signed with the New York Knicks in 2022, he walked into a dilemma. His preferred jersey number—#13, which he'd worn with the Dallas Mavericks as a tribute to Steve Nash—was already claimed by veteran Evan Fournier.

His second choice? Number 1, the number he wore while winning two national championships at Villanova. That was taken too, by Obi Toppin.

Rather than negotiate or make demands, Brunson chose #11—a number that was simply available.

"I wanted to earn things," he explained. "I didn't want to do anything to show status or anything like that."

It was a humble move for a player who easily could have flexed his status as a prized free-agent signing. But that's Brunson's style: let your game do the talking.

Over time, #11 became part of his identity in New York. As he emerged as a franchise cornerstone and All-Star, leading the Knicks back to playoff relevance, Brunson grew attached to it—especially seeing young fans wearing his jersey around Madison Square Garden.

Then something interesting happened: both Fournier and Toppin were traded. Suddenly, #13 and #1 were available again.

Brunson could have switched back. He could have reclaimed the numbers that meant something to him before New York. But he didn't.

"I stuck to it … seeing little kids wear No. 11 around the Garden, it's a special feeling and I didn't want to change my number," Brunson said.[179]

Now, #11 is more than a fallback—it's a symbol of humility, leadership, and the rise of a new Knicks era. Brunson may not have chosen it at first, but the number chose him.

DeMarvion Overshown: #0—Agent Zero Waits His Turn

For Dallas Cowboys linebacker DeMarvion Overshown, jersey #0 is more than a digit—it's a symbol of pride, history, and personal identity.

Overshown made headlines in 2025 when he became the first player in Cowboys franchise history to wear the number—a moment he called a "badge of honor."

His connection to #0 began in college, where he was the first to wear it at the University of Texas after the NCAA approved the number in 2020. The number quickly became part of his brand, earning him the nickname "Agent 0" among fans and teammates.

When the NFL changed its rules in 2023 to allow players to wear #0, Overshown had his sights set on it. But he faced a challenge: he couldn't have it. Not yet.

Initially, veteran safety Jayron Kearse was slated to wear it. Rumors also swirled that the Cowboys were reserving the number for their mascot, Rowdy, who wears #00. So Overshown wore #13 instead and quietly earned his place on the roster.

After a breakout 2024 season in which he led the team in tackles and became one of the defense's most dynamic playmakers, Overshown finally got the green light.

"As soon as they changed the policy where you can now wear No. 0 in the NFL, I just knew it was meant to be," he said. "To say I'm the first to wear No. 0 at Texas and the first to do it in Dallas Cowboys history—that's a badge of honor."[180]

Overshown's journey to #0 wasn't about entitlement—it was about patience, performance, and pride. He didn't demand it as a rookie. He earned it through his play.

Now, when he steps on the field, it's not just DeMarvion Overshown—it's Agent 0, a player rewriting history one tackle at a time.

Anthony Edwards: #1 to #5—Three Years of Patience

Anthony Edwards always wanted to wear #5. It's the number he wore in high school, in college at Georgia, and in AAU. But more than that, it's a number that carries profound personal meaning—it honors his mother and grandmother, who both died on the fifth day of the month when he was just 14 years old.

When Edwards entered the NBA and joined the Minnesota Timberwolves, he naturally wanted to continue wearing his signature

#5. Unfortunately, teammate Malik Beasley wore it and didn't want to give it up.

So Edwards wore #1 for his first three seasons in Minnesota, building himself into an All-Star while waiting for his moment. As noted in Chapter 2, #1 also represented his position in the 2020 NBA Draft—a fitting consolation.

Beasley was traded after the 2021–22 season, but #5 still remained unavailable—Kyle Anderson wore it during the 2022–23 season.

Finally, before the 2023–24 season, the opportunity arrived. Anderson preferred #1 anyway, so they swapped. After three years of patience, Edwards finally got his number.

When asked if he'd be better wearing #5 than #1, Edwards responded with a smile: "For sure. A whole different player. Just a lot of athleticism, a lot more dunks. Just, you know, a different level of play because I've got my number on my back now."[181]

For Edwards, the wait wasn't about preference—it was about honoring the two most important women in his life. Some numbers are worth waiting for, no matter how long it takes.

Cristiano Ronaldo: #9 to #7—Waiting for a Legend

When Cristiano Ronaldo made his £80 million move to Real Madrid in 2009, he faced an unexpected obstacle: his traditional #7 wasn't available.

Real Madrid legend Raúl occupied the #7 shirt, a number he had worn with distinction for years. Ronaldo had no choice but to settle for #9, a significant departure from the #7 he had defined at Manchester United as well as Portugal.[182]

Ronaldo didn't complain. He wore #9 professionally, putting together a strong first season with Real Madrid, scoring 33 goals in 35 games. But everyone knew which number he really wanted.

When Raúl joined Schalke in the summer of 2010, Ronaldo immediately reclaimed his beloved #7.

The patience paid off. Wearing #7 at Real Madrid, Ronaldo became the club's all-time leading scorer and won four Champions League titles. The one-year wait was worth it to wear the number that defined his brand and identity.

Kylian Mbappé: #29 to #7—Waiting for His Turn

When Kylian Mbappé joined Paris Saint-Germain in 2017, he wanted to wear #7—a number with prestige and history. But it belonged to Lucas Moura.

So Mbappé wore #29 during his first season, a number with no particular significance. He was professional about it, putting together a stellar debut campaign. He thrived in #29, all the while waiting for the chance to wear #7.

In July 2018, Lucas Moura left PSG to join Tottenham Hotspur. Mbappé immediately switched to #7 for the 2018–19 season.[183]

Those digits became part of his identity in Paris—a symbol of his rise to superstardom. Like Ronaldo before him, Mbappé understood that some numbers are worth waiting for, even if it's just one season.

Ricky Pearsall: #1—A Return to Familiarity

For San Francisco 49ers wide receiver Ricky Pearsall, reclaiming jersey #1 ahead of his second NFL season represented more than a return to his college number—it was a symbol of resilience after a traumatic rookie year defined by injury and a near-fatal shooting. Pearsall had worn #1 during his standout college career at Florida, where he set career highs in receptions, yards, and touchdowns.

When he entered the NFL in 2024, the number was unavailable—claimed by star receiver Deebo Samuel—so Pearsall settled for #14. Despite suffering a gunshot wound before Week 1 and the injuries that followed, he fought back to post 31 catches, 400 yards, and three touchdowns in 11 games.

With Samuel traded to Washington in the offseason, the door opened for Pearsall to reclaim #1 for the 2025–26 season.[184] The switch isn't just about comfort—it's about identity. It's the number he wore when he proved himself a playmaker in college. After surviving the shooting and grinding through injury, reclaiming #1 wasn't just about comfort—it was about reclaiming his identity and proving he belongs.

Chris Webber: #4 to #2 to #4—A Detour and Return

Chris Webber's path back to #4 took an unexpected turn when he was traded to Washington. As a rookie with the Golden State Warriors, he wore his preferred #4 throughout the 1993–94 season.

But when he was traded to the Washington Bullets in November 1994, #4 was unavailable—it belonged to veteran point guard Scott Skiles. Webber settled for #2 during his first season in Washington, a temporary compromise.

After one year, #4 opened up when Skiles joined the Philadelphia 76ers. Webber reclaimed it and wore #4 with the Bullets/Wizards from 1995–98, then carried it to Sacramento, Philadelphia, and back to Golden State.[185]

For Webber, patience meant living with a substitute until the right number returned. And when it did, he seized it.

But not everyone waits. Some players negotiate—and sometimes, the currency isn't what you'd expect.

The Cheap Deals: Beer, Suits, & Golf Clubs

Not every number negotiation breaks the bank. Sometimes the currency is simple, casual, and perfectly fitting for a locker room deal.

The Beer Deal: Mitch Williams and John Kruk for #28

In 1991, John Kruk was a beloved hitter for the Philadelphia Phillies wearing #28. When Mitch Williams joined the team, he wanted #28—the number he had worn throughout much of his career.

Kruk agreed to give it up. The cost? Legend has it: two cases of beer.[186]

Whether or not beer was the official currency, the story became a classic clubhouse anecdote—one that shows the casual, human side of sports negotiations.

Kruk switched to #29. Williams got his beloved #28. And the story lived on as a reminder that sometimes numbers are worth negotiating for—and that in sports, even a jersey number can be traded in small, memorable deals.

The Suit Deal: Steve Garvey and Tim Flannery for #6

When Steve Garvey joined the San Diego Padres in 1983, he found Tim Flannery wearing the coveted #6 that Garvey had worn for 14 seasons with the Los Angeles Dodgers.

Compared to some later deals, Garvey got off fairly cheap: buying Flannery a new suit was all it took. But it wasn't just any suit.

According to Flannery, Garvey offered to buy him any suit in the world that he wanted. His response: "OK, I want a wet suit." An avid surfer, that would suit Flannery just fine.

"But he didn't let it happen," said Flannery. "He made me go to Ralph Lauren and buy a $600 three-piece suit."[187]

Simple. Classy. Done.

A Set of Golf Clubs: Rickey Henderson and Ron Hassey for #24

When Rickey Henderson returned to the Oakland Athletics in June 1989, he had a problem: his preferred number, #24, was occupied by catcher Ron Hassey.

Henderson had worn #24 during his time with the New York Yankees, and he wanted it back. But Hassey wasn't about to just hand it over—he needed something in return.

The details vary depending on who tells the story. The most widely reported version: Henderson bought Hassey a set of golf clubs and a sharp new suit. Other accounts mention stereo equipment or an autograph session. Whatever actually changed hands, the result was the same: Hassey switched to #27, and Henderson reclaimed his #24.[188]

The Creative Deals:
Autographs, Ice Cream, & Kids

Some negotiations get wonderfully weird—involving charity donations, ice cream cones, and contractual obligations to promote amateur rock bands.

The List of Demands: Donovan McNabb and Chris Kluwe for #5

Perhaps the most creative deal in sports history comes from punter Chris Kluwe, who negotiated a fun proposition with quarterback Donovan McNabb.

Upon joining the Minnesota Vikings in 2011, McNabb wanted to wear his familiar #5, which was held by Kluwe. To acquire the number, McNabb had to do three things:[189]

> 1. Make five mentions of Kluwe's band "Tripping Icarus" in non-consecutive press conferences
> 2. Donate $5,000 to "Kick for a Cure" to benefit Duchenne Muscular Dystrophy
> 3. Buy Kluwe an ice cream cone

McNabb paid the $5,000 to charity and delivered the ice cream cone. As for the five band mentions? Kluwe joked that he only got two—but the deal was done with no hard feelings and McNabb had his number.

The deal was one of a kind—not just because it was funny, but because it showed that negotiations can be creative, charitable, and entertaining all at once.

A Babe Ruth Autograph: John Lackey and Pat Neshek for #41

In 2014, when John Lackey was traded to the St. Louis Cardinals, he wanted to keep wearing #41, the number he'd worn for most of his career. But reliever Pat Neshek was wearing it—and he wasn't just any teammate.

Neshek is a serious memorabilia collector, with a passion for autographs and baseball history. Lackey initially planned to give him a

Breitling watch, but Neshek had a better idea: He asked for a Babe Ruth-signed baseball.

Lackey delivered. The ball, authenticated and likely signed around 1926, became the crown jewel of Neshek's collection. "It's pretty awesome," Neshek said. "It's something I've always wanted. It's the best autograph I have in my collection. Man, what a gift."[190]

A College Fund: A.J. Burnett and Daniel McCutchen for #34

When A.J. Burnett joined the Pittsburgh Pirates in 2012, he wanted to wear #34, the number he'd worn with the Yankees. But Daniel McCutchen was the one wearing it in Pittsburgh.

McCutchen and his wife were expecting a baby girl, so instead of negotiating with cash or luxury goods, Burnett offered something more meaningful: he set up a college fund for McCutchen's future daughter.

The fund was a College America 529 plan, designed to grow over time and help cover tuition when the child turned 18. "He asked me what I wanted, I brought that up," McCutchen explained. "Eighteen years from now, we'll see what the market is."[191]

Burnett got his number. McCutchen got peace of mind. And a future college student got a head start. Sometimes, the best number deals aren't about ego or extravagance. They're about legacy.

A Nursery: Tom Glavine and Joe McEwing #47

When Tom Glavine joined the New York Mets in 2003, he wanted to wear #47, the number he'd worn throughout his Hall of Fame career in Atlanta. But Joe McEwing had claimed it in New York.

Rather than offer cash or a Rolex, Glavine made a more personal gesture: He financed the construction of a baby nursery in McEwing's home.[192]

McEwing and his wife were expecting a child, and Glavine's gift wasn't just generous—it was thoughtful. Every night McEwing tucked his child into bed, he had a quiet reminder of the deal: a number traded not for money, but for comfort, care, and a shared moment between teammates.

Glavine got his number. McEwing got a nursery. And the Mets got a story that still makes fans smile.

Boots, RVs, and a Mystery Deal: Madison Bumgarner and Andrew Chafin for #40

When Madison Bumgarner signed with the Arizona Diamondbacks in 2020, he wanted to keep wearing #40, the number he'd made dominant during his decade with the San Francisco Giants. But Andrew Chafin, a fellow pitcher and outdoorsman, had staked his claim to it, and he wasn't about to give it up without a little fun.

What followed was one of the quirkiest number negotiations in recent memory.

Bumgarner reportedly offered:[193]

- **A pair of cowboy boots**—Chafin's response: "There ain't a boot worth enough for that."
- **A new RV**—"I already got one of the best ones they make," Chafin said.
- **A horse**—"Everybody says, 'Horse, horse, horse,'" Chafin laughed. "I'm like, 'No.' The horse is the cheap part. Then you have to feed it, take care of it, clean up after it. It's a whole lot more work."

- **A pickup truck**—"I wish," Chafin said. "That would be nice." When asked if it had been discussed, he grinned: "I'm not at liberty to discuss."

Eventually, Bumgarner got the number. But the final terms of the deal were never disclosed. Both players kept the resolution private, leaving fans to speculate whether it was a truck, a donation, or just a handshake between two desert cowboys. Sometimes the best deals are the ones nobody talks about.

Jersey number negotiations reveal that respect takes many forms. Sometimes it's about patience—waiting your turn like Anthony Edwards or Cristiano Ronaldo. Sometimes it's creative—beer, golf clubs, ice cream cones, or college funds. And sometimes it's expensive, thoughtful, or just about being a good teammate.

The currency changes, but the principle remains: if you want something someone else has, you ask. And when someone asks you, you consider what that number means—to you, to them, and to the team.

CHAPTER 10

Brother, Do You Have the Time?

In the world of professional sports, there's an unwritten rule about jersey numbers: if a veteran wants a number that a younger player is wearing, there's usually a way to work it out.

Sometimes that involves cash. Sometimes it's about respect and asking nicely. But increasingly, there's become a standard currency for these transactions: luxury watches.

Specifically, Rolex watches.

It's become so common that it's almost a cliché. When a star player joins a new team and wants a number that's already taken, the question isn't "What will it take?" It's "What kind of Rolex do you want?"

The Rolex Pioneer: Roger Clemens

Roger Clemens and Carlos Delgado: #21

When Roger Clemens signed with the Toronto Blue Jays in 1997, he wanted to wear #21—the number that had brought him years of success with the Boston Red Sox, including multiple Cy Young Awards.

However, his new teammate, first baseman Carlos Delgado, was already wearing #21.

Clemens didn't ask. He didn't negotiate. He went straight to the solution: a Rolex watch plus $15,000 in cash.

Delgado accepted the deal and switched to #25, which he wore for the rest of his All-Star career with the Blue Jays. Clemens went on to win back-to-back Cy Young Awards in Toronto wearing #21.[186]

The transaction became groundbreaking—not just because of the amount, but because it set a precedent. For Clemens, #21 represented his peak years in Boston—multiple Cy Young Awards, dominance, identity. Bringing it to Toronto was an attempt to recreate that success, and he was willing to pay $15,000 plus a Rolex to keep that continuity alive.

From that moment on, the Rolex became the standard currency for several jersey number deals in baseball and beyond.

The Tradition Continues: Baseball's Rolex Standard

Once Clemens set the precedent, other players followed suit. The Rolex became less about showing off and more about showing respect—a way to acknowledge that you're asking someone to give up something that's theirs.

Jim Thome and Alexi Casilla: #25

When Jim Thome joined the Minnesota Twins in 2010, he wanted his familiar #25—the number he'd worn for most of his Hall of Fame career. Utility infielder Alexi Casilla was wearing it.

Following baseball's unwritten tradition, Thome gave Casilla a Rolex watch for the number. Casilla moved to #12, allowing Thome to finish out his illustrious career wearing his signature number.[194]

Adrian Beltre and Julio Borbon: #29

When Adrian Beltre signed with the Texas Rangers in 2011, he actually had it written in his contract that he would wear his lucky #29—the number he'd worn throughout his career.

Young outfielder Julio Borbon was wearing it and really didn't have a say in the matter.

However, Beltre handled the situation with class, offering Borbon a Rolex watch in exchange for the number. Borbon graciously accepted, switching to #20 so the veteran star could wear his preferred digits.[192]

Beltre went on to make #29 unforgettable in Texas, playing eight Hall of Fame-caliber seasons with the Rangers before the team retired the number in his honor in 2019.

For Borbon, a young player with little leverage, the Rolex was a gracious consolation. For Beltre, wearing #29 was essential to his identity.

Starling Marte and Jeff McNeil: #6

When Starling Marte signed with the New York Mets in 2022, he wanted to wear #6, the number he had worn for 10 seasons in Pittsburgh and Miami. But Jeff McNeil was wearing it in New York as he had for the previous three seasons.

Rather than press the issue, Marte followed baseball's Rolex tradition. He gave McNeil a Rolex watch, and McNeil moved to #1, which he has worn ever since.[195]

For Marte, it was about continuity—keeping the number that defined his career. McNeil received a luxury timepiece and a gesture that recognized what he was giving up.

The swap reinforced how the Rolex had become baseball's currency of respect.

Luis Severino and Mitch Spence: #40

When Luis Severino signed with the Oakland Athletics in 2025, he had one request: to keep wearing #40, the number he had carried through his years with the Yankees and Mets. But that number already belonged to pitcher Mitch Spence, who had just broken into the majors the previous year.

Rather than press the issue, Severino followed the unwritten tradition that had become baseball's Rolex standard. He gifted Spence a Rolex GMT Master II in exchange for the number. Spence accepted, switching to #28, while Severino took back the digits that defined his career.[196]

The deal was more than a transaction—it acknowledged what the number meant. To Severino, #40 was part of his identity, connecting him to his past triumphs. Spence gained a five-figure watch, simply because he held the number a veteran needed.

The deal echoed Clemens, Thome, Beltre, and Marte before them: a Rolex for a number, a tradition that had become shorthand for continuity and respect across Major League Baseball.

The Rolex Tribute Spreads to Hockey

Sergei Bobrovsky and Frank Vatrano: #72

When Sergei Bobrovsky signed his seven-year deal with the Florida Panthers in 2019, he wanted his familiar #72. But teammate Frank Vatrano already wore it.

Bobrovsky didn't push—he made a deal.

Vatrano revealed on social media that the goalie gave him a Rolex watch and promised a season's worth of dinners in exchange for the number.[197]

Vatrano happily switched, and Bobrovsky continued his career with the digits that had become his identity. The playful nature of the deal—a watch plus a season of dinners—showed how hockey players had adopted the Rolex tradition with their own twist, blending generosity with camaraderie.

Ilya Kovalchuk and Brett Kulak: #17

When Ilya Kovalchuk joined the Montreal Canadiens in 2020, he wanted #17, the number he had worn throughout his NHL career. Brett Kulak had it, but Kovalchuk didn't just take it.

He gave Kulak a Rolex watch engraved with "Thanks for number 17."[198]

Kulak switched to another number, and Kovalchuk restored his identity in Montreal. The gift showed how the Rolex had become more than currency—it was a symbol of gratitude and appreciation.

The personalized engraving turned Kulak's watch into a keepsake, a reminder of how even legends honor teammates when reclaiming their signature digits.

Mikko Rantanen and Jack Roslovic: #96

When Mikko Rantanen was traded to the Carolina Hurricanes in 2025, he brought with him a decade of dominance—and a deep attachment to jersey #96.

Rantanen had worn #96 throughout his career with the Colorado Avalanche, a nod to his birth year and a number that had become central to his identity. But when he arrived in Carolina, he ran into an issue: forward Jack Roslovic already had the number.

Rather than make demands or escalate the issue, Rantanen followed a now-familiar playbook in professional sports: he offered a Rolex.

Roslovic accepted the gift—a Rolex Datejust 41, reportedly valued at over $14,000—and switched to another number. Rantanen regained #96 and continued his All-Star-caliber play in a new uniform.[199]

The twist? Just weeks after gifting the Rolex to claim #96 in Carolina, Rantanen was traded again—to Dallas. His time in a Carolina jersey was short-lived, but Roslovic still enjoys the Rolex.

The Unconfirmed Legends

Some Rolex stories have become part of sports lore despite zero documentation. These are the deals that teammates whisper about, reporters reference cautiously, and fans accept as fact—even though no one can quite confirm them.

Chris Paul and Ryan Anderson: #3 (?)

Chris Paul always wore #3. It's not just his number—it's his brand. "CP3" is his identity, rooted in family (Chapter 3) and basketball legend Allen Iverson.

When he was traded to the Houston Rockets in 2017, he needed to secure #3 from teammate Ryan Anderson.

Though never officially documented, the story goes that Paul went bigger than a single Rolex—handing Anderson a collection of luxury watches and even making a charity donation in Anderson's name. It was the kind of rumored deal that set a new bar for high-stakes number negotiations.

We know that Anderson had #3 when Paul arrived, and then suddenly Anderson was wearing #33. Something happened—and given Paul's brand and resources, a collection of luxury watches plus a charity donation wouldn't be far-fetched.[200]

Emmanuel Sanders and Tre'Quan Smith: #10 (?)

When joining the New Orleans Saints, wide receiver Emmanuel Sanders supposedly wanted #10, but it belonged to Tre'Quan Smith.

Locker-room lore claims Sanders dangled a Rolex for Smith's #10. If a Rolex offer was made, Smith clearly didn't accept it. According to Pro-Football-Reference.com, Smith continued to wear #10 throughout his time with the Saints while Sanders wore #17.[201]

Mitch Richmond and Derek Fisher: #2 (?)

One more rumor places Mitch Richmond across the table from Derek Fisher, with a Rolex in play for #2. The story floats through Laker lore without proof, but the setup makes sense: Richmond had worn #2 for a decade, Fisher owned it in L.A., and Richmond ultimately switched to #23.

While not publicly disclosed, it's entirely plausible that an offer of some kind was proposed. When Richmond joined the Lakers in 2001, he had been wearing #2 consistently over the last 10 seasons with the Kings and the Wizards. Upon arriving in Los Angeles, Derek Fisher was the owner of #2 which he had worn for the previous five seasons and the only number he had worn in his career up to that point.

Even if a Rolex offer was made, Fisher must have declined it. He continued to wear #2 for the Lakers while Richmond took #23, the number he'd worn during his early years with the Golden State Warriors.[202]

Still, the fact that these stories persist shows how ingrained the "Rolex for numbers" tradition has become. Whether they happened or not, they're believable—and that tells you everything about how these deals work. In the world of professional sports, a Rolex for a number isn't just possible—it's often expected.

The tradition that Roger Clemens started in 1997 has become standard practice across professional sports. Today, a Rolex is the going rate when a star wants a number that isn't available.

Of course, not everyone has been presented with such an offer. After the Severino/Spence exchange, A's manager Mark Kotsay joked "I never had the pleasure of being able to give up my number for a Rolex. If anybody wants [my] No. 7, it's definitely negotiable for a Rolex."[196]

It's a currency that works because everyone wins: the veteran gets their identity back, the young player gets a luxury timepiece, and the team gets a star who feels at home in their new uniform—and somewhere, a watch dealer is smiling.

From Autographs to Automobiles

A Rolex is nice. Cash is straightforward. But sometimes, a jersey number is worth something more substantial—something with four wheels, leather seats, and a price tag that makes your accountant nervous.

Welcome to the world of car deals—where athletes trade luxury vehicles for one or two digits on a jersey, where car keys appear in lockers with handwritten notes, and where a $200,000 Porsche becomes a thank-you gift for surrendering a number you've worn for years.

These aren't just negotiations—they're statements: "This number means so much to me that I'm willing to give you a luxury vehicle."

The Legend:
Deion's BMW and a Very Direct Note

Deion Sanders and Alundis Brice: #21

Upon joining the Dallas Cowboys in 1995, cornerback Deion "Prime Time" Sanders wanted to continue wearing #21—a number that had become instantly recognizable for his flashy, lockdown style.

There was just one complication: his new teammate, defensive back Alundis Brice, was already wearing it.

Sanders, never one for subtlety, decided to make an offer Brice couldn't refuse.

According to Jeff Pearlman's book *Boys Will Be Boys*, Sanders randomly ran into Brice at a car dealership, where he saw his new teammate shopping for a sports car. Sanders watched Brice browse, then made a decision that would become legendary.

Without Brice's knowledge, Sanders bought him a brand-new BMW on the spot, then left the keys and a note in his locker.

The note read: "NOW GIVE ME MY DAMN JERSEY!"[203]

It's hard to turn down a number request after someone surprises you with a BMW. Brice handed Sanders #21.

Alundis Brice only lasted two seasons in the NFL, but that was long enough to get a free BMW from Deion Sanders. And Prime Time got his number back, which he wore throughout the rest of his Cowboys career.

The Epilogue: When Deion Didn't Ask

Deion wore #21 throughout his NFL career until he came out of retirement to play for the Baltimore Ravens. At that point, #21 was being worn by defensive back and Pro Bowler Chris McAlister.

This time, Deion didn't want to cause any friction by asking for the number. McAlister was an established star, not a rookie, and the dynamic was different. McAlister was excited for Sanders to join the team and would have been willing to negotiate if asked.[204]

Instead, Sanders chose #37—reflecting his age at the time.[205] And for the first time in his career, Prime Time was wearing an actual prime number.

The fact that Deion—who once bought a BMW to get his number— chose not to negotiate speaks volumes about respect, hierarchy, and knowing when a number isn't worth pursuing.

The Record Breaker:
Shohei Ohtani's Porsche

Shohei Ohtani and Joe Kelly: #17

When Shohei Ohtani joined the Los Angeles Angels in 2017, he couldn't wear #11—his number from the Hokkaido Nippon-Ham Fighters—because the Angels had retired it for Jim Fregosi. At his Angels unveiling, Ohtani joked about his second choice: "I actually wanted number 27, but someone was wearing that number."[206]

That someone was Mike Trout, the Angels' franchise player and three-time MVP. Even Ohtani wasn't about to ask Trout to give up his number.

So Ohtani settled on #17, which turned out to be fitting. In Japanese baseball tradition, ace pitchers often wear #18—a custom that began with the Yomiuri Giants in the 1960s. Ohtani's #17 sits right next to that number, close enough to honor the tradition while making it his own.

When Ohtani signed with the Los Angeles Dodgers in December 2023 on a record-breaking $700 million contract, he valued #17 so much that he gave teammate Joe Kelly a Porsche—worth somewhere between $100,000 and $200,000—as thanks for surrendering the number.[207]

Kelly's wife Ashley had even run a #Ohtake17 social media campaign to recruit Ohtani to the Dodgers, so the family was clearly all-in on making the superstar feel welcome.

The gift showed just how much the number meant to Ohtani. He wanted to keep the same number he began his MLB career with—#17 had become his trademark, his brand, his identity. Kelly walked away with a Porsche. To Ohtani, it was non-negotiable—a Porsche was a small price to pay to keep the number that defined him.

The Rookie Move:
Ashton Jeanty's Mercedes Money

Ashton Jeanty and Daniel Carlson: #2

Ashton Jeanty, the Las Vegas Raiders' first-round pick in 2025, wanted to keep wearing his college number, #2. It wasn't just a preference—it was personal.

"Yeah, so I was born on Dec. 2, so that's the day greatness was born," Jeanty said with a smile after the draft. "But also, all my family—my older brother, uncle—it's kind of like the family number. So that's the main reason I wear number 2."

The problem? Raiders kicker Daniel Carlson, an All-Pro, had worn #2 since 2020. Soon Jeanty and Carlson were trading texts, negotiating terms. Carlson kept it professional: "My big thing was, I didn't want to draw this out. If you want the number, that's fine. We can figure out what makes sense, what's fair."

A deal was reached, but the exact terms weren't shared by either party. When pressed for a dollar amount, Jeanty hinted that he'd paid about the price of a Mercedes GLE. With a starting MSRP of $61,850, the rookie had effectively paid the price of a luxury SUV to keep his family number.

Carlson later confirmed he didn't actually buy a Mercedes with the cash—half of the money went to The Hub LV, his nonprofit serving unhoused and trafficked youth in Las Vegas.[208]

To Jeanty, the deal was worth every penny. And that was worth the price of a Mercedes.

The Tahoe Thank-You: Juan Soto's Gift

Juan Soto and Brett Baty: #22

In December 2024, after signing a record-breaking 15-year, $765 million contract with the New York Mets, Juan Soto wanted to wear his preferred number, #22.

However, third baseman Brett Baty already wore it.

To acquire the number, Soto gave Baty a 2025 Chevy Tahoe, complete with a red ribbon and "Thanks for #22" painted on the rear window.[209]

The gesture reflected the growing tradition of star players compensating teammates for their jersey numbers—and doing it with style. Soto could have just handed Baty a check, but the Tahoe with the personalized message? That's showmanship.

Baty received a nice surprise. To Soto, it was worth it to wear the number that had been his throughout his career with the Washington Nationals, San Diego Padres, and New York Yankees.

The Tahoe, with an MSRP starting around $55,000–$60,000, wasn't the most expensive car deal in sports history, but it was one of the most stylish. The painted message made the whole thing unmistakable: this wasn't just a transaction—it was gratitude with a personalized touch.

The Two-Wheeled Trade:
A Custom Motorcycle

Brian Jordan and Fredi González: #33

Not every number deal ends with a car. Sometimes, it's two wheels instead of four—with chrome detailing and a price tag that turns heads.

When Brian Jordan returned to the Atlanta Braves in 2005, he wanted to reclaim #33, the number he'd worn during his first stint with the team from 1999–2001. But it was already taken—by third-base coach Fredi González.

Jordan's solution? Buy González a custom motorcycle, reportedly worth $40,000, in exchange for the number.[186]

The bike's make and model were never publicly disclosed, but the point was unmistakable: Jordan valued #33 enough to trade serious horsepower for two digits. He wore the number for the final two seasons of his 15-year career, cementing his legacy as one of the Braves' key players during their dynasty years.

The story became Braves clubhouse lore—a $40,000 motorcycle for two digits that meant everything to a veteran's legacy.

From Deion's BMW with a note to Ohtani's Porsche to Jeanty's Mercedes-level payment, the currency has evolved. A Rolex says "Thank you." A luxury vehicle says "This number is who I am."

The currency has escalated from watches to wheels, from thousands to six figures. Deion's BMW deal was shocking in 1995; by 2025, Ohtani's Porsche barely caused a stir. The principle remains the same:

when a number becomes part of your identity, no price is too high to keep it—even if that price has a steering wheel.

CHAPTER 12

Cash Is King

Players will go to extravagant lengths to get the number they want. We've seen athletes swap digits for golf clubs, designer suits, Rolex watches, and even luxury cars. But sometimes, the deal skips the gifts and goes straight to the bank. No symbolism. No subtlety. Just cold hard cash exchanged for one or two digits stitched on a jersey.

In the NBA, former guard Mario Chalmers has noted that players will sometimes pay as much as $10,000 to secure a number.[210] In basketball, that might be enough to seal the deal. But in other sports, the price climbs much higher. Here, we'll explore cash transactions ranging from Rickey Henderson's $25,000 investment in #24 to Gerald McCoy's jaw-dropping $250,000 payout for #93—stories that show just how far athletes will go to reclaim the number that defines them.

Because when you absolutely, positively need that number right now? Cash is still king.

The Initial Investment: $25,000

Rickey Henderson and Turner Ward: #24

Throughout his 25-season Hall of Fame career, Rickey Henderson was most closely associated with #24—the number he wore during his prime years with the Oakland Athletics. He originally selected it as a tribute to his idol, Willie Mays.

The number became so revered that the A's retired it in 2009, and in 2025, the team honored him posthumously by having all players wear #24 for their home opener.

But Henderson's journey through nine different MLB teams meant his number wasn't always consistent. In his first stint with the A's, he wore #35 briefly before switching to #24. When traded back to Oakland in 1989, he wore #22 for a few games before reclaiming #24.

At the 1993 trade deadline, the Toronto Blue Jays were elated to add Rickey Henderson to their roster. But there was just one minor issue: someone on the roster already had his signature #24—Turner Ward.

Henderson initially wore #14 as a placeholder while negotiations continued. After nine games—and struggling at the plate—he knew he needed his real number back.

Ward drove a hard bargain, and he had precedent to work with. Just four years earlier, Henderson had given Ron Hassey golf clubs and a suit for #24 with the Athletics (Chapter 9). Ward figured if Henderson valued the number enough to give gifts once, he could pay cash this time.

The official terms were never disclosed, but reports suggest Henderson paid around $25,000 for the rights to wear #24 with the Blue Jays.[188]

To Rickey Henderson, $25,000 wasn't much—he was making $3.55 million that year. But it was a windfall for Turner Ward, whose salary was $160,000, just barely above the league minimum in 1993.

That $25,000 was roughly 16% of Ward's entire annual salary—a massive windfall for simply changing numbers.

Henderson officially switched to #24 on August 13, 1993. To Henderson, the psychology mattered more than the statistics. Number

24 was who he was—and $25,000 was a small price to pay to feel like himself again.

The Standard Deals: $20,000-$50,000

After Rickey Henderson's rumored $25,000 payment set the tone, jersey number deals began to settle into a predictable range. Some players paid a little less, some a little more—but by the early 2000s, $20,000 to $50,000 had become the going rate for securing a number that mattered.

Lee Evans and Mark Campbell: #83—$20,000

When wide receiver Lee Evans was drafted by the Buffalo Bills in 2004, he wanted to wear #83—a nod to his college number, #3, at Wisconsin. NFL rules prohibited receivers from wearing single digits at the time, so Evans sought a number that preserved the "3" in some form. Number 83 was perfect.

However, he'd soon learn that veteran tight end Mark Campbell already had it.

Evans reportedly paid Campbell $20,000 to acquire the number[192]—a rare documented case of a rookie buying a jersey number from a veteran teammate. Campbell agreed, switching to #88.

Evans went on to wear #83 for seven seasons with the Bills and one season with the Baltimore Ravens, racking up over 6,000 receiving yards and becoming one of the league's most consistent deep threats.

Kellen Winslow Jr. and Aaron Shea: #80—Undisclosed Amount

When Kellen Winslow Jr. entered the NFL in 2004, he wanted to wear #80—the number his father, Hall of Famer Kellen Winslow Sr., had worn with the San Diego Chargers. But #80 was already taken by Browns tight end Aaron Shea.

Winslow had worn #11 during the preseason, but once his six-year, $40 million rookie contract was signed, he got serious about securing his preferred digits. After weeks of negotiations, Shea agreed to give up #80—for a price.

The exact amount was never disclosed, but Shea confirmed that Winslow met his asking price. He joked to reporters: "I didn't get a deal like Campbell got. Campbell robbed the guy."[211]

That's a direct reference to Mark Campbell's $20,000 payday from Lee Evans. Shea's comment suggests he accepted less than Campbell's $20,000—though exactly how much remains a mystery. He also quipped that Winslow had the Poston brothers (high-powered agents) negotiating for him, while Shea was "doing it all by myself."

The self-deprecating humor suggests Shea probably got between $10,000 and $20,000. Shea switched to #83, and Winslow got to wear #80, just like his dad.

Eric Decker and Jeff Cumberland: #87—$25,000 and a Steak Dinner

Wide receiver Eric Decker, upon joining the New York Jets in 2014, wanted to wear #87, a number that belonged to tight end Jeff Cumberland.

Decker reportedly paid Cumberland $25,000—plus a steak dinner—to acquire the number.[212] The dinner was a nice touch, a way to make the transaction feel less transactional and more like teammates helping each other out.

Cumberland got a nice meal and got paid $25,000 for changing the number on his shirt. Not a bad night's work.

Darrelle Revis and Mark Barron: #24—$50,000

When cornerback Darrelle Revis joined the Tampa Bay Buccaneers, he set his heart on wearing #24, a number held by safety Mark Barron.

Revis reportedly paid $50,000 to Barron to acquire the number.[213]

At the time, this was believed to be the highest price ever paid for a number in the NFL. Barron agreed to switch to a different number, allowing Revis to don his preferred digits.

To Revis, #24 was his identity—the number he'd worn as one of the league's elite shutdown corners. It was worth double what Henderson had paid two decades earlier, reflecting both salary inflation and the increasing value of personal branding.

The Mystery Deal: When Players Keep Us Guessing

Za'Darius Smith and Brodric Martin: #99—Three Zeros on the End

When Za'Darius Smith joined the Detroit Lions in 2024, he sought to wear his familiar number, #99, which was held by defensive tackle Brodric Martin.

Smith reportedly paid Martin a sum somewhere in the four- to five-figure range—and kept the exact amount vague.

When asked about it, Smith hinted cryptically: "The going rate? There's three zeros on the end of that." He elaborated, "I'm not going to tell you the exact price, but for sure, he's going to have some good money, put some gas in his car."[214] The vagueness was intentional. His phrasing could mean $1,000, $10,000, or even $99,000. Smith clearly relished keeping people guessing.

Given that Martin was just coming off his rookie season and Smith was an established veteran, it was probably closer to the lower end. But the fact that Smith was willing to pay thousands of dollars for #99 shows just how important the number was to him.

The Six-Figure Club:
When $100,000 Becomes the Price

Stefon Diggs and Jimmie Ward: #1

When wide receiver Stefon Diggs was traded to the Houston Texans in 2024, he desired to wear #1, a number held by veteran safety Jimmie Ward.

Diggs reportedly paid $100,000 to Ward to acquire the number.[215]

Ward agreed to switch back to his previous number, #20, which he had worn during his time with the San Francisco 49ers.

The six-figure payment represented a new threshold in jersey negotiations. We've gone from golf clubs and suits, to Rolexes, to cars, and now to straight-up six-figure cash deals.

However, Diggs only lasted one season in Houston before moving on to New England. So #1 is available again, and Ward is welcome to reclaim it. So far, he seems content with his new #20—and his $100,000 bonus.

The Record:
Gerald McCoy's $250,000 Deal

Gerald McCoy and Kyle Love: #93

In 2019, defensive tackle Gerald McCoy joined the Carolina Panthers and sought to wear his familiar number, #93, which was held by veteran defensive tackle Kyle Love.

McCoy reportedly paid Love $250,000 to acquire the number, making it one of the most significant known payments for a jersey number in NFL history.

Let that sink in: a quarter of a million dollars—for a number.

No sane person would turn down that kind of money, so of course, Love ended up taking it. McCoy had spent the first nine seasons of his career wearing #93 in Tampa Bay, and he wanted to keep the number after signing with Carolina.

Unfortunately, McCoy only played one season with the Panthers, wearing the number for just 16 games—roughly $15,625 per appearance.

From a pure cost-benefit perspective, it seems ridiculous. But from an identity perspective? If you've worn #93 for nine years—if it's part of your name, your brand, your identity—then maybe $250,000 starts to feel less like a price and more like preservation.

"I'd been wearing 93 since I got to college, so when I got to the Carolina Panthers, I wanted 93," McCoy said. "It cost me [$250,000]. Hey, listen, I wasn't going to do it, but my wife said, 'That's your legacy—keep it.'"[216]

From Rickey Henderson's $25,000 in 1993 to Gerald McCoy's $250,000 in 2019, the cash market for jersey numbers has inflated right alongside player salaries. What once felt outrageous—shelling out thousands for a pair of digits—now barely surprises anyone.

Six-figure deals are no longer shocking; they're expected. Rolexes are nice gestures. Cars make headlines. But when you absolutely, positively need that number right now? Cash is still king. And if you're the guy holding the number? Well, it pays to negotiate.

CHAPTER 13

For the Love of the Game

We've seen Rolexes. We've seen BMWs and Porsches. We've seen $250,000 in cold hard cash change hands for a jersey number. But sometimes, the most powerful number transactions are the ones that don't involve money at all.

Sometimes, a veteran quietly gives up his number because it's the right thing to do. Sometimes, a young player steps aside to welcome a legend. Sometimes, a player is offered a prestigious number—and respectfully declines. And sometimes, the most meaningful acts in sports happen not on the field, but in the equipment room: when someone chooses respect over compensation.

The Ultimate Respect: Making a Legend Feel Welcome

When a legend joins a new team, the jersey number they've worn for years can be part of their identity. Sometimes, teammates recognize that—and make a quiet, powerful gesture to help them feel at home.

Mike Piazza and John Franco: #31

Mike Piazza had worn #31 throughout his career, a number that became part of his identity from his early days with the Los Angeles Dodgers. When he was traded to the New York Mets in the spring of 1998, he faced a dilemma: #31 was already taken by veteran reliever John Franco, who had worn it for 15 seasons.

Piazza worried he might have to switch numbers. But when he arrived at the Mets clubhouse for the first time, he found a fresh #31 jersey with his name on it waiting for him.

Franco had voluntarily given it up, saying simply: "I wanted him to feel comfortable, to know that we wanted him to stay here."[217]

It was a classy move that set the tone for Piazza's time in New York and ensured that #31 remained his signature. Franco didn't ask for money. Didn't ask for anything. He just did what he thought was right—welcoming a new teammate and helping him feel at home. The number eventually became one of the most beloved in Mets history, and the team retired it in Piazza's honor on July 30, 2016.

Years later, both players would be honored by the Mets: Piazza's #31 was retired in 2016, and John Franco was inducted into the Mets Hall of Fame.[218] Franco's generosity with #31 became part of his legacy—proof that the most sincere gestures often happen off the field.

Tom Brady and Chris Godwin: #12

When Tom Brady joined the Tampa Bay Buccaneers in 2020, wide receiver Chris Godwin had been wearing #12 since joining the team in 2017.

But when the greatest quarterback of all time—who had worn #12 for 20 years with the New England Patriots—arrived, Godwin didn't hesitate. He offered it to Brady immediately.

Godwin explained, "I have a ton of respect for Tom and for what he's done. Because of that, I'm willing to defer that [#12] to Tom. It's out of respect for him. I'm hoping that when it's my time and somebody comes up, I get that same respect from the younger guy."[219]

Brady gratefully accepted. Godwin switched to #14, and the Buccaneers went on to win the Super Bowl that season with Brady wearing his signature #12.

Godwin could have negotiated for something in return. But he recognized that welcoming a legend was more important than keeping a number.

LeBron James and Mario Chalmers: #6

When LeBron James joined the Miami Heat in 2010, he needed a new number. His hallmark #23 was off the table—unofficially retired by the Heat in honor of Michael Jordan (Chapter 21). So LeBron chose #6, a fresh start for a new chapter.

At the time, #6 was already worn by guard Mario Chalmers, but he agreed to give it to LeBron. The switch was seamless, with no compensation and no drama—just a young player making room for a superstar joining the team. LeBron wore #6 for all four seasons in Miami, winning two championships and two MVPs.

Chalmers later clarified he had already planned to switch to #15 before LeBron arrived—a detail that made the transaction even smoother.[220]

The smoothest jersey swaps are often the ones that happen before anyone even asks—and where the player who gave up the number later clears the air to confirm there was no controversy.

The Charitable Hearts:
When Players Pay It Forward

Some players accept payment for their numbers but immediately turn around and give it all away. These stories show that generosity can take many forms.

Michael Vick and Ryan Quigley: #1—All to Charity

Back in April 2014, Michael Vick asked his Twitter followers if he should wear #3 or #8 with the New York Jets—two numbers he could have worn for free.

Instead, Vick decided to pay $10,000 to wear #1. At the time, the number belonged to Jets punter Ryan Quigley, who agreed to give it up only if the money went to charity.

"Most of the time in the NFL if a veteran requests your number, you work out a financial agreement between the two players," Quigley said. "I was not interested in the money for myself. I wanted to find a way to help some others."

Vick made the donation in Quigley's name to Teen Angel of North Myrtle Beach—Quigley's hometown—and to the Boys and Girls Club of New York.[221]

Vick was willing to pay for what he wanted—Quigley saw an opportunity to give back, and the charities reaped the reward. It was a moment that showed how players can use their platform to make a difference beyond the game.

Terrell Owens and Antonio Bryant: #81—Funding the Foundation

When Terrell Owens signed with the Cincinnati Bengals in 2010, he wanted to keep wearing his signature #81—the number he had made his own with the 49ers, Eagles, Cowboys, and Bills.

But #81 was already taken by wide receiver Antonio Bryant, who had signed with the Bengals earlier that offseason.

Rather than demand the number or let the team intervene, Owens approached Bryant directly. The two reached a quiet agreement:

Owens would donate to Bryant's youth foundation in exchange for the number.[222]

Bryant gave up #81. Owens got his number. And a charitable cause benefited in the process.

Across teams and seasons, #81 remained central to Owens' identity. But in Cincinnati, it came with something extra—not just for the player, but for the cause.

Rick Porcello and Dominic Smith: #22—A Donation for Development

When Rick Porcello signed with the New York Mets in 2020, he wanted to wear #22, the number he'd worn for the previous five years with the Boston Red Sox. But Dominic Smith already had it.

Smith agreed to switch to #2, but not for personal gain. Instead, Porcello made a donation to Baseball Generations, a nonprofit player development academy co-founded by Smith to support underserved youth in Los Angeles.[186]

The gesture was quiet, classy, and deeply personal. Smith didn't pocket the money—he passed it on to a cause that reflected his values and community ties.

Porcello got his number. Smith got to amplify his mission. And young athletes got a boost toward their dreams.

Jersey number deals aren't always about ego or luxury—they're about impact.

The Young Guns:
Rising Stars Who Step Aside

Sometimes the most impressive acts of respect come from young players who give up their numbers to welcome established veterans—even when they didn't have to.

Davante Adams and Puka Nacua: #17

When Davante Adams signed with the Los Angeles Rams in 2025, there was speculation that he would want to wear #17 as he had throughout his NFL career with the Packers, Raiders, and Jets.

However, Puka Nacua, the Rams' rising star receiver, was wearing it.

Before Adams even had a chance to speak with Nacua about wearing #17, Nacua had already decided he was changing to #12, thus freeing up #17 for his new teammate.

The move worked out for both players. Number 12 carried strong sentimental value for Nacua and his family—he wore it at BYU, and his older siblings wore it as well.

Adams clarified the transaction by stating: "For everybody out there that wants to hate me for making them buy new [Nacua] jerseys, I did not tell him. I didn't pay him. I didn't do anything. That was out of the kindness of his heart and he wore it [#12] in college so I guess it made sense."[223]

Nacua's gesture showed maturity beyond his years. He recognized that Adams had earned his number through a long career of excellence, and that sometimes being a good teammate means making things easy for others.

Russell Wilson and Deonte Banks: #3

Russell Wilson has worn #3 throughout his 13-year NFL career—in high school, college, Seattle, Denver, Pittsburgh, and now with the New York Giants.

When he joined the Giants, cornerback Deonte Banks, who previously wore #3, gave it up for Wilson without publicly asking for compensation.

Wilson expressed gratitude toward Banks on social media for relinquishing the number, posting: "Salute to my guy & young star Tae Banks! Grateful for you letting me wear #3 King! Full of gratitude."[224]

Whether Banks received any private compensation remains unknown, but the public gesture showed respect and team unity.

Banks could have negotiated publicly, making demands or holding out for payment. But instead, whatever arrangement they had was handled quietly, showing respect and team harmony.

Aaron Rodgers and Corliss Waitman: #8

When Aaron Rodgers joined the Pittsburgh Steelers in 2025, he brought with him a legacy—and a number. Rodgers had worn #8 in college and most recently with the New York Jets, and he wanted to keep it in Pittsburgh.

But in Pittsburgh, #8 belonged to Punter Corliss Waitman.

In a league where jersey number swaps often involve Rolexes, luxury cars, or five-figure payments, Waitman's response was almost unheard of.

He gave it up. No negotiation. No compensation. No drama.

Asked why he didn't ask for anything in return, Waitman shrugged it off: "We get a lot of money to play football," he said. "You know what I mean?"[225]

It was a simple statement, but it spoke volumes. Waitman recognized that Rodgers was a future Hall of Famer, that #8 was part of his identity, and that sometimes being a good teammate means doing the generous thing—no strings attached.

Rodgers got his number, and Waitman moved to #3 without hesitation. And the gesture became one of the feel-good stories of the season.

In a sport where everything has a price, Waitman reminded everyone that respect still comes free.

When Generosity Hides Darker Truths

Chad Ochocinco and Aaron Hernandez: #85

When Chad Johnson signed with the New England Patriots in 2011, his last name was still Ochocinco, so getting #85 was kind of important to his brand.

Tight end Aaron Hernandez, who was wearing #85, gave it to Johnson—for nothing.

At the time, Hernandez said: "We're playing at a high level, so all of us have a decent amount of money. I definitely should have [asked for compensation], but I didn't." Ochocinco confirmed that account by saying "It was Mr. Hernandez's way of greeting me here. He gave me the number, I didn't have to pay anything."

It seemed like a generous, team-first move. Johnson got his coveted number. Hernandez came across as a selfless teammate.

But years later, a darker story emerged. According to Hernandez's former attorney, the number wasn't given away for free. Johnson allegedly paid Hernandez $50,000, which Hernandez then used to finance illegal activities.[226]

Hernandez was later convicted of first-degree murder in 2015, sentenced to life in prison, and died by suicide in his cell in April 2017.[227]

This story isn't included to dwell on tragedy, but as a reminder that jersey number negotiations happen between real people with complex lives. Sometimes the gestures that seem noble on the surface hide complications we never see. And sometimes, the cost of choices extends far beyond jersey numbers.

When Respect Means Saying No

Sometimes the most respectful gesture isn't giving up a number—it's declining to take one, even when offered.

Joe Montana and Len Dawson: #16

When Joe Montana joined the Kansas City Chiefs in 1993, he was offered three jersey numbers to choose from:

> **#3**, which was his number at Notre Dame
> **#19**, which he wore briefly in training camp with San Francisco
> **#16**, which was his signature San Francisco 49ers number that had been retired by the Chiefs in honor of Hall of Fame quarterback Len Dawson

Dawson himself gave his blessing for Montana to wear #16. It would have been the easy choice—Montana wearing his familiar number, carrying on his identity from San Francisco.

But Montana declined.

He understood that #16 belonged to Dawson and to Kansas City history. Instead, Montana chose to wear #19, creating a fresh identity for his final chapter.[228]

Montana declined out of respect for what that number meant to Chiefs fans. He didn't need to borrow someone else's legacy—he had built his own. By wearing #19, Montana proved that true legends don't need famous numbers; they make the numbers famous.

Aaron Rodgers and Joe Namath: #12

When Aaron Rodgers joined the New York Jets in 2023, the most obvious jersey choice was the number he'd worn for 18 seasons in Green Bay: #12. But that number had long been retired by the Jets in honor of Hall of Fame quarterback Joe Namath, the man who boldly guaranteed—and delivered—a Super Bowl III victory in 1969.

Namath didn't hesitate. He publicly offered to unretire #12 so Rodgers could wear it. "If he's there, yeah, I want him to wear his number," Namath said. It was a generous gesture from one legend to another.

But Rodgers declined.

"To me, 12 is Broadway Joe," he said. "I didn't want to even go down that path." Instead, Rodgers chose #8, the number he wore in college at Cal.[162] It was a quiet nod to his roots—and a respectful distance from Namath's legacy.

Rodgers didn't need to borrow greatness. He recognized that some numbers are sacred, especially in cities where history runs deep.

Anthony Davis and LeBron James: #23

When Anthony Davis was traded to the Lakers in 2019, LeBron James made an extraordinary gesture: he offered to give Davis his signature #23.[229]

Up to that point, James had worn #23 for his entire non-Miami career, and Davis had worn the same number throughout his time in New Orleans. It seemed like a perfect fit—the star passing his signature number to the new star.

But Davis declined.

Even though James was willing, Davis decided against taking #23. When the time came for Davis to officially choose his number, he had already decided on #3, the very first number he ever wore, going back to grade school.[230]

Davis understood that #23 belonged to LeBron in Los Angeles, just as it had belonged to him in Cleveland. Taking it, even with permission, wouldn't have felt right. Some numbers are too connected to the player who wears them, and Davis respected that bond.

Tim Duncan and Dominique Wilkins: #21

When Tim Duncan was drafted by the San Antonio Spurs in 1997, Dominique Wilkins was wearing #21 for the team. Duncan wanted to wear #21—it was his number at Wake Forest—but he refused to assume it was his to take.

"If 'Nique decides to stay, I'm not going to take 21," Duncan said firmly.[231]

Wilkins played one season in San Antonio (1996–97) before going overseas to play in Italy. Only after Wilkins left did Duncan claim #21 and make it legendary in San Antonio.

Duncan honored Wilkins before ever stepping on the court, showing that even as a rookie, he understood the importance of respecting the veterans who came before him. He didn't demand the number. He didn't negotiate for it. He simply waited until it was available.

In a world where jersey numbers can cost six figures, these stories remind us of something fundamental: respect can't be bought. It's earned through gestures—small and large—that put team over self, legacy over ego, and relationships over transactions.

John Franco welcoming Mike Piazza. Chris Godwin honoring Tom Brady. Corliss Waitman stepping aside for Aaron Rodgers. Joe Montana declining Len Dawson's blessing.

These moments don't make headlines like luxury-car deals or six-figure payments, but they matter just as much. They remind us that in sports, as in life, the most valuable currency isn't always money. Sometimes, it's just doing the right thing.

CHAPTER 14

Double Deals and Double Crosses

We've seen the best of jersey negotiations—the generous gestures, the respectful exchanges, the deals that leave everyone satisfied.

Then there are the rarities: the double deals—when a player sells one number, then later sells the replacement number as well.

And in a different category altogether are the double crosses—when promises collapse, trust unravels, and the fallout becomes part of jersey lore. Both reveal the strange economics of numbers, but in very different ways.

Jeff Feagles:
The Original Double Dealer

Jeff Feagles, one of the NFL's most respected punters, became known for his willingness to negotiate over jersey numbers. Over his tenure with the New York Giants, he engaged in two notable deals—with wildly different outcomes.

Deal #1: The Eli Manning Paid Vacation for #10

When Eli Manning was drafted by the New York Giants in 2004, he wanted #10—a number he had worn in college at Ole Miss.

But that was Jeff Feagles' number.

"I said 'Listen, Eli is going to wear that number a lot longer than I am going to,'" Feagles said. "'I have no problem with it. We can work the details out later, but tell him he's going to have to come up with something."[232]

That something turned out to be an all-expenses-paid family vacation to Destin, Florida, with Manning picking up the tab. Manning got his signature number, which became a defining part of his two Super Bowl championship career. Feagles got a nice vacation. Everyone was happy.

After giving up #10, Feagles adopted #17 to honor his 17th season in the league.

Deal #2: The Broken Promise of a Plaxico Burress Outdoor Kitchen for #17

In 2005, wide receiver Plaxico Burress joined the Giants and wanted #17. His reasoning? He signed with the team on March 17th and considered the number lucky.

Feagles, having successfully negotiated once before, was open to another deal. Burress, through his agent Drew Rosenhaus, agreed to provide Feagles with a new outdoor kitchen for his home.

Feagles gave up the number. Burress started wearing #17. And then ... nothing.

The outdoor kitchen never materialized.

"I never got paid for it," Feagles said years later. "I asked [Burress] for it. Every time I went to [Burress' agent] Drew [Rosenhaus] he said, 'That's between you and Plax.' Bottom line, I never got paid. He basically stole my number."[233]

Feagles tried to collect, but Burress never delivered—and collecting proved even more challenging once Burress began serving a two-year jail sentence for a gun felony after accidentally shooting himself in the leg at a New York nightclub in 2008.

Feagles never got his kitchen. Burress wore #17 during the Giants' Super Bowl XLII championship run. And Feagles learned a hard lesson: get it in writing, and get paid upfront.

Feagles didn't conduct any other number-swapping deals after that. He quietly wore his new number, #18, for the remainder of his NFL career.

Jay Feely:
Doubling Down for a Good Cause

Jay Feely, kicker for the Arizona Cardinals, pulled off a successful double deal of his own—not for himself, but for those in need. Jersey numbers never meant much to Feely personally, so when he had the opportunity to give up his number for a donation to the Feely Family Foundation he jumped at the chance. Not once, but twice.

Deal #1: The Kevin Kolb Donation for #4

In 2010, quarterback Kevin Kolb arrived in Arizona hoping to wear #4—the number veteran kicker Jay Feely already held. Feely suggested a charitable arrangement: Kolb could take the number if he made a donation to Feely's foundation.

Kolb agreed, and the swap became more than a simple jersey exchange. Instead of a cash payment or luxury gift, the deal produced tangible support for Feely's philanthropic work, showing how a number could be turned into something meaningful off the field.

Deal #2: The Carson Palmer Donation for #3

Three years later, when Carson Palmer joined the Cardinals in 2013, he wanted to reclaim his signature #3. Once again, Feely held that number. He offered Palmer the same charitable option: donate to the foundation, and the number would be his.

Palmer agreed, and the swap was sealed—not with cash, Rolexes, or cars, but with a philanthropic gesture. Feely switched to a new number, Palmer got his #3, and a good cause benefited in the process.

"It really didn't matter to me," Feely said. "[The number] is an irrelevant thing to me in the grand scheme of things. If I can use that to build a couple of homes, great."[234] The homes he spoke of were in Haiti, where his foundation supported long-term rebuilding efforts for families in need.

Troy Hill: Taking It to the Bank

Troy Hill pulled off a successful double deal while with the Los Angeles Rams, changing his jersey number twice and cashing in both times. There was perfect symmetry to Hill's price points—each number sold for its face value in thousands.

Deal #1: Eric Weddle—$32,000 for #32

In 2019, Troy Hill was wearing #32 with the Rams. When veteran safety Eric Weddle joined the team and wanted the number, Hill sold it to him for $32,000 and switched to #20.

Deal #2: Jalen Ramsey—$20,000 for #20

Later that same season, when All-Pro cornerback Jalen Ramsey was traded to the Rams and wanted #20, Hill sold that number to Ramsey for $20,000 and switched to #22.

Total earnings from selling two jersey numbers in one year: $52,000. Not a bad side hustle for changing your shirt twice.[235]

The Lawsuit:
Clinton Portis vs. Ifeanyi Ohalete

Perhaps the most dramatic jersey number dispute in NFL history ended with lawyers, a written contract, and a settlement the day before trial.

After signing with the Washington Redskins in 2004, running back Clinton Portis wanted to wear #26—the number he had worn with the Denver Broncos. But the number was already assigned to Ifeanyi Ohalete, a defensive back.

Portis and Ohalete reached an agreement: Portis would pay $40,000 for the rights to the number.

Ohalete gave up #26 and switched to #30. Portis promptly paid Ohalete $20,000 upfront, with the two agreeing that the rest would be paid by Christmas.

Then Ohalete got released from the team.

With Ohalete off the roster, Portis apparently decided he was no longer under any obligation to pay him. But Ohalete had one thing going in his favor: a written contract with the terms of the deal.

Ohalete sued. The day before trial, Portis settled, paying an additional $18,000.

Final tally: Ohalete received $38,000 of the $40,000 owed—the missing $2,000 likely went to legal costs.[236]

Ohalete's written contract saved him. Without it, he would have had no legal recourse when Portis stopped paying.

Feagles gave up two numbers and only got paid for one. Portis tried to back out and ended up paying almost the full amount anyway, plus legal fees. Burress got his number but damaged his reputation. Jay Feely and Troy Hill? They got it right. Two deals each, and everyone delivered on their promises.

Jersey number deals are business transactions—and like any deal, they work best when both parties honor commitments, put terms in writing, and deliver on their word. In sports, your word should be your bond. But as Feagles learned and Ohalete proved, the safest bond is the one written in ink.

CHAPTER 15

The Hidden Costs

We've seen athletes pay teammates hundreds of thousands of dollars for jersey numbers. Porsches, Rolexes, BMWs changing hands. Deals succeeding, failing, ending in lawsuits. But there's a cost no one talks about: the league's cut.

When you change your number, someone has to buy all those jerseys sitting in warehouses. And the league has decided that someone is the player.

The NFL's New Rules and Massive Buyout Fees

In 2021, the NFL announced a rule change: defensive backs and linebackers could now wear single-digit numbers. Players were thrilled—until they saw the price tag.

Want to change your number? Buy out every jersey with your old number still sitting in warehouses, team stores, and retail outlets across the country.

We're not talking hundreds of jerseys. We're talking thousands—and the costs were staggering.

Jalen Ramsey: $330,000 to Wear #5

In 2021, Jalen Ramsey decided to switch from #20 to #5. To make the change, he had to pay approximately $330,000 to buy out the inventory of existing Ramsey #20 jerseys.

Ramsey had previously paid Troy Hill $20,000 to acquire #20 (Chapter 14). But when the NFL rule change allowed single digits, Ramsey decided #5 suited him better—and the league required him to clear out the remaining #20 stock, on top of what he'd already paid just to wear the number.[237]

Total cost for Ramsey to change jersey numbers twice in three seasons:

> $ 20,000 to Troy Hill for #20 in 2019
> $330,000 to the NFL for the #20 jersey inventory in 2021
> **$350,000 total**

When asked why #5, Ramsey was cryptic: "Just because of certain little meanings that I have internally about the number five."

Many speculate #5 represents where he was picked in the 2016 NFL Draft, but Ramsey hasn't confirmed it. Whatever those internal meanings were, they were important enough for him to pay $330,000.

Jaylon Smith: $100,000 to Be Himself

Dallas Cowboys linebacker Jaylon Smith didn't just want to wear #9 in 2021—he was determined to reclaim it. It was the number he'd worn at Notre Dame, and it held deep personal meaning. But reclaiming it came at a steep price.

Because of the NFL's jersey inventory rules, Smith had to buy out every one of his #54 jerseys in stock. The cost? Over $100,000.

Most players would've balked. Smith didn't blink. He paid the fee, got the blessing of Tony Romo (the last Cowboy to wear #9), and made the switch—a reminder that for some players, the emotional value of a number outweighs the financial cost.[238]

Many Others Wrote the Check

Dozens of players changed their numbers for the 2021 season—almost all seeking single digits—and unless they were joining a new team, they all paid the buyout costs. The exact amounts aren't made public, but given the inventory involved, some high-profile players could have faced seven-figure buyout costs.[239]

> **Julio Jones**—Tennessee Titans, #11 to #2
> **Leonard Fournette**—Tampa Bay Buccaneers, #28 to #7
> **Darius Slay**—Philadelphia Eagles, #24 to #2
> **Budda Baker**—Arizona Cardinals, #32 to #3
> **Ja'Whaun Bentley**—New England Patriots, #51 to #8

Patience is a Virtue

Many players like Dalvin Cook looked at the buyout costs and decided to wait a year. If players waited until the next off-season to change their numbers, they could change at no cost.

Dalvin Cook: Over a Million Dollars? No Thanks.

Minnesota Vikings running back Dalvin Cook wanted to switch to a single-digit number in 2021 until he saw the buyout cost. He checked the price: $1.5 million to buy out his existing jerseys.[240]

Cook decided he was perfectly content in his double-digit #33 for another year.

By waiting a year to make the change and providing advance notice to the league, Cook successfully changed his jersey to #4 for the 2022 season without being subject to the $1.5 million buyout cost.

Cam Akers: Half a Million? Still, No Thanks.

Adam Schefter reported via social media that Akers planned to switch to #3 in 2021, but the buyout cost would have been $500,000, so he waited until 2022 to make his move (at no cost).[241]

The Time Is Money Club

Several other players followed the same approach as Cook and Akers and avoided the buyout costs by waiting a year. These are just a few members of the Time Is Money Club:[242]

> **Rashod Bateman**—Baltimore Ravens, #12 to #7
> **Cam Dantzler**—Minnesota Vikings, #27 to #3
> **Anthony Brown**—Dallas Cowboys, #30 to #3
> **Jourdan Lewis**—Dallas Cowboys, #26 to #2
> **Isaiah McKenzie**—Buffalo Bills, #19 to #6

MLB's July 31 Deadline: Miss It and Pay, Sometimes

The NFL charges by inventory. Major League Baseball uses a deadline: request your number change by July 31, or pay to buy out every jersey with your old number on it.

For popular players, that typically means a buyout of $225,000 or more in unsold merchandise.

Carlos Santana: The $225,000 Number He Never Got

In 2024, veteran Carlos Santana joined the Minnesota Twins. Pitcher Joe Ryan intended to give his #41 jersey to Santana, generously offering to switch numbers.

But they missed the July 31 deadline. The cost to buy out all existing #41 Joe Ryan merchandise? More than $225,000.

Santana looked at the price tag and said forget it. He wore a different number instead.

Ryan's generous gesture was rendered meaningless by league rules and merchandise inventory.[243]

Santana isn't alone. Carlos Correa has also commented on an attempted number change halted by MLB during his time in Houston because the league had too much merchandise with his #1 on it.[244]

Juan Soto: The Loophole Master

When Juan Soto signed with the New York Mets, he wanted #22. Brett Baty had it, and Soto had missed the July 31 deadline—triggering a potential $225,000 buyout.

Soto gave Baty a Chevy Tahoe worth $92,000 (Chapter 11). Baty switched. The league approved it. Whether Soto paid any buyout fee to MLB isn't publicly known, but the transaction went through smoothly.[245]

Compare that to Carlos Santana, who also missed the deadline. When Joe Ryan tried to give Santana #41, MLB cited the $225,000+ buyout cost, and the deal fell apart. Why one transaction succeeded and another didn't remains unclear—different circumstances, different negotiations, or simply a different interpretation of the same rules.

Gary Sánchez: The Mystery Waiver

When catcher Gary Sánchez was traded to the Twins in 2022, he wanted #24. Outfielder Trevor Larnach had the number, and MLB initially cited a $25,000 buyout of jerseys as the reason to block the switch.

But after the Twins objected and lawyers got involved, the league eventually waived the fee, allowing Sánchez to wear #24.[244]

The details of why the fee was waived weren't disclosed. It's possible Sánchez's jersey sales were lower, making the inventory minimal. It's possible the Twins negotiated terms we don't know about. It's possible there were circumstances that made this case different from others.

What's clear is that these situations aren't always straightforward, and the publicly available information doesn't tell the whole story.

Anthony Rendon: "I Actually Hate #6"

Washington Nationals third baseman Anthony Rendon was brutally honest about his number situation:

"I actually hate the #6, but they gave it to me when I got here. I was 23 in college, and I was always 24 growing up for [Ken] Griffey [Jr.]. But 24 was taken in college, so they gave me the closest number. Everywhere we used to go, they called me Jordan. My birthday's in June, so there are some ties to six. I don't hate it, it's just not my favorite. It's a single number, too. That's weird. I've never had a single number."

"I was going to switch for this year. I could've taken 24, but MLB makes you buy all of the inventory, and it would've been like 40 grand. I told them, 'Don't make any more then. Just sell it and get the total down, and maybe I'll change it next year.'"[246]

Rendon's candid admission reveals something important: not every player loves their number. Some are stuck with digits they never wanted because the cost to change is more than they're willing to pay.

The Michael Jordan Fine:
The Bulls Pay $100,000 for Him to Be Himself

Before the NFL and MLB started charging players hundreds of thousands to buy out jersey inventory, the NBA had a simpler system: if you switch numbers without permission, we fine you per game.

Michael Jordan and the Chicago Bulls learned this the hard way in 1995.

When Michael Jordan left the Chicago Bulls after the 1993 season to pursue professional baseball, he wore #45 with the Birmingham Barons—his original favorite number and the one his older brother Larry had worn.

After baseball didn't work out, Jordan returned to the Bulls in March 1995 and initially stuck with #45 instead of his iconic #23.

But in the 1995 Eastern Conference semifinals against the Orlando Magic, things went poorly. After a dismal performance and a Game 1 loss, Magic guard Nick Anderson infamously commented: "number 45 ain't what 23 used to be."

The quote stung. Jordan knew it was true.

Before Game 2, Jordan switched back to #23, saying simply: "#23 is me, so why try to be something else?"

But league officials were furious about the sudden change. They threatened to fine the Bulls for every game that Jordan didn't wear #45.

The Bulls supported Jordan and allowed him to continue wearing #23 throughout the playoffs, but it came at a cost. How much? A $100,000 fine.[247]

And it didn't even help—the Bulls were eliminated by the Magic in that same series.

But Jordan had made his point: #23 was who he was, and the Bulls were willing to pay whatever it cost for him to be himself again.

The Bulls' fine wasn't about buying jerseys—it was about defying the league on Jordan's behalf. But it set a precedent: if you want to change your number, it's going to cost you. The only question is whether you're paying the league in fines or in inventory buyouts.

The hidden cost of jersey numbers isn't always visible in the headlines. We see the Rolex, the Porsche, the $100,000 handshake. But behind the scenes, leagues are charging hundreds of thousands—sometimes millions—just to change the number on your back.

And it's not every league. The NBA and NHL don't appear to charge players for unsold inventory when changing jersey numbers—or if they do, those costs are kept private. This is primarily an NFL problem, with MLB running a close second.

Why? Volume and revenue. NFL jersey sales dwarf other leagues, meaning more inventory at risk when a player changes numbers. When Jalen Ramsey switches from #20 to #5, that's potentially hundreds of thousands of unsold jerseys. In the NBA or NHL, the numbers are smaller—meaning either lower buyout costs or no buyouts at all.

In the NFL and MLB, changing your number mid-career isn't just about identity—it's about inventory. And someone has to pay for all those warehouses full of the wrong jerseys.

For some players, it's worth it. Jalen Ramsey paid $330,000 to wear #5. Jaylon Smith paid six figures to reclaim #9. They decided the number mattered more than the money.

For others, like Dalvin Cook, the price was too high—so they waited. And then there's Anthony Rendon, stuck with a number he hates because $40,000 seemed like too much to escape it.

As Michael Jordan showed us, sometimes the most expensive part of being yourself is convincing the league to let you be yourself.

CHAPTER 16

When No Means No

We've seen successful negotiations—Rolexes, cars, cash, and generous free gestures. We've seen deals gone wrong—broken promises, double-crosses, and lawsuits. But sometimes, negotiations never happen at all. Sometimes, no amount of money, no luxury gift, no pleading can convince someone to give up their number.

Sometimes, a player simply says: "No. This is mine."

Manute Bol and Tim Hardaway
The $500,000 Joke

During his time with the Golden State Warriors, Manute Bol wore jersey #10, a number that became part of a humorous and memorable story.

When rookie Tim Hardaway joined the Warriors in 1989, he hoped to wear #10—the number he'd worn since high school. But Bol already had it.

When Hardaway asked what it would take to get the number, Bol set the price at $500,000.

Hardaway said, "What? C'mon man, that's my whole contract."

Bol responded, "Exactly. That shows me if you want it real bad, give me your whole contract."[248]

Hardaway laughed and settled for #5 instead.

Bol's response wasn't serious—it was delivered with the dry wit that made him beloved by teammates and coaches alike. But the message was clear: some numbers aren't for sale at any price. Or at least, not at a price a rookie could afford.

To Bol, #10 reflected his personality: unexpected, humorous, and entirely his own.

Hardaway eventually got the coveted #10 a year later when Bol was traded to the Philadelphia 76ers. He continued to wear it for the next 11 seasons with four different teams. Fortunately for Hardaway, Bol wasn't waiting for him on any of those rosters.

Cam Newton and Jimmy Clausen
The $1,000,000 No-Joke

When Cam Newton was drafted first overall by the Carolina Panthers in 2011, he had one simple request: to keep wearing #2, the number he'd worn at Auburn while winning a national championship and the Heisman Trophy.

But Jimmy Clausen already wore #2 for the Panthers and wasn't going to give it up cheap.

When Newton asked what it would take to get the number, Clausen set the price at $1,000,000.

Newton thought he was joking. He laughed it off. But Clausen came back with a counteroffer:

"OK, bro, I talked to my people, we'll do it for $750,000."

That's when Newton abruptly broke off negotiations.

"I said, 'Boy, kiss my ass. A million dollars for a number? People don't make that in a lifetime.'"

Newton called the equipment manager and said he'd wear #1 instead. Then he made a vow:

"That will be the last time Jimmy Clausen is ever heard of in Carolina."[25]

And he delivered. Newton went on to win Offensive Rookie of the Year, NFL MVP, and led the Panthers to a Super Bowl. Clausen never started another game for the team.

Dwight Gooden and Frank Viola
"He Can Even Have My Wife…"

When the New York Mets acquired reigning AL Cy Young Award winner Frank Viola in 1989, he hoped to keep wearing #16, the number he'd worn with the Minnesota Twins.

Unfortunately for Viola, Dwight Gooden already had it—and after winning Rookie of the Year and establishing himself as a Mets icon while wearing #16, he wasn't about to give it up.

Gooden made his stance crystal clear in a quote that became instant clubhouse legend:

"I don't care how much money he makes. He can have my locker, I'll take him to all the best restaurants and show him New York. He can even have my wife, but he can't have my number. No way."[249]

Viola settled for #26, and Gooden kept his number—and his legacy—intact.

It was one of the most emphatic refusals in jersey number history, delivered with humor, bravado, and a firm grip on identity.

Dirk Nowitzki and Robert Pack
The Need to Flip Digits

When Dirk Nowitzki arrived in Dallas in 1998, he had one number in mind: #14. It was the number he wore in Germany, inspired by his idol Charles Barkley, who rocked it during the 1992 Olympics. For Dirk, #14 wasn't just a number—it was a tribute.

However, Robert Pack already wore it for the Mavericks, and he wasn't about to hand it over to a rookie.

When Dirk asked, Pack didn't hesitate: "Hell no, rookie. You're not getting my number."[121]

So Dirk improvised. He flipped the digits and chose #41—a quiet workaround that would define his legacy. Over the next 21 seasons, #41 became a lasting symbol of loyalty, humility, and greatness. Dirk won an MVP, a Finals MVP, and a championship, perfecting the fadeaway that became his signature—all while wearing the number he landed on by circumstance.

Pack's refusal wasn't cruel—it was classic locker room swagger. And in the end, it gave birth to one of the most memorable jersey numbers in NBA history.

Jaxson Dart and Deonte Banks
Too Rich for My Blood

Sometimes negotiations break down before they even begin—because the asking price is simply too high.

Rookie quarterback Jaxson Dart, who previously wore #2 at Ole Miss, considered acquiring the number from New York Giants cornerback Deonte Banks when he joined the team.

But after hearing what it might cost, Dart decided against pursuing it.

Banks never revealed the exact figure, but given that other deals were going for $50,000-$100,000 or more, Dart decided to try a different number. He went with #6.[250]

Sometimes negotiations fail not because someone refuses to sell, but because the buyer can't (or won't) pay the asking price.

Sometimes the smartest negotiation is the one you walk away from.

Carlos Correa and Nick Gordon
The Number That Got Away

When Carlos Correa signed with the Twins in 2022, he hoped to reclaim his old number—#1, the jersey he'd worn throughout his career with the Astros. But Nick Gordon already had it in Minnesota.

Gordon was ready to negotiate. "I don't know if I really want a car, you know?" he said. "I'm more of a cash guy."

But Gordon's approach—casually throwing out cars, cash, dreaming about what he could extract—turned Correa off entirely. Correa, seeking a fresh start, chose not to pursue the number and instead opted to wear #4 as the Twins' new shortstop.[251]

Sometimes negotiations fail not because of the price, but because of the approach.

Davante Adams and Malachi Corley
The Million Dollar Demand

When Davante Adams was traded to the New York Jets in 2024, he wanted to wear his familiar #17—the number he'd worn throughout his NFL career with both the Packers and the Raiders.

When he arrived in New York, Malachi Corley, a rookie, was wearing #17.

Adams, being a veteran and a professional, wasn't going to just take the number without asking. He believed he had a fair offer for the rookie: $17,000 in exchange for #17.

Corley's response? "Hey man, it's good to have you. Happy to have you on the squad. But I need a million."

Adams, who had not yet met Corley face-to-face, figured the Jets rookie was joking. But when Adams pressed the issue—noting that #14 was available—Corley had the audacity to respond:

"14 would look good on you, I think."

Adams was stunned. Here was a rookie with virtually no NFL experience telling a six-time Pro Bowler which number would look good on him.

Adams took the issue to the team, and they quickly intervened. "I got 17 and there was no exchange of money at all once that happened," Adams explained. "The money stayed in my pocket because I felt disrespected at the time."

Adams got #17. Corley got reassigned to a different number. And no money changed hands—but Adams made it clear that Corley's overzealous negotiation had backfired spectacularly.

"I'm laughing about it now because it's funny now," Adams said, "but at the time I was like, '14 would look good?' All that? Damn."[252]

Corley had misread the situation entirely. A rookie demanding a million dollars from a six-time Pro Bowler then suggesting an alternate number? That's not negotiating—that's misunderstanding leverage.

He could have taken the $17,000, been gracious, and built goodwill with his new star teammate. Instead, he overplayed his hand and lost the number with zero compensation.

Terrell Owens and James Hardy
The Power Play

When Terrell Owens joined the Buffalo Bills in 2009, he wanted to keep wearing his signature #81—the number he had worn throughout his career with the 49ers, Eagles, and Cowboys.

But the number was already assigned to James Hardy, a second-year wide receiver.

Rather than negotiate directly with Hardy, Owens made it clear in interviews that #81 "belongs to him."

Hardy was quietly reassigned to #84. Owens got his preferred number.[253]

There's no confirmed report that Owens explicitly demanded the change. He didn't need to. His public comments made his expectations clear, and the team made it happen. That's what leverage looks like.

It wasn't a negotiation. It was a power move. Owens didn't ask Hardy—he essentially told the team he expected #81, and they delivered.

Hardy had no leverage. Owens was the star. The decision was made.

These stories reveal an uncomfortable truth about jersey number negotiations: sometimes they aren't really negotiations at all. When leverage is unequal—rookie vs. star, unproven vs. icon—the outcome is often predetermined.

The players who succeed in these situations are the ones who read the room correctly. Hardaway laughed and moved on. Newton chose #1 and held a grudge. Dart walked away before overpaying.

But the players who fail? They either demand too much (Corley), refuse to understand their position (Hardy), or forget that in professional sports, power matters more than principle. Sometimes "no" is the only answer you'll get. And sometimes, you don't even get to ask the question.

CHAPTER 17

When Higher Powers Say No

In the previous chapter, players said no to each other. Teammates refused. Asking prices were too high. Leverage didn't exist. But sometimes, you don't even get to negotiate with your teammate. The decision is already made—by the team, the league, or the legend whose number you're asking for.

When higher powers say no, there's no counteroffer. There's no second chance. There's just finding another number.

When Teams Protect Numbers

Some teams retire numbers permanently. Others keep them "unofficially retired"—not formally honored, but quietly protected out of respect for legends who wore them. And some teams just have rules against players wearing certain numbers.

Todd Frazier and Paul O'Neill's #21

Todd Frazier grew up in Toms River, New Jersey, idolizing Paul O'Neill. He wore #21 his entire career as a tribute. When he signed with the Yankees in 2017, he hoped to wear his hero's number in his hero's stadium.

But the Yankees had unofficially retired #21 for O'Neill, the beloved right fielder who was a key part of four World Series championship teams in the 1990s.

Frazier hoped to speak with O'Neill for permission, but never made the call. Whether the Yankees shut down the idea or Frazier saw the fan backlash on social media, it was clear that #21 was off-limits.

Frazier settled for the number he was issued, #29. "At the end of the day, it doesn't really bother me that much," Frazier said. "I would have liked to have the number [21], but at the same time, I think #29 is a good number, too."[254]

The Yankees made it official in 2022, formally retiring #21 for O'Neill—confirming what everyone already knew in 2017.

Paige Bueckers and UConn's #1

When Paige Bueckers arrived at UConn as the nation's top recruit, she hoped to wear the same number she'd worn in high school—#1. It fit her perfectly—confident, competitive, and unafraid to take the spotlight.

But when she got to Storrs, she learned that UConn has a long-standing policy: players can't wear 1, 0, or 00. Coach Geno Auriemma believes these numbers draw unnecessary attention to individual players over team identity.[255]

Unable to keep her trademark #1, Bueckers chose #5 instead—a number she had worn while representing Team USA. It was a quiet tribute to her international experience and a symbol of her ability to adapt and lead on any stage.

She went on to make #5 matter at UConn, leading the Huskies to a National Championship, winning National Player of the Year honors, and becoming one of the most accomplished athletes in program history.

Desmond Bane and Nick Anderson's #22

When Desmond Bane joined the Orlando Magic in 2025, he wanted #22, the number he wore in Memphis during his first five years in the league. However, in Orlando, #22 was retired in honor of Nick Anderson, a franchise icon who played a key role in the Magic's early success.

Team policy meant Bane had to choose another number. He settled for #3 instead.[256]

No discussion. No exceptions. Some numbers are simply off-limits.

When Legends Refuse Permission

Abdul Carter's Double Denial: Lawrence Taylor and Phil Simms

When Abdul Carter was selected third overall by the New York Giants in the 2025 NFL Draft, he had high hopes of wearing a number steeped in tradition.

Carter wore #11 throughout his career at Penn State, where he became one of college football's most dominant pass rushers. He also admired Lawrence Taylor's signature #56—the number that defined Giants defense. However, the Giants had retired both numbers: #11 for quarterback Phil Simms and #56 for Lawrence Taylor.

So he did what any confident rookie would do—he asked for permission to wear one of these retired numbers.

First attempt: Lawrence Taylor's #56. That was a hard no from LT himself. No discussion. No negotiation. No chance.

Second attempt: Phil Simms' #11. After a lengthy and enthusiastic debate among the Simms family, that request was ultimately denied as well.

Two storied numbers. Two denials. Upon hearing the news, Carter joked he would "be out there with just my last name on my jersey, no number."[257]

Carter ultimately chose #51, deciding to create his own legacy rather than trying to wear someone else's.

When the League Says No

Sometimes it's not about a specific legend or team policy. Sometimes the league itself has rules that prevent athletes from wearing the numbers they want—no matter how much those numbers mean to them.

Dennis Rodman and #69: The Conservative Ban

During the 1999–2000 season, Dennis Rodman joined the Dallas Mavericks and requested to wear #69. Of course he did—this was Rodman, the man who showed up to book signings in a wedding dress.

The NBA said no. Sexual connotations. Standards. Decency.[258]

Rodman wore #70 instead, which satisfied the league but missed the entire point. He wanted #69 precisely because it would provoke. The NBA gave him #70, which provoked absolutely nothing.

It remains one of the most talked-about number denials in sports history—not because of legacy or respect, but because the league decided the number itself was inappropriate.

Reggie Bush and #5: The Single-Digit Ban

Reggie Bush was electric in college at USC wearing #5. It became part of his identity when he won the Heisman Trophy.

But when he entered the NFL in 2006, running backs weren't allowed to wear single-digit numbers. The NFL competition committee took up the matter, but after two conference calls, decided against granting Bush an exception to the league's positional numbering rules and forced him to change.[259]

Bush reluctantly took #25—a number that never looked quite right.

By the time the NFL changed its rules to allow single digits in 2021, Bush had been retired for four years. He never got to wear his true number at the pro level—a casualty of a rule that no longer exists. He was just ahead of his time.

Brian Bosworth and #44: The Restraining Order

At Oklahoma, Brian "The Boz" Bosworth made #44 his trademark. It was flashy, bold, and central to his larger-than-life persona.

But when he joined the Seattle Seahawks in 1987, the league told him linebackers couldn't wear numbers in the 40s. He was forced to switch to #55.

Bosworth didn't go quietly. He filed a restraining order, wore #44 in preseason, and even got to wear it for one regular-season game before the NFL forced him back to #55.

"It made me feel better," Bosworth said after the one game he was allowed to wear #44. "I felt more confident out there. The number thing may not be a big deal to anybody else, but it's a big deal to me. I'm very superstitious about my number, the way I approach the game, the way I do things."[260]

Though he didn't win the fight, Bosworth's battle over #44 became one of the most memorable jersey number controversies in NFL history.

In 2015, the NFL finally allowed linebackers to wear numbers in the 40s—a quiet vindication of the Boz's bold stand decades earlier. He eventually won the war—just 28 years too late to wear it himself.[261]

And sometimes, the higher power isn't the league or the legend—it's the team that chooses not to step in.

When Current Players Say No to Legends

Reggie Jackson and Mike Gallego's #9

When Reggie Jackson returned to the Oakland Athletics in 1987 for his final season, he wanted to reclaim #9—the number he'd worn during his first stint with the team in the early '70s, before #44 became inseparably tied to "Mr. October."

But Mike Gallego, a younger player in just his third season, was already wearing #9—and he refused to give it up. Gallego had worn #9 since his 1985 debut, building his own identity with the number. He wasn't about to surrender it, not even for a Hall of Famer.

No negotiation. No amount of respect for Jackson's career could change Gallego's mind. There were surely discussions, but according to the A's general manager, Sandy Alderson, "He wouldn't give it up."[262] The A's could have intervened, but they didn't—and that silence was the real decision, the higher power saying no.

Jackson ultimately wore #44 for his final season, marking a rare instance where a Hall of Famer couldn't reclaim his original number.

It's a reminder that sometimes tenure and possession matter more than legacy.

When higher powers say no—whether it's a team protecting legacy, a league enforcing rules, or a legend guarding his place in history— there's no negotiation. There's no counteroffer. There's just acceptance. Some athletes thrive anyway, like Paige Bueckers making #5 resonate at UConn.

Others fight back, like Brian Bosworth turning rejection into rebellion. And some, like Reggie Bush, never get the chance to wear the number that defined them.

CHAPTER 18

You May Have the Wrong Number

Athletes obsess over their numbers. They pay teammates six figures. They negotiate for months. They choose digits that represent family, legacy, tribute, superstition. But sometimes, none of that matters. Sometimes you wear the wrong number because your girlfriend miscounted. Sometimes your jersey gets misplaced. Sometimes a fortune-teller tells you to switch.

These are the stories of numbers that didn't go according to plan.

When Numbers Actually Change How You Feel

In the 1970s, Danny Buggs wore #86 and #88 with the New York Giants, but he always preferred the single digit #8. "I wore it in college ... It's psychological or something. I don't know. I feel *lighter* in 8."[263]

When Jeff Smoker reported to Rams mini-camp in 2005, he found a newly assigned #15 jersey waiting for him in his locker as opposed to his customary #9. He wasn't pleased. "I think it makes me look fat, the two digits," said Smoker. "I liked just the one digit. It kept me looking more slender and athletic."[264]

They both sounded ridiculous. They weren't wrong.

Eric Dickerson: #25 Was "Too Slow"

When Eric Dickerson was drafted second overall by the Los Angeles Rams in 1983, they handed him jersey #25 on draft day. He smiled for the cameras, held up the jersey, and later told his best friend what number he had chosen.

"He said, 'What number did you take?' I said, 'I took 25.' He said, '25?! Why'd you take that slow number? That's a slow number!' So I'm like, 'Man, you're right. That number does seem slow!'"

He couldn't explain it rationally, but he felt it. The number 25 should have been fine—plenty of great running backs had worn it. But to Dickerson, it felt heavy, sluggish, wrong. He wanted a number that felt fast.

So the next day, Dickerson requested a switch to the speedier-looking #29.[265]

The change worked. Wearing #29, Dickerson rushed for 1,808 yards his rookie season—an NFL rookie rushing record that still stands. The following year, he shattered O.J. Simpson's single-season rushing record with 2,105 yards, a mark that remains unbroken four decades later.

Would Dickerson have been just as fast in #25? Probably. But Dickerson didn't feel fast in #25. And in sports, feeling matters as much as reality.

The Rams retired #29 in his honor. No one remembers #25.

Dickerson wasn't crazy. And he wasn't alone.

Backed by Science

A 2023 UCLA study proved it: observers consistently perceive athletes with low jersey numbers as more slender than athletes with high numbers—even when the digits take up identical visual space.[266]

The researchers' hypothesis? "This effect results from learned associations between numbers and size attributes of objects in daily life." We see numbers on flour bags showing weight, on saw blades showing size, on weights showing mass. Our brains unconsciously link bigger numbers with bigger objects.

And that unconscious association affects how we see athletes.

It's not just players who noticed. NHL coaches started using it strategically. When Mikael Backlund played for the Calgary Flames in 2010, GM Darryl Sutter gave him #11 instead of his requested #8 or #19, saying he wanted Backlund to look taller with the vertical numbers. James van Riemsdyk and Toronto Maple Leafs GM Lou Lamoriello picked #25 to make him look bigger.[267]

Even Derrick Rose understood this instinctively. While many assumed he chose #1 because he was the first overall pick, the real reason ran deeper. As explained in Chapter 6, Rose's "Alter Ego Theory" showed how wearing #1 triggered a more aggressive, dominant version of himself—the player he was in AAU rather than the more passive playmaker he became in high school wearing #25.[26] The number literally altered his perception of who he was on the court, proving that digits can shape psychology just as much as psychology shapes digit choice.

Allen Iverson felt the same pull. When he joined the Pistons in 2008 and had to switch from his lifelong #3 to #1, he admitted later that it affected his overall performance and happiness. "Every time I put my jersey on, that s**t didn't feel right."[268] And it showed. Iverson only played in 54 games that season while battling various injuries. The wrong number disrupted his rhythm, showing how digits can unsettle even the most confident stars.

So when Deion Sanders signed with the Baltimore Ravens in 2004 after coming out of retirement and chose to wear #37 to represent his age,[205] he wasn't being superstitious. His brain was processing that higher number as heavier, older, less dynamic. It actually affected how people saw him—and how he saw himself. He played two seasons with the Ravens, contributing as a situational cornerback and mentor, but not at his Hall of Fame level.

Nearly a decade later, Derek Fisher made the same choice with the Oklahoma City Thunder, donning #37 to symbolize his age. The results were striking: he appeared in only 24 games, and his field-goal percentage dropped to .333, the lowest of his career.[269] Maybe it was simply age catching up with him. Maybe wearing his age had its own psychological effect. In both cases, the number itself seemed to reinforce the perception of decline.

Sometimes numbers feel wrong because they change your perception. And your opponents'. And the fans'.

The math is simple: Lower numbers look lighter, faster, more dynamic. Higher numbers look heavier, slower, more powerful. It's not superstition. It's neuroscience. Which explains why some numbers feel wrong from the start—and why athletes will do almost anything to change them.

This also explains why 79% of NFL receivers had switched to teen numbers by 2019, after the league changed the rules in 2004,[267] and then dozens of additional players switched to single digits beginning in 2021 when the league again relaxed the numbering restrictions (Chapter 15). They weren't just following fashion—they were following their instincts. And science proves those instincts are correct.

The Miscount That Became a Brand

Amon-Ra St. Brown: #14 Should Have Been #16

When the Detroit Lions drafted wide receiver Amon-Ra St. Brown in 2021, he carried a massive chip on his shoulder. He'd been passed over repeatedly in the draft, watching receiver after receiver get selected before him.

St. Brown wanted to remember exactly how many receivers had been taken ahead of him. To keep that number close—to use it as fuel, as motivation, as a constant reminder—he asked his girlfriend, Brooklyn Adams, to track it during the draft.

She told him: 14 receivers were taken before you.

So he chose to wear #14 for the Lions—a badge of disrespect, a symbol of being overlooked. Every catch, every touchdown would be proof that those 14 teams had made a mistake.

The number became his identity—his brand, his motivation.

Except ... later, his girlfriend admitted something: she'd lost count.

"He'll never admit this, but he asked me to count the amount of receivers [drafted] before him and that was gonna be his number, and I messed up," Adams said on Netflix's *Quarterback*. "And it's not 14 and I told him it was 14. And so that's why he's 14."[270]

The real number was 16.

By then, it was too late. The jerseys were made. The promotional materials were printed. Number 14 had already become identified with

Amon-Ra St. Brown, the overlooked receiver with something to prove.

And ironically, #14 has now become his brand—a symbol of his underdog mentality and chip-on-the-shoulder attitude. It doesn't matter that the math was wrong. The meaning stuck.

A number might be chosen for accuracy. It might be chosen for feeling. And occasionally, you build your entire identity on a number that was based on a miscount—and it works anyway.

The One-Night Stands: When Legends Had to Improvise

For whatever reason—loss, damage, or theft—sometimes the right jersey hasn't always been available. Prior to the expansive team shops and same-day delivery, the only option in the past was to wear something else. Sometimes, this even happened to the best of players.

Michael Jordan: #12—On February 14, 1990, Michael Jordan walked onto the court against the Orlando Magic wearing #12 instead of his customary #23. No nameplate. No explanation. Just Jordan in the wrong number. Magic security later found Jordan's #23 jersey hidden in the ceiling tiles—someone was hoping to sell a piece of history.[271]

Kareem Abdul-Jabbar #40 and #50—Kareem was spotted on two occasions wearing something other than his customary #33 jersey. On November 23 and 24, 1976, Kareem Abdul-Jabbar wore #40 against the Denver Nuggets, and almost ten years later on January 20, 1986, he donned #50 as a replacement against the Chicago Bulls. In both cases, the explanation was simply that his original jersey was unavailable.[272]

James Worthy: #00—On December 11, 1987, James Worthy wore a substitution #00 jersey because, according to TBS reporter, Bob Neal, "[Worthy's customary #42] jersey was lost at the dry cleaners."[167]

Isiah Thomas: #42—On May 8, 1985, in Game 5 of the second-round playoff series between the Pistons and Celtics, Isiah Thomas' #11 jersey was unavailable. As the only alternative, he donned a nameless #42 jersey which apparently affected his performance, scoring just 18 points in the contest. Thomas later reflected, "The leprechaun [Celtic mascot] took my #11 jersey that night in Boston."[273]

Elgin Baylor: #34—Hall of Fame Laker and 11-time All-Star Elgin Baylor goes down as perhaps the finest player in the NBA to wear #22 (sorry, Clyde Drexler), which he donned for his entire 14-year career with the exception of one half of one very important game. On April 9, 1959, in Game 4 of the NBA Finals against the Boston Celtics, rookie Elgin Baylor took the court wearing #34 instead of his customary #22. He played the first half in the alternate jersey before switching back to #22 for the second half.[274] Perhaps misplaced or in need of repair at the beginning of the game, the brief jersey mishap remains one of the earliest examples of a superstar appearing in the "wrong" number on basketball's biggest stage.

Even the best players sometimes have to improvise. They just make it look good when they do.

When Your New Number Doesn't Live up to the Hype

Nicklas Bendtner: #52—The Fortune-Teller's Advice

In 2009, Nicklas Bendtner changed from #26 to #52 at Arsenal based on advice from a fortune-teller his mother knew. The clairvoyant said

26 was unlucky (2 + 6 = 8, his "bad number"), while 7 was his lucky number. But #7 was already taken, and #25 (2 + 5 = 7) was also taken, so he settled on #52 (5 + 2 = 7). Coincidentally, some fans thought it was a tribute to his salary of £52,000 a week. Others suggested that he doubled his number from #26 to #52 in response to his manager's request for twice the effort from him. By Bendtner's own account, the fortune-teller numerology was the true reason for the switch.[275]

Bendtner even offered to reimburse fans who'd bought his old #26 jersey.

The result? In 64 appearances wearing #52, he scored 21 goals—right on par with his performance before the number change (15 goals in 50 appearances). Following the 2009–10 season, his role at Arsenal diminished, and he spent his remaining years with the club primarily in cup games or as a substitute.

The fortune-teller didn't seem to help. The number didn't seem to matter.

Deion Sanders: #21—The Owner's Prank

"Prime Time" Deion Sanders always wore #21. It was his signature. His brand. His identity.

So when he signed with the Washington Redskins in 2000, there was never any question what number he'd wear. Owner Dan Snyder knew it. Everyone knew it.

But Snyder couldn't resist having a little fun.

During the signing, Snyder pulled out a jersey—but it wasn't #21. Sanders's face dropped. He was furious. After everything, after the negotiations, after choosing Washington, they were going to make him wear a different number?

Deion was ready to walk out.

Then Snyder started laughing and pulled out the real jersey: #21, exactly as promised.[276]

It was a prank—harmless in hindsight, but it revealed something deeper. For an athlete like Sanders, the number wasn't just decoration. It was identity. It was legacy. The prank only worked because Snyder understood that—and knew threatening it, even as a joke, would provoke a genuine reaction.

John Davidson: #00—Looking for Shutouts

John Davidson was a solid goaltender for the New York Rangers during the 1970s, typically wearing #30. But heading into the 1977–78 season, he decided to make a change that seemed brilliant in theory.

Davidson switched to #00—double zero. For a goaltender, the logic was undeniable: zeros represent shutouts, the ultimate achievement for any netminder. What better way to manifest success than to wear your goal on your back?

His teammate Phil Esposito, who wore #77, encouraged the move. Teammate Ken Hodge wore #88. The Rangers would have a trio of matching double-digit numbers, and Davidson would be draped in the symbolism of perfection.[277]

The result? One shutout. In 34 games wearing #00, Davidson recorded exactly one shutout.

It was the opposite of what he hoped for. The number that was supposed to bring shutouts brought just one—an ironic twist that defeated the entire purpose.

Davidson switched back to #30 the following season, and #00 faded into NHL history as a cautionary tale: sometimes the number you choose to inspire greatness becomes a reminder of irony instead.[14]

Before They Became Legends

Some of the all-time greats didn't start their careers wearing the numbers we remember them by. Hammerin' Hank wore #5. Sweetness wore #21. Clemente wore #13. For brief moments— sometimes just days—these legends wore numbers that weren't quite right, numbers they were waiting to outgrow.

Here are just some of the stories of legendary players wearing numbers that are barely footnotes in sports history.

Hank Aaron: #5 Before He Was #44

Hank Aaron and #44 are inseparable. He hit 44 home runs in four different seasons. He broke Babe Ruth's record in the fourth inning of the fourth month against a pitcher wearing #44. The number was destiny.

But when Aaron arrived for his 1954 rookie season with the Milwaukee Braves, the equipment manager simply told him to keep wearing what he'd had all spring: #5.

Aaron didn't complain. He wore #5 professionally, finishing fourth in NL Rookie of the Year voting. But when the 1955 season arrived, he switched to #44 and never looked back.[98]

What followed was one of the most fitting number-player connections in sports history. Hammerin' Hank became #44, and #44 became Hammerin' Hank—a bond so powerful that the number itself seemed to predict his destiny.

Reggie White: #91 Before He Was #92

Known as the Minister of Defense, Reggie White's jersey identity was remarkably consistent. At the University of Tennessee he wore #92, and he carried that number into the USFL with the Memphis Showboats.

But when he joined the Philadelphia Eagles in 1985, #92 was already taken, so he was temporarily assigned #91.[278]

As soon as #92 became available the following season, White reclaimed it—deliberately—and wore it for the rest of his Hall of Fame career with the Eagles, Packers, and Panthers.

The one-year detour into #91 was pure roster logistics. White's true number was always #92, and both the Eagles and Packers eventually retired it in his honor.

Roberto Clemente: #13 Before He Was #21

Roberto Clemente's #21 became sacred in Pittsburgh. The right-field fence at PNC Park stands 21 feet high in tribute. Stars from Carlos Delgado to Sammy Sosa to Paul O'Neill wore it in his honor.

Clemente wanted #21 from the start—21 letters in Roberto Clemente Walker. But at the time, Earl Smith had it.

So Clemente wore #13. Just for a few days—so briefly that photos hardly exist.[98]

Then Smith was sent back to the minors after recording just one hit in, appropriately, 21 at-bats. The number was available.

Clemente claimed #21 and made sure no one else ever wore it in Pittsburgh again. His 3,000th hit, his World Series heroics, his Hall of Fame career—all accomplished wearing #21. When he died in 1972 delivering aid to earthquake victims in Nicaragua, the number became a memorial to both his baseball excellence and his humanitarian legacy.

Sometimes a number becomes so intertwined with a player's legacy that it's impossible to imagine them wearing anything else. For

Clemente, #21 wasn't just a number—it was his name, his identity, his immortality.

Walter Payton: #21 Before He Was #34

Walter Payton's greatness is forever stitched into #34. It's the number retired by the Bears, the number whispered whenever "Sweetness" is invoked. But what a lot of people don't know is that when he first arrived in Chicago as the fourth overall pick in the 1975 draft, he was initially assigned #21.[279]

That assignment never made it past the paperwork. Payton switched numbers prior to the season, and the record books only know Sweetness as wearing #34.

Those record books show a lot more than that. At the time of his retirement, Payton held the NFL records for carries (3,838), rushing yards (16,726), rushing touchdowns (110), receptions by a running back (492), receiving yards by a running back (4,538), and total yards from scrimmage (21,264). He was the league MVP in 1977, and a Super Bowl champion with the Bears in 1985.

By the time his career ended, #34 was more than a jersey. It was shorthand for toughness, elegance, and relentless drive. Retired by the Bears, immortalized in Canton, and remembered by generations, #34 remains the purest symbol of Sweetness.[280]

Mickey Mantle: #6 Before He Was #7

When the Yankees brought 19-year-old Mickey Mantle to the majors in 1951, the hype was unprecedented. "The greatest prospect I've seen in my time, and I go back quite a ways," said Yankees coach Bill Dickey, a Hall of Famer who'd played alongside Ruth and Gehrig.

New York assigned him #6,[98] positioning him as the next in a formidable sequence: Ruth (#3), Gehrig (#4), DiMaggio (#5), and now Mantle (#6). The symbolism was intentional. The expectations were crushing.

And Mantle crumbled under them.

He hit just .260/.341/.423 over his first 76 games. The Yankees sent him down to Triple-A Kansas City in July, and he continued to struggle so badly he nearly quit baseball entirely. Only a now-famous pep talk from his father convinced him to persevere.

The slump finally ended. When Mantle returned to the big club in late August, third baseman Bobby Brown was wearing #6.

So Mantle took #7 instead.

Maybe it was the number change. Maybe it was the demotion. Maybe it was his father's words. But something shifted. Mantle became the player everyone expected—just not in the number they expected.

The wrong number at the wrong time can lead to the right number at the right moment. Getting out from under the weight of expectation can mean getting out from under the number that carried it.

The wrong number might be an accidental miscount, a stolen jersey, a prank. It might be a placeholder before you earn the one you want. Or it's wrong because your brain perceives it as heavier, slower, or just not who you are.

Numbers are identity, psychology, and perception wrapped into one or two digits. Get the wrong one, and it doesn't just feel wrong—it actually changes how you move, how you play, how others see you.

Which is why athletes obsess over them. And why, when they finally get the right number, everything clicks into place.

CHAPTER 19

Quirky Numbers

While many athletes choose digits that honor family, faith, or fallen heroes, others pick numbers purely because they're unusual, funny, or just plain weird. These quirky numbers stand out not because they honor tradition, but because they defy it. They're chosen for puns, personality, humor, or simple defiance of convention. They make you do a double-take—like spotting a personalized license plate. Sometimes you get it immediately. Sometimes you're left wondering what they're trying to say.

The Pun Masters

Some athletes looked at their jersey number as an opportunity for wordplay. And it's always a fan favorite.

Heinz 57: A Saucy Selection

In the gritty world of professional hockey, jersey numbers often carry weight—legacy, superstition, or personal meaning. But for two players, #57 was all about the sauce.

Steve Heinze wanted #57 in Boston as a play on his name, but the Bruins said no.[281] He finally got it in Columbus in 2000 and continued to wear it for the rest of his career with the Buffalo Sabres and Los Angeles Kings.[282]

Shawn Heins wore #57 with Pittsburgh in 2002–03—perfect for the city where Heinz was founded. Swap the "s" for a "z," and the pun is complete.[14]

Two players. One number. One brand.

Andrei Kirilenko: #47—"AK-47"

When Andrei Kirilenko joined the Utah Jazz in 2001, he wanted #13—the number his mother wore during her playing days—but it was taken by John Amaechi. Teammate Quincy Lewis had a better idea: "Andrei Kirilenko—AK, that's your initials. AK-47 is the most famous machine gun. You have to pick 47."[283]

The nickname stuck instantly. Not only did it match his initials and jersey number, but it also connected to Kirilenko's Russian heritage—the AK-47 rifle was invented in his hometown of Izhevsk.

Kirilenko embraced the number and the nickname, which became widely known throughout his NBA career. Known for his defensive versatility and high-energy play, "AK-47" became more than a clever moniker—it was a symbol of identity, intensity, and international impact.

Natasha Cloud: #9—"Cloud 9"

Sometimes the perfect pun is already in your name—you just need the right number to unlock it.

WNBA guard Natasha Cloud wears #9, creating the effortless wordplay "Cloud 9"—the idiom for extreme happiness or bliss. Unlike the elaborate formula of AK-47, Cloud's connection is simple and obvious. But obvious doesn't mean less effective.

"Cloud 9" became such a natural fit that *SLAM Magazine* titled their 2025 feature on her move to the New York Liberty "Back on Cloud 9."[284]

The phrase appears on merchandise, social media, and in fan conversations—a perfect example of a number that transforms a surname into a brand-ready catchphrase. Cloud didn't have to force it or build a business empire around it. Sometimes the best number stories are the ones that just work.

Chad Johnson: #85—Ochocinco

Chad Johnson publicly changed his name to Ochocinco in 2008 to reflect his jersey number #85 and his larger-than-life personality.

But there's more to the story.

Johnson first used the name in 2006 during Hispanic Heritage Month, coming out of the tunnel with a Velcro nameplate that said "Ochocinco." Quarterback Carson Palmer ripped the label off before the game, but Johnson was fined $5,000 anyway.

Johnson liked the name so much that he legally changed his surname in 2008 to Ochocinco. But he waited until 2009 to wear it on his jersey to avoid having to buy out all of the #85 Johnson jerseys (Chapter 15).

The funny thing is, "Ochocinco" doesn't actually mean 85. It means "eight five." The correct Spanish translation for 85 is "ochenta y cinco"—but maybe that was too many letters for the back of a jersey.

The change lasted until 2012 when he legally switched back to Chad Johnson, but he kept Ochocinco as his middle name.[285]

Still, Chad Ochocinco remains one of the most memorable name-number combinations in NFL history—a perfect blend of personality, branding, and linguistic chaos.

Ochocinco changed his name to match his number. But for some athletes, the process worked in reverse—they chose their numbers to match the names they already had.

The Name Games

Some athletes chose numbers that literally spelled out their names or identities.

Jim Otto: #00—"Aught-O"

Wearing #0 is one thing, but double zero is a rarity—only four players in NFL history have ever worn it.

Jim Otto, Hall of Fame center for the Oakland Raiders, wore #00 throughout his AFL and NFL careers. His reasoning? "Aught" is an old-fashioned way of saying "oh," so "aught-oh" = "oh-oh" = 00.

It made sense to him, if not to everyone else.

Otto wore #00 through his entire 15-year career in the AFL and NFL. Even though the NFL banned the issuance of #00 in 1973, he was able to wear it until his retirement in 1974. He was inducted into the Hall of Fame in 1980.[286]

Adam Ottavino: #0—"O" for Ottavino

Adam Ottavino is one of only two pitchers in MLB history to wear #0. His reasoning? The zero looks like the letter "O" and "O" is for Ottavino.

He'd worn it since Little League, but his first MLB team, the St. Louis Cardinals, wouldn't allow it. He's since worn #0 with the Rockies, Yankees, Red Sox, and Mets. Sometimes the quirkiest numbers are the most personal.[287]

When Your Name IS the Number

Deron Quint wore #5 with the Winnipeg Jets and the Phoenix Coyotes. The reason? "Quint" is a Latin prefix meaning "five." When your surname does the work, why complicate it?

Scott Lachance wore #7 with the New York Islanders and the Columbus Blue Jackets for similar reasons. "La chance" means "the luck" in French, but it also contains "chance"—historically associated with dice games. The lucky number? Seven.

Two defensemen, two names, two obvious choices.[14]

Neil Sheehy: #0—Adding the Missing "O" in O'Sheehy

Neil Sheehy played defense in the NHL during the 1980s and early 1990s, and wore #0 when he played for the Hartford Whalers in 1987–88.

His choice of #0 had a clever backstory: Sheehy's family name was originally spelled "O'Sheehy" before the "O" was dropped generations earlier.[14]

By wearing #0, Sheehy paid tribute to the missing letter in his family's name—a subtle nod to Irish heritage and a creative way to reclaim a piece of family history that had been lost over time.

It was one of the more thoughtful number choices in hockey history, hiding a genealogical Easter egg in plain sight on the back of his jersey.

Jordin Tootoo: #22—Just Like It Sounds

Jordin Tootoo made history as the first player of Inuit descent to play in the NHL, skating for teams including the Nashville Predators, Detroit Red Wings, New Jersey Devils, and Chicago Blackhawks over his 13-year career.

His jersey number, which he wore for every team he played for, was the most obvious choice imaginable: #22, matching his surname perfectly.[14]

Tootoo wore the number with pride throughout his career, and it became instantly recognizable. Fans loved the synchronicity—it was simple, memorable, and impossible to forget.

In a league where most numbers require explanation, Tootoo's needed none. His name was his number, his number was his name, and #22 became one of the most distinctive jersey identities in modern hockey.

What Could Have Been—Missed Opportunities

Not every player embraces the obvious. Mike Commodore, whose last name screamed for #64 (a nod to the nostalgic Commodore 64 computer), passed on the opportunity and never adopted the number. Miroslav Satan, whose surname offered the perfect setup for #6 (a total of three 6's on his jersey if you count the sleeves), never wore it. Sometimes the best number stories are the ones players choose—and sometimes they're the ones we can only imagine.[14]

While some numbers come from names, others come from physical attributes.

Size Matters

Some athletes didn't choose their numbers for meaning or legacy— they chose them because of simple mathematics: how tall they stood, how much they weighed, or how small a jersey they needed to fit their frame.

Derek Jeter: #2—The Smallest Jersey

When Jeter joined the Yankees, he wanted #13—the number his father wore. But the clubhouse had a different plan. "[They] just gave it to me, man," Jeter later explained on the *Drink Champs* podcast. "I think it was the smallest jersey. I really do."

And the measurements backed him up. At 18, Jeter checked in at 6'2", 154 pounds—dressed. He was so skinny that #2 was simply the jersey that fit him best.

"There's all these rumors of why they gave me No. 2," Jeter said. "I just think No. 2 was the smallest jersey they had, man."[288]

Over two decades, that "smallest jersey" became a symbol of clutch postseason performance, professionalism, and championship pedigree. One of the most storied numbers in Yankees history exists because a skinny kid needed a jersey that wouldn't swallow him whole.

Brett Butler: #22—Too Small to Matter

At 5'10" and 160 pounds, Brett Butler heard it constantly throughout his baseball career: he was too small to make it. Scouts doubted him. Coaches questioned him. But Butler turned that skepticism into motivation—and into his jersey number.

"I really chose 2 because I am little, and I needed the littlest number and the littlest uniform that they had," Butler explained.[107] He wore #2 or #22 for the majority of his 17-year MLB career as a reminder of how many times he was told he was "2 small" to play in the major leagues.

Butler proved them all wrong. He was an All-Star, stole 558 bases, and collected 2,375 hits. Every time he stepped to the plate wearing #2, it was a quiet declaration: size doesn't determine success.

Shawn Bradley: #76—Perfect Alignment

Shawn Bradley stood 7'6"—one of the tallest players in NBA history. When he was drafted second overall by the Philadelphia 76ers in 1993, the jersey number choice seemed almost predestined.

Bradley chose #76, creating a perfect triple alignment: his height (7'6"), his team's name (the 76ers), and the number itself.[289] It was too perfect to pass up—a convergence of physical reality, franchise identity, and numerical symmetry. It was a walking reminder that sometimes the most obvious choice is also the perfect choice.

It wasn't just a jersey number—it was destiny wearing shorts.

Dellin Betances: #68—Standing Tall on the Mound

When Dellin Betances made his debut with the New York Yankees in 2011, he was listed at 6'8"—an imposing height for any pitcher, let alone a reliever. The number choice was obvious.

Just like Bradley, Betances opted to wear his height on his back: #68.[107]

Betances transformed #68 during his Yankees tenure, becoming a four-time All-Star and one of the most dominant relievers in baseball. His towering frame made him intimidating on the mound, and his jersey number made sure everyone knew exactly how tall he stood. After leaving the Yankees, Betances also wore #68 with the Mets.

Bixente Lizarazu: #69—Using the Metric System

When French soccer legend Bixente Lizarazu returned to Bayern Munich for his second stint in 2005, he chose #69—a number that raised eyebrows across Europe.

But Lizarazu quickly clarified it wasn't what people thought.

Not only was he born in 1969, but he was 1.69 meters tall, and weighed 69 kilograms. Three different measurements, all resulting in the same number—69.[290]

It was a mathematical coincidence too perfect to ignore. Lizarazu wore #69 during his final seasons with Bayern, winning two more Bundesliga titles and cementing his legacy as one of soccer's elite left-backs. The number that seemed scandalous was actually just simple arithmetic—sometimes a player's dimensions define their digits.

Mathematical Minds

Iván Zamorano: #18—1 + 8 = 9

When Iván Zamorano joined Inter Milan, he initially wore his familiar #9—a number he cherished throughout his career.

But in 1998, after the arrival of Brazilian superstar Ronaldo Nazário, Zamorano graciously offered up the coveted #9 to Ronaldo. Rather than forsake his identity and legacy, Zamorano asked for a creative solution. With the approval of club management (and reportedly the Italian federation), he switched to #18, but insisted on placing a "+" sign between the digits—creating the jersey "1+8." The math was simple: 1 + 8 = 9.

"At first we used tape and made a sign, but after the fourth or fifth match, the sports manufacturer who made Inter's shirts started sending them with the 1+8."[291]

Over the next seasons, that jersey became iconic: part humor, part historical footnote, and the best-selling shirt in the history of Italian football.

Aron Baynes: #46—A Family Equation

When Aron Baynes joined the Boston Celtics in 2017, he chose #46— a number almost no one else in the league had worn.

The choice wasn't arbitrary. Baynes explained that 46 was the sum of his son's birthday digits (month + day + year), and later added that when he combined the numbers tied to his three children and even his wife, the totals all came out to 46.[292]

For Baynes, the jersey became a kind of equation: family expressed as math, stitched onto his back. He carried #46 through Boston, Phoenix, and Toronto, turning an unusual number into a family crest.

Dennis Rodman: #91 & #73—The Ten Man

Dennis Rodman wore #10 with the Detroit Pistons, a number he elevated through rebounding, defense, and pure personality. When he joined the Chicago Bulls, #10 was retired for Bob Love. He then asked for #0 and was denied.

Rodman then chose #91, reasoning it was about as far from zero as he could get—an act of defiance that perfectly suited his persona.[293] But true to form, he didn't stop there. He offered two other explanations for the number:

- 9 + 1 = 10—a nod to his original Pistons number.
- 91 as the first two digits of 911—a playful nod to emergencies and chaos on the court.

When he later joined the Lakers, he chose #73: 7 + 3 = 10. He stated the number also symbolically represented his seven rebounding titles and three championships at that point in his career.

Other than Rodman's last stint in Dallas, where he wore #70 after being denied #69 (Chapter 17), Rodman's numbers were always either #10 or digits that added up to 10.[294]

Kenyon Martin: #6—Unconfirmed, but the Math Works

Kenyon Martin wore #6 with the New Jersey Nets, Denver Nuggets, and Milwaukee Bucks.

Born on December 30 (12/30), fans noticed an intriguing mathematical coincidence: $1 + 2 + 3 + 0 = 6$. The theory circulated online and in sports forums, but Martin himself has never confirmed or denied it.[295]

It's possible the connection is purely coincidental. Or maybe he quietly chose #6 as a personal tribute to his birthdate. Without confirmation, it remains one of the NBA's unsolved number mysteries.

The Double-Digit Workarounds

Phil Esposito & Ken Hodge: #77 and #88

In the early days of the NHL, jersey numbers above 40 were rare. But that began to change in the 1970s as players sought more individuality—and two New York Rangers helped lead the way.

When the Rangers acquired Phil Esposito and Ken Hodge from the Boston Bruins, they ran into a numbers problem. Esposito had long worn #7, and Hodge wore #8. But in New York, those numbers were already taken.

Rather than pick something random, they got creative:[296]

> Esposito chose #77
> Hodge took #88

It was a clever workaround—doubling their original digits to keep the spirit of their numbers alive. At the time, it was unusual, even bold. But it helped pave the way for the era of high-numbered stars and personalized jerseys that would soon follow.

The Superstitious Minded

Turk Wendell: #99—Not Just a Jersey Number, but a Way of Life

Turk Wendell, a quirky relief pitcher, became forever linked to #99 during his tenure with the New York Mets, Philadelphia Phillies, and Colorado Rockies.

But Wendell didn't stop at his jersey. He incorporated 99 into his contracts as a matter of superstition, signing deals worth amounts like:

> $1,200,000.99
> $9,999,999.99

Wendell explained that he told his agent beforehand, "If I could ever get all nines, let's do it."[297]

His unusual number and his contract quirks made him one of baseball's most memorable characters—a reminder that some superstitions go beyond the field and into the bank account.

The Bold Statements

Gilbert Arenas: #0—"Agent Zero"

Lots of athletes have worn the number 0, but Gilbert "Agent Zero" Arenas made it memorable with his reasoning.

Arenas wore #25 in high school, but when he got to the University of Arizona, the number was retired—previously worn by Steve Kerr. He wasn't good enough at the time to force the number out of retirement, and people had no problem telling him that.

So he chose a different number—and a new motivation.

"When I seen that zero, I was like, 'Man, that was how many minutes they said I would play in Arizona.'"[298]

That year, he ended up playing more than 32 minutes a game for the Wildcats and went on to become an All-Star in the NBA. The nickname "Agent Zero" stuck, and #0 became a trademark of his explosive scoring and fearless confidence.

Manny Ramirez: #99—The Mannywood Era

When Manny Ramirez joined the Dodgers in 2008, he wanted #34 as a tribute to Fernando Valenzuela. The team said no. He also considered #28, briefly wore #66, then switched to #99—a number he debuted on August 1, 2008.[299]

Though the number wasn't his first choice, it matched his outsized personality and helped define his "Mannywood" era in Los Angeles. He continued to wear #99 with the Chicago White Sox, cementing it as a signature part of his late-career reinvention.[300]

The Tributes Disguised as Quirks

Kevyn Adams: #42—The Answer to Everything

In Chapter 2 we saw that Ron Artest wore #37 because that was the number of weeks Michael Jackson's *Thriller* topped the charts. But Artest isn't the only athlete in tune with pop culture.

When Kevyn Adams joined the Toronto Maple Leafs, he chose #42—a number that puzzled teammates and fans alike.

The reason had nothing to do with hockey history or family tradition. Kevyn was a devoted fan of Douglas Adams's science fiction comedy *The Hitchhiker's Guide to the Galaxy*, in which a supercomputer calculates that the number 42 is the answer to the ultimate question of life, the universe, and everything.[14]

For Kevyn Adams, wearing #42 was a tribute to one of literature's most beloved inside jokes—a number that represents the search for meaning in an absurd universe. It was nerdy, philosophical, and deeply personal.

Sometimes the quirkiest numbers are the ones that make you smile.

Triple Digits

Most jersey numbers fit comfortably between 0 and 99. But every once in a while, someone breaks through the century mark—and the results are always memorable.

Scott Meyer: #100—When the Roster Gets Too Big

In spring training 1989, the Oakland A's had a problem: they had 100 players in camp. Equipment managers typically issue numbers sequentially, and when they reached the 100th player, minor league pitcher Scott Meyer, they did the only logical thing—they gave him #100.[107]

Meyer never made it to the big league roster, and #100 never appeared in an actual MLB game. But for a few weeks in Arizona, baseball had its first-ever three-digit jersey number, a quiet piece of spring training history that exists only in camp photos and fan scorecards.

Tommy Oar: #121—They Didn't Think He'd Play

When Australian midfielder Tommy Oar made his international debut in an Asian World Cup qualifier against Indonesia in 2010, he wore a rather unorthodox three-digit jersey: #121.[290]

The number wasn't the result of Oar's personal choice. The Asian Football Confederation requires all players in a qualifying campaign to be assigned a number they keep throughout, regardless of whether they're likely to play.

The most likely scenario is that the Socceroos coach Pim Verbeek didn't believe Oar would see any playing time during the campaign, and so the unorthodox number on the roster was a harmless administrative detail. However, Oar did take the pitch and made history wearing what remains one of the most ridiculous jersey numbers ever worn in international play.

Edson Alvarez: #282—The Triple-Digit Tradition

In Mexico's Liga MX, three-digit numbers became a quirky tradition for young players at Club América. Midfielder Edson Alvarez wore #282 during his debut with the club in 2016 when he was just 19 years old.[290]

The number had no personal significance—it was simply part of Club América's system for assigning unusual numbers to squad players and youth prospects. Other young players wore #301, #340, and similarly absurd digits, creating a brief era where Mexican soccer embraced numerical chaos.

Alvarez eventually graduated to more traditional numbers, but #282 remains a badge of his early career, where he quickly rose to stardom while retaining his three-digit number—proof that sometimes the strangest numbers mark the start of something great.

Rogério Ceni: #618—A Milestone Number

Rogério Ceni, the legendary São Paulo goalkeeper, is best known for wearing the traditional #1 jersey throughout his career. But on one special occasion, he wore a unique number to commemorate a major milestone.

In 2005, Ceni wore #618 for his record-breaking 618th appearance for São Paulo.[301]

The number was a one-time tribute to commemorate his record-breaking match, reflecting his remarkable consistency and the deep connection he had with São Paulo that would span over two decades and 1,237 total appearances.

The Most Bizarre Numbers

Eddie Gaedel: #1/8—The Only Fraction

Eddie Gaedel was a 26-year-old, 3-foot-7-inch performer who signed with the St. Louis Browns on August 17, 1951, and played in a game two days later. He was assigned the jersey number 1/8—part visual gag, part reference to his diminutive stature.[302]

Gaedel stepped up to the plate in the second game of a doubleheader against the Detroit Tigers and was walked on four straight pitches. With Gaedel's extremely small strike zone, throwing a strike was nearly impossible. Browns owner Bill Veeck had orchestrated the stunt to generate publicity for the team and Falstaff Beer, instructing Gaedel to crouch and never swing.

Gaedel remains the only recorded player in professional sports history to wear a fraction as a jersey number—and one of the few whose entire career consisted of a single plate appearance.

The Leading Zero Royals—When Single Digits Were Double Digits

In the early 1950s, the Rochester Royals pulled off one of the strangest numbering experiments in NBA history. Jack McMahon wore #03, Paul Noel wore #07, and Bobby Wanzer wore #09—the only players ever to take the court with a leading zero on their jerseys.[167]

It wasn't a fashion statement or a tribute; most likely it was a printing quirk from the uniform supplier. Whatever the reason, no other franchise has repeated it.

Outside of the familiar #00, the Royals remain the only team to issue numbers with a leading zero, a bizarre footnote in basketball's numbering lore.

Andy Messersmith: #17—Station Identification

In the mid-1970s, Atlanta Braves owner Ted Turner was operating on a shoestring budget when he signed pitcher Andy Messersmith to one of baseball's first megabucks free-agent contracts.

Turner's UHF station in Atlanta, WTCG, was struggling to attract viewers, so Turner decided to turn Messersmith into a human billboard.

Messersmith wore #17 on the back of his jersey. Above it was the word "Channel."[303]

Channel 17. It was peak 1970s promotional brilliance.

Messersmith became a walking billboard, and "Channel 17" became one of baseball's oddest jersey combinations.

Mika Lehkosuo: #96.2—Radio Waves

Perhaps taking a marketing lesson from Ted Turner, decades later in Finland, midfielder Mika Lehkosuo turned his jersey into a broadcast frequency. Playing for HJK Helsinki in the 1990s, he wore the number 96.2—matching the dial of a local radio station with whom he had a sponsorship deal.[290]

It was one of the strangest numbers ever seen on a football pitch, complete with a decimal point, and it blurred the line between sport and advertising.

However, the deal was short-lived and came to an end when UEFA regulations prohibited Lehkosuo from wearing his unsanctioned shirt in Champions League games.

Jared Allen: #69—The Joke That Became Historic

When defensive end Jared Allen was drafted by the Kansas City Chiefs in 2004, they gave him #69—an offensive lineman's number. His reaction? "Great, they're definitely cutting me."

Another lineman in camp also wore #69. Allen joked: "We can't both make it." When that player got cut, Allen kept the number.

The Chiefs' equipment manager offered him a more traditional number in the 90s, but Allen's defensive line coach convinced him to keep it: "You're an old-school player. That's an old-school number. You keep it and make it cool."[304]

Allen did just that. He wore #69 for all 12 seasons of his NFL career across four teams and became the first Hall of Famer to ever wear the number. His contract with the Minnesota Vikings even included a playful nod—$73,260,069—with the last two digits added as a joke.

For Allen, #69 started as a joke but became a symbol of his throwback mentality, humor, and dominance. With 136 career sacks and a Hall of Fame induction in 2025, he made #69 not just cool—but historic.

Quirky numbers exist because athletes refuse to be boring. They turn digits into puns, personalities into brands, and jersey choices into inside jokes that last decades. Some wear fractions and decimals. Some wear their height. Some wear steak-sauce references. And all of them prove the same thing: in sports, there's no such thing as "just a number."

CHAPTER 20

A Brand in a Number

A jersey number used to be something you wore. Now it's something you sell. In the modern era of sports, some of the most valuable marketing real estate isn't on a billboard or in a stadium—it's on an athlete's back. One or two digits can become a trademark, a business empire, and a legacy worth hundreds of millions of dollars.

When Digits Become Empires

Tom Brady didn't want #12. Cristiano Ronaldo inherited #7 from Manchester United legends. Neither number was their first choice—but both became empires—businesses worth hundreds of millions of dollars.

TB12. CR7. These aren't just jersey numbers anymore. They're trademarks, product lines, and global brands. In modern sports, a number isn't just what you wear. It's what you build, defend, and monetize.

This is the blueprint they followed—and the one every athlete now tries to replicate.

Jordan's 23: The Original Number Brand

Before TB12, before CR7, before PG13 or CP3 or any modern athlete who turned their number into a business, there was Michael Jordan's #23.[305]

Jordan didn't set out to create a brand. He just wanted to wear half of his brother Larry's number—Larry wore #45, so Michael chose #23. Simple math. No grand strategy.

But Nike saw something else. The Air Jordan line launched in 1984, and #23 became woven into every product—shoes, apparel, the Jumpman logo itself. The number wasn't just Jordan's identity—it became one of Nike's most valuable assets.[306]

Today, the Air Jordan brand generates over $5 billion annually. You see people wearing #23 jerseys who've never watched a Bulls game. The number transcended sport to become a cultural symbol—greatness, competitiveness, the idea that through hard work, you can achieve the impossible.

Jordan didn't build TB12-style wellness centers or CR7 hotels. He didn't need to. Nike built the empire for him.

But here's what matters: before Jordan, jersey numbers were just identifiers. After Jordan, they became brands. Every athlete in this chapter—Brady, Ronaldo, Paul, George—is following the blueprint MJ created.

Number 23 proved that a number could be worth billions. Everything else followed.

Gretzky's 99: The Untouchable Number

Wayne Gretzky didn't just wear #99—he trademarked it. "The Great One" and "99" became legally protected intellectual property, licensed for merchandise, memorabilia, and marketing deals.[307]

When he joined the Phoenix Coyotes' ownership group, the marketing value of "99" was part of his appeal. The number itself had equity.

Gretzky didn't build a wellness empire or clothing line. His #99 brand was about legacy and memorabilia. But he proved something crucial:

jersey numbers could be assets—not just on the ice, but in the marketplace.

Jordan showed numbers could transcend sport. Gretzky showed they could be trademarked and monetized. Together, they created the roadmap every modern athlete follows.

44 Boz: The Pioneer Brand

Before TB12, before CR7, before any modern athlete built a business empire around their number, there was Brian Bosworth—and he did it in 1987.

Bosworth, the controversial Oklahoma linebacker known as "The Boz," didn't wait until he became a star to monetize his number. Before he even signed his $11 million contract with the Seattle Seahawks, Bosworth had already incorporated as "44 Boz Inc." to market himself and his number.

The company produced "44 Boz Blues" sunglasses and "44 Blues" jeans, turning his college number into a merchandise line before he played a single NFL down.[260]

However, as we saw in Chapter 17, NFL rules prohibited linebackers from wearing numbers in the 40s. Bosworth sued the league for the right to wear #44. The Seahawks even petitioned for a rules change. Both failed.

Forced to wear #55, Bosworth didn't give up on his brand. Instead, he painted "44" and "44 Blues" on his shoes for games—turning his protest into marketing genius. Every game became a walking advertisement for his company.

Bosworth's NFL career lasted only three seasons before shoulder injuries ended it early. But "44 Boz Inc." proved something crucial:

athletes could turn their numbers into businesses, even when the league said no.

He was decades ahead of his time. TB12, CR7, and every modern number brand owes something to The Boz—the first athlete to turn two digits into a company. Bosworth proved it could be done—Brady and Ronaldo proved how big it could get.

The Modern Brands

Jordan and Gretzky showed it was possible. Bosworth showed it could be done even when the system said no. But Tom Brady and Cristiano Ronaldo proved that jersey numbers could become something even bigger: global business empires worth hundreds of millions of dollars.

These weren't just endorsement deals or merchandise lines. They were verticals—wellness centers, hotels, clothing brands, and lifestyle philosophies all built around the numbers they wore. TB12 and CR7 didn't just sell products. They sold identities.

This is where number branding went from clever marketing to legitimate business strategy.

TB12: The Wellness Empire

Tom Brady didn't want #12. He wanted #10—his Michigan number. But punter Lee Johnson had it, so Brady got what was in his locker: #12.

When the Patriots cut Johnson three weeks after Brady became the starting quarterback, he considered switching. "I thought about going back to 10," Brady said. "But I just stuck with 12."[308]

That decision built an empire.

After building a Hall of Fame career, Brady embraced #12 completely. It became inseparable from his identity—six Super Bowls in New England, one more in Tampa Bay, and a legacy as arguably the greatest quarterback of all time.

But TB12 became more than football excellence. It evolved into a wellness empire—representing Brady's training methodology, nutrition philosophy, and approach to longevity. The TB12 brand is valued at tens of millions of dollars, with room to grow, and includes:[309]

- A bestselling book (*The TB12 Method*)
- TB12 Performance & Recovery Centers
- Supplements, nutritional products, and training equipment

The number 12 became a symbol not just of championships, but of discipline, reinvention, and longevity. Brady turned a jersey number he didn't even want into a brand that will long outlast his playing career.

CR7: The Global Phenomenon

Cristiano Ronaldo was assigned #7 early in his career at Manchester United and it became much more than a jersey number—it became one of the most powerful personal brands in sports history, with an estimated value of over $500 million.

When Ronaldo joined Manchester United at age 18, he inherited #7—George Best's number, Eric Cantona's number, David Beckham's number. The weight of that legacy was immense.

But over time, he transformed #7 into "CR7"—blending his initials with the number to create something entirely his own.

Today, CR7 represents a vast empire:[310]

- Clothing lines and fragrances
- Hotels (Pestana CR7)
- Fitness centers and footwear
- CR7-branded products in dozens of categories

The CR7 brand exists independently of whatever team he plays for. He's worn #7 at Manchester United, Real Madrid, Juventus, and with Portugal—making it his portable identity across clubs and countries.

The number 7 is now synonymous with Ronaldo himself, symbolizing excellence, style, ambition, and a relentless drive to be the best. CR7 isn't just a brand—it's a lifestyle.

The Next Generation: Lessons in Number Branding

Not every number brand follows the TB12 or CR7 playbook. Some emerge accidentally. Some represent creative expression rather than commerce. And some serve as cautionary tales—reminders that building a brand requires more than one great season.

CP3: The Point Guard Brand

Chris Paul is CP3—not just because he wears #3, but because he shares initials with his father and older brother (CP1 and CP2). The number is literally his family lineage.

But CP3 evolved from tribute to empire.

His partnership with Jordan Brand launched the CP3 signature shoe line—13 models over 15 years, making it one of the most successful point guard shoes in history.[311] The shoes weren't just about on-court performance; they represented his cerebral, hyper-controlled style of play.

CP3 appears on everything from basketball camps to merchandise to his broader business portfolio. The brand represents leadership, precision playmaking, and basketball IQ—everything Chris Paul embodies on the court.

The number 3 isn't just his identity—it's his empire, built on the foundation of family, basketball excellence, and strategic branding that made CP3 one of the most recognizable names in the sport.

CC22: The New Standard

Caitlin Clark didn't just break scoring records—she broke the business model for women's basketball.

While still in college, Clark built a brand valued at more than three times the WNBA's top salary. Her NIL (Name, Image, and Likeness) partnerships were valued at $818,000, making her the fifth-most valuable female college athlete in the country. Meanwhile, the WNBA's top salary at the time maxed out at $250,000.

The numbers were absurd. The message was clear: her brand was already outpacing what the WNBA could offer.[312]

Clark operates through CC22 Ventures LLC, trademarking everything from her foundation to her merchandise. She runs caitlinclark22.com, selling apparel that moves faster than her crossover. When Wilson released her first signature basketball in September 2024, it sold out in under 40 minutes.

Then came the Nike deal: eight years, $28 million—the largest sponsorship contract for a women's basketball player in history. It includes her own signature shoe and logo, both currently in development.

CC22 isn't just a jersey number. It's a business model that proves female athletes can build brands as valuable as any man's—sometimes more valuable than the leagues they play in.

For decades, women's sports struggled with the "prove it first" mentality. Clark flipped the script. She proved her value before entering the pros, then used that leverage to redefine what's possible.

TB12, CR7, and CP3 built empires after establishing themselves professionally. CC22 built hers before her first WNBA game. That's the new blueprint.

PG13: The Clever Rebrand

Paul George began his NBA career wearing #24, honoring his idol Kobe Bryant. But in 2014, he made a strategic change to #13.

Why? To create the nickname "PG13"—a clever play on his initials and the movie rating that implies excitement and high stakes.

The change was suggested by Bill Simmons and Jimmy Kimmel. George embraced it. Critics called it "giving yourself your own nickname"—but in the NBA, where personal brand matters as much as performance, it was genius.

The number 13, typically unlucky, became his trademark. Nike built a shoe line around it. Social media ran with it. And PG13 became one of the most marketable identities in the league—not despite the self-given nickname, but because of it.

PG13 didn't just catch on—it became a product ecosystem. The branding extended into his signature shoe line, where the PG series became one of Nike's most accessible and consistently popular guard models.[313] It showed how a self-made nickname could translate into a commercial lane all its own.

For George, #13 evolved from a clever rebrand into a full identity—one that blended style, swagger, and marketability into a single, unmistakable number.

Not every number brand is built on wordplay—some are built on much deeper meaning.

KD35: The Tribute Brand

Kevin Durant's KD35 brand with Nike has been consistently strong. What makes it authentic is the story behind it—he chose 35 to honor his youth coach Charles Craig, who was murdered at age 35. The number carries deep personal meaning that adds authenticity to the brand.

The KD line of shoes has become one of Nike's most successful signature lines, and #35 is inseparable from Durant's identity—a number that honors his mentor and anchors his brand.[314]

Durant showed that a number brand can be powerful not because it sells something, but because it stands for something.

The Challenges

Building a number brand is one thing. Sustaining it is another. And in the modern era of sports business, success brings new problems athletes never had to face before.

Some brands collapse when performance declines. Others end up in courtrooms when competitors claim the same digits. The empires of TB12 and CR7 make it look easy, but the reality is more complicated.

Not every number brand succeeds. And even the successful ones must be defended.

RG3: The Reality Check

Robert Griffin III's 2012 rookie season was electric. RG3 merchandise flew off shelves. Adidas invested heavily. Subway commercials. Magazine covers. The brand was everywhere.

Then came the injuries. Griffin's career took a different path than expected, and the brand momentum that seemed unstoppable in 2012 faded as his on-field opportunities diminished.[315]

What distinguishes branding success is longevity. Brady played 23 seasons. Ronaldo played at an elite level for two decades. Gretzky dominated for 20 years.

One magical season creates buzz. Two decades build empires.

When Brands Collide

When jersey numbers become valuable intellectual property, the battles move from the field to the courtroom. In 2025, Lamar Jackson successfully blocked Dale Earnhardt Jr.'s attempt to trademark a stylized version of the number 8, arguing it conflicted with his own "ERA 8" brand registrations. Jackson is also locked in an ongoing dispute with Troy Aikman over the word "EIGHT."[316]

The disputes reveal how competitive number branding has become. It's not enough to build a brand—you have to legally defend it. Numbers that were once just identifiers are now assets worth fighting for—sometimes against multiple opponents at once.

The Future of Branding

The landscape of number branding has changed forever. What started with Jordan's #23, transitioned to Gretzky's trademarking, and evolved into Brady's wellness empire has now become standard practice for athletes at every level.

The next generation doesn't wait to go pro. They trademark their numbers in college, launch brands before their first professional game, and arrive at the highest levels of sport with business plans already in place.

The future of number branding isn't just bigger—it's earlier, more accessible, and more inventive than ever before.

Zero Fears: The Perfect Pun

When Jeremiah Fears entered the NBA, he chose #0. On the back of his jersey: "FEARS 0."[317]

It wasn't just clever—it was perfect. "Zero Fears" became more than a pun; it was a mantra. A declaration that he plays without hesitation, without doubt, without fear.

For a young guard entering the league, it was bold. For fans, it was unforgettable. Time will tell if "Zero Fears" becomes a lasting brand. But if branding is about making people remember you, Fears has already won.

The number creates immediate brand recognition, generates merchandise interest, and tells a story in just two words. Yes, it's also a pun—but it's a pun with a purpose. That's branding done right.

From Jordan's #23 to Fears' "Zero Fears," jersey numbers have evolved from identifiers to intellectual property.

The NIL Revolution: Every Athlete Is a Brand Now

Brian Bosworth had to fight the system. He sued the NFL, defied the rules, and painted his brand on his shoes when they wouldn't let him wear his number.

Today's athletes don't have to fight. They just file the paperwork.

In 2021, the NCAA allowed college athletes to profit from their Name, Image, and Likeness (NIL). What was once reserved for superstars is now available to every college athlete with a social media account.

The numbers tell the story:

Arch Manning continues to gain endorsement deals and partnerships while playing for the Texas Longhorns.[318] Shedeur Sanders launched SS2LEGENDARY, his own merchandise line, at Colorado.[319] And Bronny James's NIL deals earned him nearly six million dollars while attending USC.[320] Caitlin Clark entered the WNBA with a fully formed brand—something most players spend years trying to build.

This isn't just about superstars anymore. Thousands of college athletes now run LLCs, trademark their brands, and sell merchandise. Some make millions. Most make thousands. But all of them understand something Bosworth knew in 1987: your number is intellectual property.

The difference? Bosworth was punished for it. Today's athletes are rewarded.

The future of number branding isn't one or two athletes turning digits into empires. It's thousands treating their numbers as business assets from day one—because now, they can.[321] Bosworth was ahead of his time. Today's athletes are simply catching up.

Fifty years ago, jersey numbers were assigned by equipment managers. Players wore what they were given and felt grateful to have a roster spot.

Twenty-five years ago, Michael Jordan proved numbers could transcend sport and become cultural symbols worth billions.

Today, college freshmen trademark their numbers before playing a single game. Athletes build LLCs, launch product lines, and turn one or two digits into empires worth hundreds of millions of dollars.

TB12. CR7. PG13. CP3. CC22. These aren't just jersey numbers anymore—they're logos, companies, and legacies that will outlast the athletes who wear them.

The number on your back isn't just who you are—it's what you build, defend, and ultimately leave behind.

CHAPTER 21

Forever Numbers

Having a jersey number retired by a team is one of the highest distinctions an athlete can receive. More than a tribute—it becomes a permanent symbol of greatness.

When a number is retired, no future player on that team will ever wear it again. This is the team's way of saying: "You made history here, and your impact will never be forgotten."

But retirement isn't the only way teams celebrate numbers. Some programs reserve certain numbers for select players who embody specific values—not retiring them permanently, but treating them as select honors passed from one worthy athlete to the next.

Permanently Retired Numbers

The most absolute form of honor is permanent retirement—when a team decides that a number will never be worn again. These are the figures who didn't just excel; they reshaped their franchises, their sports, or society itself. Once retired, these numbers become monuments—visible reminders that greatness leaves a permanent mark.

Lou Gehrig: #4—The First Retired Number

On July 4, 1939, in front of a packed Yankee Stadium, Lou Gehrig delivered one of the most enduring speeches in sports history, declaring himself "the luckiest man on the face of the earth."

That day, the New York Yankees retired his jersey number #4, making it the first number ever retired in Major League Baseball—and among the first in all of professional sports.[322]

Gehrig's retirement wasn't just about honoring his incredible career, which included six World Series titles and a streak of 2,130 consecutive games played. It was a response to his diagnosis with ALS, a disease that would later bear his name and take his life just two years later at age 37.

The Yankees' decision to retire #4 set a precedent for how teams honor their legends, turning jersey retirement into one of the highest tributes an athlete can receive.

That tradition continues today across every major sport, rooted in what the Yankees did for Lou Gehrig in 1939.

Jackie Robinson: #42—The Ultimate Honor

Every baseball fan has heard of Jackie Robinson and his #42. Robinson broke Major League Baseball's color barrier in 1947 with the Brooklyn Dodgers, wearing #42 and enduring unimaginable racism, threats, and pressure while revolutionizing the game.

To commemorate his legacy, MLB retired #42 across all teams in 1997—no player can wear it except on one special day each year. Every April 15th is Jackie Robinson Day, when every player on every team wears #42 in his honor.[323] The entire league—from superstars to rookies, from veterans to managers—dons the same number, creating a striking visual tribute to Robinson's courage and impact.

The number 42 doesn't just belong to the Dodgers. It belongs to the sport itself.

Other League-Wide Retirements

In addition to Jackie Robinson, only two other numbers in all of professional sports have been retired league-wide.

Wayne Gretzky: #99—The Great One

The NHL retired "The Great One's" #99 across the entire league in 2000.[324] Partly because he is considered the greatest player in league history, but mostly because his name and his number became inseparable. The Hockey Hall of Fame center held or shared 61 NHL records when he retired in 1999, including 894 career goals and 1,963 assists. He was a 15-time All-Star and won the Hart Trophy as the NHL's most valuable player a record nine times.

Bill Russell: #6—The Quiet Champion

In 2022, the NBA retired Bill Russell's #6 across the entire league.[325] Russell's résumé is staggering: 11 championships in 13 seasons, five MVP awards, and 12 All-Star selections. Russell was named to all four NBA anniversary teams (25th, 35th, 50th, and 75th) and inducted into the Basketball Hall of Fame in 1975. He wasn't just a dominant center; he was also the league's first Black head coach and a powerful voice for civil rights.

Multi-Team Legends
Numbers Retired by Multiple Franchises

While league-wide retirements are reserved for transcendent figures, having your number retired by multiple teams is its own elite honor— proof that you left a permanent mark in multiple cities.

Baseball: The Multi-Team Legends

Having your number retired by one team is an extreme honor and has happened over 150 times in MLB history. Even more impressive is that eight players have had their number retired by two teams. But only two players have had their numbers retired by three:[326]

Nolan Ryan's #30 was retired by the Angels, and his #34 was retired by the Astros and Rangers—honoring a Hall of Fame career across multiple decades and organizations.

Frank Robinson's #20 was retired by the Reds, Orioles, and Indians—honoring the Hall of Famer who was the first player to win MVP awards in both leagues.

Of the eight players who have had their number retired by two teams, the most interesting is Carlton Fisk, whose #27 hangs in Boston and whose #72 hangs in Chicago. When Fisk left the Red Sox and joined the White Sox, he flipped his digits while changing his "Sox"—creating two separate legacies marked by numbers in perfect reverse.

Basketball: When Greatness Spans Cities

In the NBA, there are nearly 200 retired numbers across the 30 teams in the league. Similar to baseball, only two players have had that honor bestowed on them by three teams:[327]

Wilt Chamberlain's #13 hangs in the arenas of the Lakers, 76ers, and Warriors. His dominance was so complete that three franchises claim him as their own.

Pete Maravich also has numbers retired by three NBA teams—#44 by the Hawks, and #7 by both the Jazz and Pelicans. His unmatched flair and impact earned a permanent tribute from three organizations.

There are currently 14 other players who have had their number retired by two teams, but the most unusual two-team retirement belongs to Michael Jordan. The Bulls, of course, retired Jordan's #23, but the Miami Heat did as well, despite Jordan never playing for the team. Heat president Pat Riley called it "a reminder of what greatness is all about," acknowledging that some athletes transcend the teams they played for.

Hockey: Numbers That Skated Into Double-Retirement

There are currently 184 retired numbers across the NHL, but not counting Gretzky, who also had his #99 retired by two teams (Edmonton and Los Angeles) prior to his league-wide retirement, eight other players have had their numbers retired by two franchises:[328]

> **Mark Messier's #11** hangs in both Edmonton and New York
>
> **Patrick Roy's #33** is retired by Montreal and Colorado
>
> **Ray Bourque's #77** is retired by Boston and Colorado
>
> **Gordie Howe's #9** is retired by Detroit and Hartford
>
> **Tim Horton's #7** is retired by Buffalo and Toronto
>
> **Red Kelly's #4** hangs in Detroit and Toronto
>
> **Scott Niedermayer's #27** is retired by New Jersey and Anaheim
>
> **Bobby Hull's #9** is retired by Chicago and Winnipeg

Hockey culture emphasizes longevity and franchise loyalty, and players who earn multi-team honors typically spent significant portions of their careers with each organization, winning championships and transforming franchises in the process.

Football: Being Conservative With Retiring Numbers

The NFL currently has 163 retired numbers across the league, and Reggie White is the only player to have his number officially retired by two NFL teams. White's #92 was retired by both the Green Bay Packers and Philadelphia Eagles, honoring his dominance as "The Minister of Defense" and his role in revitalizing both franchises.

Peyton Manning's #18 holds a unique distinction: it was officially retired by the Indianapolis Colts in 2017. The situation in Denver is more complex—the Broncos had originally retired #18 for Frank Tripucka in 1963, but unretired it so Manning could wear it from 2012 to 2015. When they re-retired the number in 2016, they gave Manning 'special acknowledgment' alongside Tripucka. While it's not a traditional dual retirement like White's, Manning's legacy is recognized by both franchises where he won Super Bowls.

The NFL's conservative approach to retiring numbers is partly practical. NFL teams carry 53-player rosters—nearly four times larger than the NBA's 15-man rosters, double the NHL's 23, and twice MLB's 26. With more roster spots to fill and strict positional numbering rules limiting which players can wear which numbers, teams risk running out of available digits. The NFL rulebook even requires teams to make retired numbers available again if they exhaust all options at a position—a safeguard against numerical scarcity.[329]

Some NFL teams take this conservatism to the extreme. The Dallas Cowboys, for instance, have never officially retired a number despite their storied history. Instead, they maintain a Ring of Honor to celebrate franchise legends, but the numbers keep circulating. For example, Tony Dorsett's #33 has been reissued eight times since he last wore it for the Cowboys.[330] Other teams with no retired numbers include the Oakland/Las Vegas Raiders, Jacksonville Jaguars, and

Atlanta Falcons, with each choosing alternative methods like rings of honor or honor rolls to celebrate their most revered players.[331]

When All the Good Numbers Are Taken

Blake Griffin and the Boston Number Crunch

When Blake Griffin signed with the Boston Celtics in 2022, he faced a problem that only exists in a handful of NBA cities: finding an available number.

Griffin had worn #32 with the Clippers, #23 with the Pistons, and #2 with the Nets. But in Boston, all three numbers were retired.

"You know how many numbers are retired in Boston?" Griffin joked. At the time, the Celtics had 23 retired numbers hanging in the rafters— by far the most in the NBA.[332]

Griffin scrolled through available options with a friend, who suggested #91 as a tribute to Dennis Rodman and his championship years with the Chicago Bulls.

"You know what? F**k it. I'll stand by the Boston 91," Griffin said.

With that decision, Griffin became just the fifth player in NBA history to wear #91, joining a small fraternity of players who embraced the rarely-used number.

The Celtics' numerical scarcity isn't just about honoring legends—it's a testament to the franchise's unparalleled history. With 18 championships and a century of basketball excellence, Boston has more retired numbers than some teams have had All-Star appearances.

For Griffin, #91 wasn't his first choice, or his second, or even his third. But it became a badge of humor and tribute—proof that sometimes the best stories come from the numbers nobody wants.

A Sign of Respect—Asking for Permission

Some of the most powerful jersey retirement stories aren't about the ceremonies themselves—they're about the conversations that happen before a number is ever worn.

Mariano Rivera and Rachel Robinson: #42

Mariano Rivera continued to wear #42 even after it was retired league-wide for Jackie Robinson. When MLB retired the number in 1997, thirteen active players were grandfathered in to keep wearing it.

Rivera was the last player to ever wear the number before his retirement in 2013. He had personally met Jackie's widow, Rachel Robinson, multiple times, and it's been widely speculated that he asked her permission to keep wearing the number. While that hasn't been publicly confirmed, Rachel Robinson clearly respected Rivera's stewardship of #42.

"I've always been proud and pleased that Mariano was the [last player] to wear that number because I think he brought something special to it," Rachel Robinson said. "He carried himself with dignity and grace, and that made carrying the number a tribute to Jack."[333]

Rivera's respectful approach earned him widespread admiration and reinforced the significance of Jackie Robinson's place in history. He didn't just wear the number—he honored it.

Ichiro Suzuki and Randy Johnson: #51

When Ichiro Suzuki joined the Seattle Mariners in 2001, he wanted to wear #51—the same number he wore in Japan with the Orix BlueWave.

But in Seattle, that number had a history. Randy Johnson had worn #51 during his dominant nine seasons with the Mariners from 1989 to 1998, becoming one of the most feared pitchers in baseball.

Out of respect, Ichiro didn't simply take it. He personally asked Johnson for permission. Johnson agreed, handing the number over with a gesture of respect and trust.[334]

Ichiro's #51 became sacred in Seattle—a number tied forever to his unique style of play. But it began with a conversation, a quiet request that became part of a larger story of legacy and respect.

To honor both Hall of Famers, the Seattle Mariners retired "Ichiro's #51" in 2025 and announced plans to retire "Johnson's #51" during a ceremony in 2026.

Two legends. One number. Shared with respect.

Molly Bent and Sue Bird: #10

When Molly Bent arrived at UConn in 2016, she faced an intimidating decision: ask one of basketball's premier point guards for permission to wear her number, which no one had worn since her 2002 national Player of the Year season.

Bent had worn #10 ever since she could remember. She loved the number. But at UConn, #10 belonged to Sue Bird—four-time WNBA champion, five-time Olympic gold medalist, and an icon whose legacy loomed large over the program.

Bent finally got her chance when the Seattle Storm held a practice nearby. "When they practiced at Werth, I had to ask Sue if I could wear it," Bent said. "Sue was really nice about it. I was a little nervous. She said to, 'Wear it proudly and do it proud.' It was nice."[335]

Bird could have said no. She could have kept #10 sacred, untouchable. But instead, she passed it forward—trusting a young player to honor it through her own hard work and dedication.

For Bent, wearing #10 became more than just a number—it became a responsibility, but one earned out of respect.

That's what great numbers do. They don't just commemorate the past—they inspire the future.

Phil Esposito and Ray Bourque: #7

In one of the most heartfelt moments in hockey history, the Boston Bruins planned to retire Phil Esposito's #7 in 1987 to honor his Hall of Fame career.

Interestingly, #7 was being retired for Esposito while the team's star defenseman, Ray Bourque, was currently wearing the same number on the ice.

Rather than let the situation diminish the ceremony, Bourque orchestrated a surprise. During the retirement event, he skated over to Esposito, removed his own #7 jersey, and revealed a new one underneath: #77, which he would wear for the rest of his Hall of Fame career.[336]

The gesture stunned Esposito and the crowd, turning the night into one of the most moving tributes in NHL history.

The Bruins officially retired #7 for Esposito, and later #77 for Bourque—two numbers, two legends, one selfless moment that connected them forever.

A shining example of sportsmanship and respect between two generations of greatness.

A Salute to Service—Pat Tillman: #40

Pat Tillman holds a special place in NFL history—a standout safety for the Arizona Cardinals who made headlines not just for his play but for his profound sacrifice.

After the 9/11 attacks, Tillman left a promising NFL career and a multimillion-dollar contract to enlist in the U.S. Army, where he served as an Army Ranger.

Tragically, Tillman was killed in action in Afghanistan in 2004.

That same year, the Cardinals retired his jersey number, #40, in honor of his courage, selflessness, and legacy.[337] This stands as one of the most powerful and emotional jersey retirements in NFL history.

Tillman's #40 represents more than football—it embodies service, sacrifice, and the values that transcend sports.

Honored College Numbers— Reserved for Greatness

Not all celebrated numbers are permanently retired. Some programs have created a different tradition: honored numbers that are reserved for select athletes who embody specific values, passed from one worthy player to the next.

These numbers aren't taken out of circulation—they're kept alive, awarded annually or periodically to players who earn the right to wear them. A living tribute that connects past greatness to present excellence.

The most recognized example might be Syracuse's #44—though calling it merely "honored" doesn't capture the full story.

Syracuse's #44: The Legendary Legacy

Some jersey numbers fade into history. Others become legends. And then there's Syracuse's #44—a number so revered that an entire university rewrote its address to honor it.

The number belonged to Jim Brown, Ernie Davis, and Floyd Little—three running backs who didn't just dominate college football; they changed it. Brown became one of the most influential athletes in American history. Davis was the first Black player to win the Heisman Trophy. Little carried on the legacy with grace and power.

Together, they made #44 untouchable.

But Syracuse didn't stop at retiring the number. They went further.

The university changed its zip code from 13210 to 13244 and switched the phone exchange from 423 to 443. Every phone number on campus now begins with 44. The number is hung in the rafters and embedded in the very infrastructure of the institution.[338]

It's not just nostalgia—it's identity.

Most retired numbers live in memory. Syracuse's #44 lives in the mail you send, the calls you make, and the address you write. It serves as a reminder that some athletes don't just play for a school—they become the school. And the school becomes them.

And sometimes, honoring a legacy means changing more than a jersey—it means changing the institution itself.

Ohio State's #0: The Block O Jersey

At The Ohio State University, #0—affectionately known as the Block O jersey—is not given out casually. It is an honor reserved for a player who exemplifies leadership, character, and excellence both on and off the field.

The tradition began in 2020, with #0 awarded annually to a player who embodies the spirit of Bill Willis—toughness, accountability, and character.[339] Willis was a pioneering African American player who broke the color barrier in the NFL in 1946 with the Cleveland Browns.

For the chosen player, wearing #0 is a mark of recognition—a sign that they have earned the trust and respect of the program and carry the tradition of those who wore it before them.

Ole Miss' #38: The Chucky Mullins Courage Award

At Ole Miss, the #38 jersey carries a story far deeper than football—it honors the life and spirit of Chucky Mullins, a defensive back whose career was tragically cut short by a paralyzing injury during a game in 1989.

To preserve his legacy, the university created the Chucky Mullins Courage Award, given annually to the defensive player who best embodies Mullins' grit, heart, and leadership.[340] That player earns the right to wear #38 for the following season—a number that has become a symbol of resilience, honor, and the power of the human spirit.

Wearing #38 isn't just about athletic performance; it's about character. It's a visible reminder that football is more than a game—it's a platform for perseverance, unity, and tribute. Each time #38 takes the field, it tells the story of a young man who faced unimaginable adversity and responded with grace, strength, and hope.

LSU's #18: Annual Leadership Award

At LSU, the #18 jersey is more than a number—it's an emblem of leadership, selflessness, and excellence both on and off the field. The tradition began in 2003 with quarterback Matt Mauck, who helped lead the Tigers to a national championship. Since then, the jersey has been passed down to players who embody the same qualities that defined Mauck's impact: character, toughness, and team-first mentality.[341]

Over the years, #18 has been worn by standout leaders such as Jacob Hester, Tre'Davious White, and Damone Clark—each leaving their own mark on the program while carrying forward the legacy of the number. The selection is made by coaches and teammates, making it one of the most meaningful honors a Tiger can receive.

In 2025, fifth-year senior quarterback Garrett Nussmeier was honored with #18, becoming the first quarterback to wear it since Mauck.

Honored Numbers Across the Globe

Soccer's Sacred #10

By now, you understand #10's evolution—from positional marker to Pelé's random assignment to the symbol of a playmaker. But there's one more layer: how individual clubs and nations have transformed it into sacred tradition.[12]

At FC Barcelona, #10 became synonymous with Lionel Messi for nearly two decades, representing not just individual artistry but the club's entire philosophy of beautiful, creative play. When Messi left in 2021, Barcelona initially retired the number—that's how deeply #10 had become intertwined with identity.

In Brazil's national team, #10 carries the weight of an entire nation's expectations. The lineage—Pelé, Zico, Ronaldinho, Neymar—represents more than great players. It represents *jogo bonito*, the "beautiful game" itself. Wearing #10 for Brazil means you're not just playing soccer; you're carrying the soul of Brazilian football on your back.

Across Europe and South America, clubs reserve #10 for their most creative player, often their captain or designated leader. It's frequently the last number assigned in preseason—a deliberate ceremony, not a casual decision.

What began as a formation position, immortalized by an unknowing teenager, and evolved into the playmaker's symbol, has become something even larger: a living contract between player, team, and history. When you wear #10 at certain clubs, you're not just promising to play well. You're promising to honor everyone who wore it before you and to leave it better for whoever comes next.

That's not pressure. That's legacy.

Japan's Ace Pitcher #18

In Japanese professional baseball, #18 is traditionally reserved for the team's ace pitcher. This practice began in the 1930s when Tadashi Wakabayashi switched from #4—considered unlucky because it sounds like 'death' in Japanese—to #18. The number's prestige also draws from Kabuki theater, where the number 18 represents the pinnacle of artistic excellence.[342]

This custom took root with the Yomiuri Giants and has become a respected tradition throughout Nippon Professional Baseball (NPB). Wearing #18 is a mark of honor and responsibility—the player wearing it is expected to lead the pitching staff and deliver top performances. It connects modern players to a decades-long tradition that carries the weight of expectation.

The tradition has been so powerful that it has followed Japanese pitchers to Major League Baseball. As of 2024, thirteen Japanese pitchers have worn #18 in the Major Leagues, including Daisuke Matsuzaka (Boston Red Sox), Hiroki Kuroda (Los Angeles Dodgers, New York Yankees), Hisashi Iwakuma (Seattle Mariners), Kenta

Maeda (Los Angeles Dodgers, Minnesota Twins, Detroit Tigers), Yusei Kikuchi (Seattle Mariners), Yoshinobu Yamamoto (Los Angeles Dodgers), and Shota Imanaga (Chicago Cubs).

The tradition is so respected that when Masahiro Tanaka joined the New York Yankees in 2014, he had to wear #19 instead of his preferred #18, since Hiroki Kuroda already wore the number.[343]

Whether permanently retired or passed down as living honors, jersey numbers represent sports' highest tributes—symbols that say, 'You made history here, and your legacy will never be forgotten.'

From Lou Gehrig's #4 to Jackie Robinson's league-wide #42, from Syracuse's #44 to Ohio State's #0, these numbers transcend statistics.

They represent courage, sacrifice, and impact that extends far beyond the field. They honor something greater than the game itself—the people who shaped it, elevated it, and left it better than they found it.

CHAPTER 22

When Retired Numbers Return

Retiring a jersey number is supposed to be permanent—a forever honor that ensures no one will ever wear that number again. It's the ultimate tribute, a way to say: "This number belongs to history now."

But sometimes, retired numbers come back.

Sometimes it's with permission and grace. Other times it's controversial. Occasionally it's because of franchise relocation or changing circumstances. And in some cases, outrage forces teams to change course. The reasons vary, but each un-retirement tells us something about how organizations value tradition versus pragmatism, and whether numbers truly belong to individuals or to the institutions that honor them.

The Gracious Returns:
When Legends Give Permission

Not every un-retirement is controversial. Sometimes, the original honoree personally blesses the return of their number—creating shared legacies instead of erasing old ones.

Malik Nabers and Ray Flaherty's #1

When the New York Giants drafted wide receiver Malik Nabers sixth overall in 2024, he wanted to wear #1—a number with deep roots in NFL history.

The Giants had retired #1 in 1935 for Ray Flaherty, making it the first retired number in professional football history. For 89 years, no Giant had worn it.

But Nabers was persistent. He asked team president John Mara if it was possible. Mara's response: "Only if the Flaherty family was okay with it."

The family initially said no. But after conversations with Mara and learning more about Nabers, they reconsidered. When they agreed, Nabers immediately called Ray Flaherty Jr. personally.

"I really appreciate you letting me wear your father's retired jersey," Nabers told him. "I'm gonna wear it with honor. I'm gonna do my best when I'm out there on the field to represent y'all the right way."[344]

Flaherty Jr. was moved by the gesture. "He seems like a fine young man," he said. "I feel really good about it after he made the call."

The team made it clear, however, that when Nabers' Giants career is over, #1 will return to retired status in honor of Flaherty.

A remarkable instance where the first retired number in football history came back—not to erase the past, but to create a bridge between generations.

Peyton Manning and Frank Tripucka's #18

When the Denver Broncos retired #18 in honor of quarterback Frank Tripucka in 1963, it was a tribute to his role in the franchise's early years during the AFL.

But in 2012, the Broncos signed Peyton Manning, one of the game's elite quarterbacks—and Manning had worn #18 throughout his storied career with the Colts.

At Tripucka's insistence, the Broncos un-retired #18 for Manning. Tripucka had just one request: "Go out and win a Super Bowl for me."[345]

And Peyton did. In 2016, he won Super Bowl 50 wearing #18, honoring both his brother, for whom he originally wore the number (Chapter 3), and the quarterback who had already left a legacy in Denver.[346]

A notable example of shared legacy through a reissued retired number—two great quarterbacks, one number, and mutual respect.

Omar Vizquel and Luis Aparicio's #11

In 1984, the Chicago White Sox retired #11 to honor Hall of Fame shortstop Luis Aparicio.

But in 2010, the number made a rare return when Omar Vizquel, a fellow defensive wizard and admirer of Aparicio, joined the team.

Vizquel had long admired Aparicio's defensive artistry and saw #11 as a direct link to baseball's heritage. The White Sox reached out to Aparicio, who not only approved but embraced the idea—honored that another defensive-minded shortstop would carry the number forward.

With Aparicio's personal blessing, Vizquel wore #11 as a tribute—not to replace the legend, but to honor his legacy. "For me, it's like a huge celebration, trying to keep his name alive and trying to spread the word of Venezuelan shortstops."[347]

It remains one of the very limited instances in MLB history where a retired number was temporarily reissued with the mutual respect of the players involved.

Grant Hill and Alvan Adams' #33

In 1988, the Phoenix Suns retired #33 for Alvan Adams, who had spent his entire 13-year career with the franchise. Nearly two decades later, when Grant Hill joined the team in 2007, he quickly realized #33 was already part of Suns history: he'd worn #33 his entire career in Detroit and Orlando, but it was retired in Phoenix.

The Suns reached out to Adams, who gave his blessing without hesitation.

"To me, it's not my number—it's Jerry Colangelo's," Adams said, referring to the Phoenix Suns' owner. "I think of 33 as belonging more to him, the fans, and Suns history. The past is great, but the most important thing is this franchise winning a championship. If I can make a small contribution by making Hill's transition to Phoenix a smooth one, then I'm all for it."[348]

The connection ran deeper than either initially realized: both had chosen #33 as tributes to legends they admired. Adams wore it for Kareem Abdul-Jabbar—another branch on the Kareem Tree (Chapter 5), and Hill wore it for Magic Johnson, who wore #33 during his collegiate career.

Hill wore #33 in Phoenix from 2007 to 2012, honoring both Adams and the legends who inspired them both.

Brett Hull and Bobby Hull's #9

When Brett Hull signed with the Phoenix Coyotes in 2005 for what would be the final games of his Hall of Fame career, he wanted to wear the same number his Hall of Fame father had worn with the Winnipeg Jets. However, Bobby Hull's #9 had been officially retired in Winnipeg in 1989 and subsequently carried forward in Phoenix as an "honored" number, never reissued.

In an extraordinary move, the Coyotes agreed to unretire #9 so Brett could wear it—a symbolic passing of the torch from father to son. Brett, himself a 741-goal scorer and future Hall of Famer, skated his last five NHL games in his father's number, a tribute that linked their legacies.

After Brett's retirement, the Coyotes returned #9 to its place of honor, this time recognizing both Bobby and Brett Hull.[349] Two legends. One number. One family legacy.

This highlights the nuance between "retired" and "honored" numbers: Bobby's #9 was formally retired in Winnipeg, but only honored in Phoenix. Franchise relocations complicate the record, as we'll explore later in this chapter.

The Controversial Returns:
When Permission Wasn't Asked

Not every un-retirement happens with grace. Sometimes teams make decisions that anger fans, dishonor families, and spark lasting controversy.

Mark Messier and Wayne Maki's #11

When Mark Messier joined the Vancouver Canucks in 1997, he brought six Stanley Cups and a Hall of Fame résumé. But he also brought a demand that would ignite one of the most emotional controversies in franchise history: the right to wear #11.[350]

That number had been unofficially retired by the Canucks in honor of Wayne Maki, a beloved player who tragically died of brain cancer in 1974. Though never formally retired, #11 had been kept out of circulation for over two decades as a quiet tribute.

Messier's contract reportedly included a clause guaranteeing him the number, leaving the team legally unable to deny the request.

The Maki family was left completely out of the decision. They were blindsided when Messier unveiled the jersey at his press conference, expressing deep hurt and disappointment.

The controversy didn't end there. Messier's tenure in Vancouver was marred by poor performance, locker room tension, and disputes with management. Fans viewed his time with the Canucks as a low point in both his career and franchise history.

For Messier, #11 represented continuity and personal legacy. For Vancouver fans, it became a mark of disrespect and broken trust.

The number is one of the most emotionally charged in Canucks history—proof that even the greatest players can leave complicated legacies.

Guy Lapointe and Dit Clapper's #5

The Boston Bruins retired Aubrey "Dit" Clapper's #5 in 1981, honoring a player who spent 20 seasons with the team and was the first living inductee into the Hockey Hall of Fame.

But in 1983, the Bruins signed Guy Lapointe, a Hall of Fame defenseman who had worn #5 throughout his career with the Montreal Canadiens.

Without consulting Clapper's family or the public, Bruins GM Harry Sinden—who had a reputation for prioritizing on-ice talent over tradition—allowed Lapointe to wear the number, apparently viewing it as a way to honor another Hall of Famer.

The decision triggered immediate backlash. Fans, media, and even Bruins legend Bobby Orr criticized the move.

Lapointe, unaware of the controversy, was taken aback by the public reaction and quickly switched to #27 after just a handful of games.[351]

One of the most unusual cases in NHL history where a retired number was reissued, then retracted. It reinforced the sacredness of jersey retirements and the enduring respect for Dit Clapper's contributions to the game.

The San Diego Chargers and Ron Mix's #74

In one of the most unusual stories in professional sports, Ron Mix, a Hall of Fame offensive lineman, had his number retired—and then un-retired by the same team.

The San Diego Chargers retired Mix's #74 in 1969, honoring his stellar career. But in 1971, Mix came out of retirement and joined the Oakland Raiders, one of the Chargers' fiercest rivals.

The Chargers felt betrayed. In response, the team quietly un-retired #74—putting the number back into circulation as if the honor had never happened.[352]

There was no press release, no ceremony—just the number quietly reissued.

Unlike other cases where teams later reinstated retired numbers, the Chargers never re-retired #74—even after Mix was inducted into the Chargers Hall of Fame in 1978 and the Pro Football Hall of Fame in 1979. Old grudges die hard.

An extraordinary case where a retired number was permanently revoked—a stark illustration of how personal and symbolic jersey honors can be.

The Cincinnati Reds and Willard Hershberger's #5

In August 1940, Cincinnati Reds backup catcher Willard Hershberger tragically took his own life—the only major-league player to date to die by suicide during the season. The 30-year-old had been struggling with depression, blaming himself for losses, convinced he was letting his team down.

His devastated teammates rallied to win both the pennant and World Series, voting Hershberger a full share of their championship earnings for his mother. To honor their fallen teammate, the Reds temporarily retired his #5.[353]

But in 1942—just two years later—the team quietly reactivated the number. Over the next several decades, various players wore #5 in Cincinnati, with Johnny Bench being the most notable and the last to wear it throughout his Hall of Fame career from 1967 to 1983.

On August 11, 1984, the Reds permanently retired #5—this time for Bench.

Unlike other controversial un-retirements, this one happened quietly in an era before jersey retirements carried modern weight. No family was consulted. No announcement was made. The number simply returned to circulation.

Today, when fans see #5 honored at Great American Ball Park, they think of Johnny Bench. Few remember Willard Hershberger—whose number was retired in grief, un-retired without ceremony, and retired again for a legend.

The Franchise Relocations:
When History Gets Left Behind

When teams relocate, one of the most difficult questions is: What happens to retired numbers?

Some teams honor the past. Others make a clean break. And fans are left to decide whether those numbers truly belonged to the franchise—or to the city.

The answers vary wildly from sport to sport and team to team.

Baltimore Colts to Indianapolis: The Quiet Reset

During their storied tenure in Baltimore, the Colts retired three numbers to honor franchise legends:

> **#19—Johnny Unitas**
> **#24—Lenny Moore**
> **#82—Raymond Berry**

These numbers held deep emotional weight for Baltimore fans. But when the team abruptly relocated to Indianapolis in 1984, the Colts made no formal announcement about the status of their retired numbers. There was no ceremony, no public reaffirmation—just silence.

The ambiguity created confusion. In 2011, the Colts issued #19 to wide receiver Kole Heckendorf—sparking outrage among Baltimore fans who saw it as disrespecting Unitas' legacy. Though Heckendorf wore #19 only in practices and was released before ever playing in a game, the incident made clear that Indianapolis had never formally addressed the status of the Baltimore retirements.[354]

It wasn't until years later that the Colts began to retroactively honor their Baltimore legends, officially retiring numbers like #19, #24, and

#82 again. But for decades, the move to Indianapolis functioned as a soft reset—a moment when the status of even the most sacred numbers remained unclear.

Montreal Expos to Washington Nationals: Erasing History

Before relocating to Washington, D.C., the Montreal Expos retired jersey numbers for four beloved players:

> **#8—Gary Carter**
> **#10—Rusty Staub and Andre Dawson**
> **#30—Tim Raines**

When the team became the Washington Nationals in 2005, the organization made a controversial decision: it returned all Expos-retired numbers to circulation, except for the league-wide retired #42 in honor of Jackie Robinson.

Several Nationals players have worn #8, #10, and #30 in the years since the relocation, effectively ending their retired status.

While the Nationals later created a Ring of Honor to acknowledge these Expos legends, the jersey numbers themselves were never re-retired.[355]

Seattle SuperSonics to Oklahoma City Thunder: No Legacy Transferred

The Seattle SuperSonics retired six jersey numbers, yet none of them carried their retirement honors to Oklahoma City:

> **#1—Gus Williams**
> **#10—Nate McMillan**
> **#19—Lenny Wilkins**
> **#24—Spencer Haywood**

#32—Fred Brown

#43—Jack Sikma

When the franchise relocated to Oklahoma City in 2008 and became the Thunder, the team made a clean break. The Thunder did not adopt the SuperSonics' retired numbers. There was no ceremony, no transfer, no jerseys hanging in the rafters.[356]

However, those numbers have remained out of circulation in Oklahoma City. Players haven't worn them, suggesting an informal respect or internal policy—even if not publicly acknowledged.[357]

To date, the only number retired by the Thunder has been #4 in honor of Nick Collison, who initially played for the SuperSonics but spent the majority of his career with the Thunder.[358]

The previously retired SuperSonics' numbers, and the legacy, remain separate—preserved by fans and the city of Seattle, but not formally recognized by the current franchise.

Cleveland Browns: The Exception to Relocation

When the Cleveland Browns relocated to Baltimore in 1996, the move sparked controversy. But unlike other relocations, this one came with a unique legal compromise.

The NFL brokered a deal: the Browns' name, colors, history, and retired numbers would remain in Cleveland, while Art Modell's team would be considered a new franchise—the Baltimore Ravens.[359]

None of the Browns' five retired numbers were affected. They remained part of the reactivated Browns franchise when it returned in 1999.

One of the most unusual and respectful examples of a relocation where a team's legacy—including its retired numbers—was preserved intact.

The Fall from Grace:
When Legacies Are Revoked

Sometimes retired numbers are taken down not because of relocation or permission, but because the athlete's legacy is fundamentally reconsidered.

Roberto Alomar's #12 in Toronto

In 2011, the Toronto Blue Jays retired #12 to honor Roberto Alomar, the Hall of Fame second baseman who helped lead the team to back-to-back World Series titles.

However, in 2021, following an MLB investigation into credible sexual misconduct allegations from a former MLB employee, the Blue Jays severed ties with Alomar and removed his number from display.[360]

Number 12 is no longer honored at Rogers Centre and has been returned to circulation—an extraordinary reversal that reflects how legacies can be reevaluated as circumstances change.

Reggie Bush's #5 at USC

Reggie Bush electrified college football wearing #5 for USC from 2003 to 2005, winning the 2005 Heisman Trophy.

Then, in 2010, following an NCAA investigation that found Bush had received improper benefits:

- Bush voluntarily forfeited his Heisman Trophy.
- USC was forced to disassociate from Bush.
- His #5 jersey was removed from display at the Los Angeles Memorial Coliseum.

Despite the removal, USC never reissued #5 to another player—keeping it unofficially out of circulation.

In 2024, after changes to NCAA rules on Name, Image, and Likeness (NIL), the Heisman Trust reinstated Bush's trophy. With that, USC formally re-retired #5, restoring it to its place of honor.[361]

Bush's #5 now hangs once again in the Coliseum—a testament to both his athletic brilliance and the evolving landscape of college sports. His story suggests that in the modern era, even "permanent" revocations may not be final—and what once seemed unforgivable under one era's rules can be reconsidered—and even restored under another.

When Tragedy Forces Retirement— And Family Brings It Back

The Reluctant Un-Retirement: Dale Earnhardt's #3

After Dale Earnhardt Sr. tragically died in the 2001 Daytona 500, his iconic #3 car—the black Chevrolet he drove to six of his seven NASCAR Cup Series championships—was retired from competition by Richard Childress Racing (RCR).

While NASCAR doesn't officially retire numbers, RCR chose to withhold #3 from use out of respect for Earnhardt's legacy.

For nearly a decade, the number remained unused. But in 2010, Earnhardt's son, Dale Earnhardt Jr., brought the number back— briefly—in a Nationwide Series race at Daytona, driving a #3 Chevrolet with a classic Wrangler paint scheme.

Junior won the race in an emotional tribute to his father. "This is it. No more 3 for me," he said in Victory Lane.[362]

The number remained shelved in the Cup Series until 2014, when Richard Childress reintroduced it—not for Dale Jr., but for his own grandson, Austin Dillon.

The move was controversial, but it had the blessing of the Earnhardt family, including Dale Jr., who said, "It's your car, you own the number. We were all for it."

Earnhardt's #3 shows that retired numbers can return—but only when handled with respect, family approval, and a clear understanding of the weight that number holds.

When retired numbers return—whether through grace, controversy, or relocation—they reveal how fragile even sacred honors can be. Some legends bless the return. Some franchises ignore the families. Some cities lose their history when teams move. And sometimes, legacies are revoked entirely.

These stories remind us that jersey retirements aren't just about the past—they're about how we choose to honor—or mishandle—that past in the present. And as sports continue to evolve—with franchises relocating, NIL reshaping college athletics, and cultural standards shifting—the question of what makes a number retirement truly "permanent" will only grow more complex.

CHAPTER 23

The Unusual Retirements

Most retired numbers honor exceptional athletes—players who dominated their sport, led their teams to championships, and left a mark that endures.

But some retired numbers tell different stories.

Some honor fans. Some honor lives lost. Some recognize two players at once. Others retire names instead of numbers. And some honor people who never played the sport at all.

The Dual Retirements

Sometimes a number is so revered that teams retire it for two legends. And sometimes a single legend is so revered that two numbers are retired in their honor.

New York Yankees: #8 for Bill Dickey and Yogi Berra

The New York Yankees did something almost unheard of in sports history—they retired the same number twice.

Number 8 was first worn by Bill Dickey, the masterful catcher who anchored the Yankees from 1928 to 1946. Years later, that same number passed to Yogi Berra, a three-time MVP and 10-time World Series champion who became one of the most beloved figures in baseball.

Rather than choose between them, the Yankees retired #8 for both men, creating a rare dual retirement in 1972.[363]

Today, the number is displayed in Monument Park with both names beside it—a tribute to two legends who defined excellence behind the plate.

Chicago Cubs: #31 for Ferguson Jenkins and Greg Maddux

The Chicago Cubs retired jersey #31 for two Hall of Fame pitchers: Ferguson Jenkins and Greg Maddux.

Jenkins wore #31 for his dominant run with the Cubs from 1966 to 1973, and again from 1982 to 1983. Years later, Maddux donned the same number during his two stints with the Cubs from 1986 to 1992 and again from 2004 to 2006.

In 2009, the Cubs retired #31 in honor of both pitchers—recognizing the number's legacy across generations.[364]

Montreal Expos: #10 for Rusty Staub and Andre Dawson

The Montreal Expos also created an unusual situation when they retired #10 twice—first for Rusty Staub in 1993, then for Andre Dawson just four years later.

Staub played just three seasons for the Expos from 1969 to 1971, with a brief encore later, but was considered 'The Original Expo'—winning the franchise's first Player of the Year Award and making the All-Star team each of those first three seasons. Staub's #10 was the first number ever retired by the Expos.

Hall of Famer Andre Dawson played with the Expos for 11 seasons including 1977, when he won Rookie of the Year honors. He was still active in the majors when the Expos retired #10 for Staub, but the team retired it again for Dawson shortly after his retirement.[355]

Los Angeles Lakers: #8 and #24 for Kobe Bryant

Kobe Bryant is the only player in NBA history to have two numbers retired by the same team.

After starting his career wearing #8, Bryant later switched to #24, symbolizing a new chapter in his relentless pursuit of greatness. Both numbers saw championships, All-Star appearances, and unforgettable moments.

In a historic move, the Lakers retired both #8 and #24—making Bryant's dual retirement a tribute to a career that spanned eras.[365]

It's not a shared retirement between two players—it's a recognition that one player's legacy was so vast that it required two numbers to capture it.

Jerry Sloan: #4 and #1223

Jerry Sloan is the only person in professional sports to have both a traditional jersey number and a statistical milestone retired in his honor.

The Chicago Bulls retired Sloan's #4 for his playing career—10 seasons as a tenacious guard who embodied toughness and became the franchise's first star player.

Years later, the Utah Jazz retired #1223 for Sloan's coaching career—representing his 1,223 victories across 23 seasons as head coach from 1988 to 2011.[366] It's not a jersey number anyone could wear—it's a monument to longevity, consistency, and impact that goes beyond traditional digits.

Two franchises, two retirements, and two different ways of honoring the same man—one number for the player he was, one number for the coach he became. From player to coach, from #4 to #1223, Sloan's legacy spans eras, roles, and redefines what a retired number can represent.

Honoring Players Who Never Wore Numbers

Baseball's numbering system didn't become standard until 1929, meaning generations of baseball's early greats never wore digits on their backs. Teams have handled this by retiring their *names* instead, displaying them alongside numbered jerseys with the same stadium honors.[367]

Christy Mathewson and John McGraw, both Hall of Famers whose careers ended before jersey numbers existed, are honored by the San Francisco Giants. Their names are prominently displayed on the outfield wall as permanent tributes, equal in status to any retired number.

Rogers Hornsby, one of the most accomplished hitters in baseball history, whose career spanned the pre-number era, is similarly honored by the St. Louis Cardinals.

Chuck Klein and Grover Cleveland Alexander are both honored by the Philadelphia Phillies in the same manner, ensuring their legacies remain visible despite never wearing numbered jerseys.

Ty Cobb and the Detroit Tigers' Dilemma

The Tigers faced a unique challenge: Ty Cobb, widely considered "The Greatest Tiger of All," never wore a number. For decades, the franchise refused to retire *any* player's number, reasoning that if the team couldn't honor Cobb with a retired number, it would be unfair to honor anyone else.

That policy finally changed in 1980 when the Tigers retired Al Kaline's #6. Cobb's legacy is now preserved in Detroit with a statue, a historical plaque, and his name displayed on the outfield wall, but without a number—recognizing his greatness without the need for digits.

These name retirements remind us that jersey numbers are a relatively modern invention. The pioneers who played before numbering existed receive equal honor—their names alone carry the weight of history.

These honors aren't exceptions—they're reminders that the idea of a "retired number" had to evolve to include pioneers who played before jersey numbers existed.

But every once in a while, a player who *did* wear a number asks that it not be retired and put on display, but rather reissued to future players in order to bridge generations.

"LOSCY" and the Boston Celtics

Not every player wants a number retired. Jim Loscutoff, a rugged forward who won seven championships with the Boston Celtics from 1955 to 1964, specifically requested that his #18 not be retired at all.

Loscutoff believed the number should remain in circulation for future Celtics to wear. He wanted young players to have the opportunity to make their own legacy with #18, rather than having it permanently removed from use.

The Celtics honored his wishes—yet still found a way to celebrate him. Instead of retiring #18, they hung a banner with his nickname "LOSCY" in the rafters, ensuring his legacy was recognized without removing the number from circulation.[368]

As a result, several players wore #18 after Loscutoff, most notably Dave Cowens, who was later inducted into the Hall of Fame.

Loscutoff's decision was about more than humility—it was about believing that numbers belong to the future, not just the past. Sometimes the greatest honor isn't removing a number—it's letting the next generation try to live up to it.

When Athletes Become Leaders

Some retired numbers honor athletes who went on to achieve greatness far beyond the playing field—using their sports experience to lead in ways that changed the world.

University of Michigan: #48 for Gerald Ford

The University of Michigan retired #48 for Gerald Ford, the 38th President of the United States—honoring both his athletic excellence and his historic journey from the football field to the Oval Office.[369]

Ford was a standout center and linebacker for Michigan from 1932 to 1934, helping lead the Wolverines to back-to-back undefeated seasons and national championships in 1932 and 1933. He was named team MVP in 1934.

After college, Ford turned down offers from both the Detroit Lions and Green Bay Packers to attend Yale Law School, eventually entering politics and becoming the 38th President following Richard Nixon's resignation.

Michigan's retirement of #48 celebrates both achievements—the qualities Ford demonstrated on the field and the historic path those qualities helped forge. The lessons learned in sports can shape leaders who change nations.

Seattle Seahawks: #80 for Steve Largent

Steve Largent had a Hall of Fame career as a wide receiver for the Seattle Seahawks, earning his #80 retirement in 1992. But Largent's post-football career took an unexpected turn: he became a U.S. Congressman, serving Oklahoma's 1st congressional district from 1994 to 2002, and later running for Governor of Oklahoma.[370]

Like President Ford, Largent's retired number honors both his athletic excellence and his transition to public service. The Seahawks' retirement of #80 celebrates not just his seven Pro Bowls and Hall of Fame induction, but the traits that took him from the gridiron to the halls of Congress.

Once again, athletic excellence provided the foundation for leadership that served the nation.

Honoring Athletes Who Never Played for the Team

Miami Heat: #23 for Michael Jordan

The Miami Heat officially retired #23 for Michael Jordan, even though he never played for the Heat.

It was a fitting tribute to Jordan's impact on basketball and sports culture—an acknowledgment that some athletes are so transformative that their influence reaches beyond the teams they actually played for.

Team president Pat Riley explained that they wanted every Heat player to understand that the number represented the highest standard of basketball excellence—a symbol of talent, effort, and success. It remains one of the rare cases where a team retired a number purely out of respect, not affiliation.[371]

New Orleans Hornets: #7 for Pete Maravich

When the Hornets relocated from Charlotte to New Orleans in 2002, the franchise sought to anchor itself in the city's basketball heritage. They chose to retire #7 in honor of Pete "Pistol" Maravich, the dazzling scorer and showman who had starred for the New Orleans Jazz in the 1970s.

Maravich never played for the Hornets, but his artistry, charisma, and deep connection to New Orleans made him the ideal figure to bridge the team's new identity with the city's basketball past. Retiring his number was less about franchise lineage than about honoring a local legend whose impact transcended team boundaries.[371]

Honoring People Who Never Played

Boston Celtics: #1 for Walter Brown, #2 for Red Auerbach

The Boston Celtics retired #1 to honor Walter Brown, the founder of the team, and #2 to honor Arnold "Red" Auerbach, the team's renowned coach, general manager, and president.

Neither number was retired for a player—they were retired to honor two men who never wore them but helped build the Celtics dynasty.[372]

Honoring Voices
When Teams Retire More Than Numbers

Some retired honors don't commemorate players—they celebrate the voices that made the game come alive for generations of fans.

Robert Merrill: #1½—The Yankees' Voice

Opera legend Robert Merrill became a beloved fixture at Yankee Stadium, where he sang the national anthem for decades. To honor him, Yankees owner George Steinbrenner gave Merrill an official team jersey with the custom #1½—a playful nod to his honorary status: not quite a player, but more than a fan.

The Yankees later presented Merrill with the New York Yankees Lifetime Achievement Award in 2003, cementing his place in franchise history.[373]

Though never retired in the traditional sense, #1½ remains one of the most charming and unique numbers in baseball history—a creative way to celebrate a voice that became a defining part of Yankees tradition.

Dave Zinkoff: The Voice Immortalized

On March 25, 1986, the Philadelphia 76ers faced an unprecedented situation: they wanted to honor Dave Zinkoff, their celebrated public address announcer who had served the franchise for 22 seasons before his death on Christmas Day 1985. But Zinkoff never wore a jersey number—he wore a microphone.

So the 76ers became the first professional sports franchise to retire a microphone symbol, hanging it in the rafters alongside retired numbers of their greatest players.

The tradition caught on. Today, retiring a microphone has become a common practice across the NBA and Major League Baseball—honoring voices that connected fans to the game for decades.[374]

Retiring Numbers for Fans

Several teams have retired jersey numbers to honor their fans, recognizing their passionate support as an essential part of the game.

Seattle Seahawks: #12—The 12th Man

The Seattle Seahawks retired #12 to honor their fans as the "12th Man"—symbolizing that fans act as an extra player on the field.

The crowd noise at Seattle's stadium is legendary, often disrupting opposing teams' communication and creating one of the most intimidating home-field advantages in the NFL.

By retiring #12, the Seahawks acknowledged that their success isn't just about the players on the field—it's about the roar of 70,000 fans making every home game feel like a playoff atmosphere.[375]

NBA: #6—The 6th Man

Before the league-wide retirement of #6 for Bill Russell, both the Sacramento Kings and Orlando Magic had already retired #6 to honor their fans as the "Sixth Man"—acknowledging the energy and impact fans bring during games.

In basketball, where home-court advantage can swing playoff series, the crowd becomes part of the team's strategy. By retiring #6, these franchises recognized that fans aren't just spectators—they're participants.[376]

California Angels: #26—Gene Autry, the 26th Man

In 1982, the California Angels (now the Los Angeles Angels) retired #26 in honor of team founder, the Singing Cowboy, Gene Autry, calling him the "26th man" to represent fans and ownership support when rosters had 25 active players.

It's a creative way to honor someone who wasn't a player but whose vision and leadership made the franchise possible.[377]

Atlanta United FC: #17—The Inaugural Season

Atlanta United reserved and effectively retired #17 as a tribute to its supporters and to the club's inaugural 2017 season.

Rather than honoring a player, the number celebrates the birth of the franchise and the fans who helped make Atlanta one of MLS's most vibrant soccer markets.

Even prior to establishing any on-field history, #17 became a symbolic "first chapter" hanging in the rafters.[378]

Seattle Kraken: #32—The League's Newest Franchise

The Seattle Kraken retired #32—not for a player, but for their fans and the city.

The number honors the more than 32,000 fans who placed season-ticket deposits on day one, while also marking Seattle as the NHL's 32nd franchise.

As with Atlanta United, this retirement reflects a modern trend: new franchises using symbolic numbers to build identity before they have players worthy of traditional honors.[379]

Cleveland Indians: #455—The Sellout Streak

The Cleveland Indians (now the Guardians) retired the number 455 to honor their fans and commemorate a remarkable achievement: 455 consecutive sellout games at Jacobs Field from 1995 to 2001.

This streak symbolized the city's passionate support during one of the most exciting eras in franchise history.

Unlike traditional number retirements for players, this one was a tribute to the fans themselves—recognizing their role as the heartbeat of the team during those unforgettable seasons.[380]

Honoring Lives and Community

Some retired numbers transcend sports entirely, honoring those lost to tragedy and communities that endured.

Vegas Golden Knights: #58

The Vegas Golden Knights retired #58 to honor the 58 victims of the 2017 Las Vegas shooting—one of the deadliest mass shootings in American history.

The number serves as a permanent memorial, ensuring that the victims are remembered every time the team takes the ice. It's not a tribute to athletic achievement—it's a tribute to lives lost and a community that came together in the aftermath of unspeakable tragedy.

It's a reminder that some numbers represent not just athletic achievement, but collective grief—and the strength of a community that endured it.[381]

Marshall University: #75

On November 14, 1970, Southern Airways Flight 932 crashed near Huntington, West Virginia, killing all seventy-five people onboard—including nearly the entire Marshall football team, as well as coaches, staff, and supporters. It remains the deadliest tragedy in American sports history.

In the years that followed, Marshall rebuilt its football program, but the memory of "The 75" became inseparable from the school's identity. To ensure those lives were never forgotten, the university permanently removed the number 75 from circulation.

Marshall often describes the gesture as a *memorial* rather than a formal retirement, but the effect is the same: no player will ever wear #75 again. The number stands as a symbol of resilience and remembrance, woven into the Memorial Fountain ceremonies each November.[382]

Most retired numbers honor remarkable athletes. But some recognize fans, those we've lost, people who never played, and legacies too complex for traditional categories. These numbers prove that sports' impact extends beyond statistics—into community, remembrance, and the moments that shape who we are.

But even with all these categories, some retirements never happen at all—despite a player's greatness.

Sometimes even worthy numbers can slip through the cracks when timing and circumstances collide. Consider Gary Payton, a Hall of Famer who played 13 seasons for the Seattle SuperSonics with nine All-Star selections. But he never had his number retired—not because he wasn't deserving, but because the team relocated to Oklahoma City before it could happen. Payton has been vocal about not wanting his number retired by a franchise he never played for, leaving his legacy in limbo.[356] His story shows that retired numbers aren't just about greatness—they're about belonging.

CONCLUSION

What's in a Number?

This book has taken you across 23 chapters and hundreds of stories, from Eddie Gaedel's #1/8 to Gretzky's league-wide retired #99, from Derrick Rose's alter ego in #1 to the 58 victims honored by the Vegas Golden Knights, from two cases of beer to a quarter-million dollars in cash.

After such a wide range of stories spanning more than a century of sports history, one truth emerges: numbers are whatever we make them.

For Lou Gehrig, #4 was a testament to consistency and courage in the face of ALS. For Larry Walker, #33 was a religion—complete with alarm clocks set to 8:03 and a wedding at 3:33 p.m. For Jackie Robinson, #42 became a symbol of breaking barriers that transcended baseball itself.

For Tom Brady, #12 wasn't his choice—but it became a wellness empire. For Amon-Ra St. Brown, #14 was based on a miscount—but it became his motivation. For Jim Otto, #00 was a pun on his name that made him one of the few players in NFL history to wear double zero.

Numbers can be chosen with intention or fall into your lap by accident—but once they're yours, they take on a life of their own.

Athletes have waited three years for their number (Anthony Edwards), paid $250,000 for it (Gerald McCoy), or given it away for free (John Franco, Chris Godwin). Some declined revered numbers out of respect (Joe Montana, Anthony Davis, Tim Duncan). Negotiations have succeeded with Rolexes, BMWs, and ice cream cones. They've failed when rookies demanded millions or when legends simply said "no." Numbers have been stolen before games, miscounted by girlfriends, and changed because science proved they affected perception.

Identity has a price—and that price varies wildly.

Two cases of beer got Mitch Williams #28. A Porsche worth $200,000 got Shohei Ohtani his #17. Corliss Waitman gave up #8 to Aaron Rodgers simply because it was the right thing to do. Some numbers cost your dignity in a fictitious arm-wrestling match. Some cost $1.5 million in inventory buyouts that even NFL stars couldn't afford.

Numbers connect us across time.

When Francisco Lindor wears #12, a number tied to his family and to Roberto Clemente's legacy, we see how inspiration flows through generations. When Patrick Ewing wore #33 to honor Kareem, who wore it to honor Mel Triplett, we see a family tree of respect. When every player in baseball wears #42 on Jackie Robinson Day, we see how one number can unite an entire sport.

Some numbers transcend the game entirely.

The Vegas Golden Knights' #58 remembers tragedy. Pat Tillman's #40 honors sacrifice. The Cleveland Guardians' #455 honors fans who showed up for 455 straight games. Gerald Ford's #48 honors a path that ran from the football field to the White House.

Science, superstition, and psychology all play a role.

Danny Buggs and Jeff Smoker knew instinctively that higher numbers made them look bigger—decades before UCLA proved they were right. Derrick Rose understood that #1 triggered an "alter ego" version of himself.

Wade Boggs ate chicken before every game and wore #26 like a talisman. Turk Wendell put 99 cents at the end of his contracts because he loved the number that much.

Red Grange didn't ask for #77—he just happened to be behind #76 in line. Pete Maravich averaged 44.2 points per game wearing #44 in one of the most uncanny alignments in sports history. Michael Jordan wore #12 for one game because someone stole his jersey, and he still dominated.

Brett Favre was told "the only number we have left is 4," and he said, "Hell, I was just happy to have any jersey at all." That throwaway number became one of the most well-known in football history.

The number doesn't make you great. What you do while wearing it does.

The Stories Left Untold

This book contains hundreds of stories, but thousands more exist. Every athlete has a number story—some dramatic, some mundane, some hilarious, some heartbreaking.

There are hundreds of retired numbers we didn't cover. Countless negotiations that happened quietly in locker rooms. Superstitions that could fill entire chapters (Larry Walker alone could supply one).

All these stories reveal one thing: behind every number is a story. And behind every story is a human being trying to forge an identity in a world that will remember them by one or two digits on their back. Now you know how to find those stories.

The Future of Numbers

As sports evolve, so will the stories of numbers.

Will we see more six-figure cash deals? More teams retiring numbers for tragedy and community? More science showing how digits shape perception? Almost certainly. Because as long as sports exist, numbers will matter. They'll be chosen, negotiated, stolen, retired, honored, and even turned into global brands. They'll represent hope, legacy, superstition, and identity.

New legends will emerge, and they'll make their numbers famous.

Someone will wear #0 and redefine what it means. Someone will turn a "bad" number into a Hall of Fame career. Someone will wait patiently for years to finally wear the number they've always wanted. Someone will decline a number rich with history out of respect and forge their own path.

And somewhere, right now, a young athlete is choosing a number for the first time.

Maybe they'll pick it to honor a parent. Maybe they'll choose their birthday. Maybe they'll take what's available and make it memorable through sheer force of will. Maybe they'll negotiate for it, pay for it, wait for it, or turn it down when offered.

Whatever they choose, that number will become part of their story.

It might hang in a childhood bedroom or appear in a high school gym. For some, it will be stitched onto a college jersey. For a select few, it will make it onto a professional uniform. Fans will wear it. Commentators will reference it. Teammates will remember it. And maybe one day it will hang in the rafters or be retired forever.

Because that's what numbers do. They tell stories. They create legends. They become immortal.

Final Thoughts

Players have always had a special bond with their numbers. You see athletes wearing them on gold chains, and fans wearing them on their backs. Across all sports, a number isn't just a marker—it becomes part of a player's identity, something supporters will always connect to that individual.

So if you've learned anything from this book, it should be this:

The next time you see an athlete wearing a number, pause. Behind those digits lies a story—a tribute, a negotiation, a superstition, a brand, a legacy.

There's always a story.

And now you know how to find it.

These 23 chapters reveal what athletes have always known: the number on your back isn't decoration—it's a declaration. It announces who you honor, what you believe, how you see yourself, and the legacy you're building.

Your number may come from family or faith, calculation or chance, negotiation or assignment. But once you put it on, once you perform in it, once you make it yours—it becomes permanent. Not in the rafters, perhaps, but in memory. In the minds of those who watched you wear it.

That's the power of numbers in sports—the way they turn fabric into meaning.

And that's why this book exists—to preserve these stories before they fade, to honor the meaning behind the digits, and to remind us that in sports, as in life, identity isn't given. It's chosen, earned, fought for, and made meaningful by what you do while wearing it.

Thank you for reading *It's All About the Numbers.*

PLAYER INDEX

A

Aaron, Hank – Chapters 2, 18
Abdul-Jabbar, Kareem – Chapters 5, 18
Adams, Alvan – Chapter 22
Adams, Davante – Chapters 13, 16
Adams, Kevyn – Chapter 19
Akers, Cam – Chapter 15
Allen, Jared – Chapter 19
Alomar, Roberto – Chapter 22
Alvarez, Edson – Chapter 19
Anderson, Nick – Chapter 17
Anderson, Ryan – Chapter 10
Antetokounmpo, Giannis – Chapter 3
Antetokounmpo, Thanasis – Chapter 3
Anthony, Carmelo – Chapter 3
Aparicio, Luis – Chapter 22
Arenas, Gilbert – Chapter 19
Artest, Ron (Metta World Peace) –
Chapters 2, 5
Auerbach, Red – Chapter 23
Autry, Gene – Chapter 23

B

Bane, Desmond – Chapter 17
Banks, Deonte – Chapters 13, 16
Barkley, Charles – Chapter 5
Barron, Mark – Chapter 12
Baty, Brett – Chapter 11
Baylor, Elgin – Chapter 18
Baynes, Aron – Chapter 19
Beckham, David – Chapter 5
Beimel, Joe – Chapter 3
Belichick, Bill – Chapter 8
Beltre, Adrian – Chapter 10
Bembry, DeAndre – Chapter 3
Bench, Johnny – Chapter 22
Bendtner, Nicklas – Chapter 18
Bent, Molly – Chapter 21
Berra, Yogi – Chapter 23
Betances, Dellin – Chapter 19
Betts, Mookie – Chapter 6

Bird, Larry – Chapter 3
Bird, Sue – Chapter 21
Bobrovsky, Sergei – Chapter 10
Boggs, Wade – Chapter 6
Bogaerts, Xander – Chapter 5
Bol, Manute – Chapter 16
Bony, Wilfried – Chapter 2
Borbon, Julio – Chapter 10
Bosworth, Brian – Chapters 17, 20
Bourque, Ray – Chapter 21
Bradley, Shawn – Chapter 19
Brady, Tom – Chapters 13, 20
Brice, Alundis – Chapter 11
Brown, Walter – Chapter 23
Brunson, Jalen – Chapter 9
Bryant, Antonio – Chapter 13
Bryant, Kobe – Chapters 2, 5, 23
Bueckers, Paige – Chapter 17
Bumgarner, Madison – Chapter 9
Bure, Pavel – Chapter 4
Burnett, A.J. – Chapter 9
Burress, Plaxico – Chapter 14
Bush, Reggie – Chapter 17, 22
Butler, Brett – Chapter 19

C

Cammalleri, Mike – Chapter 6
Campbell, Earl – Chapter 8
Campbell, Mark – Chapter 12
Casilla, Alexi – Chapter 10
Carlson, Daniel – Chapter 11
Carter, Abdul – Chapter 17
Ceni, Rogério – Chapter 19
Chafin, Andrew – Chapter 9
Chalmers, Mario – Chapter 13
Chamberlain, Wilt – Chapters 6, 21
Chosen, Robbie – Chapter 7
Clapper, Dit – Chapter 22
Clark, Caitlin – Chapters 4, 20
Clausen, Jimmy – Chapter 16
Clemens, Roger – Chapters 6, 10
Clemente, Roberto – Chapters 5, 18

STORY INDEX

Chapter 3: All in the Family

Chapter 6: Superstitions, Rituals, and Obsessions

Chapter 7: Guided by Faith

Chapter 8: When the Number Chooses You

Chapter 9: Let the Bidding Begin

Chapter 10: Brother, Do You Have the Time?

-     o   Elgin Baylor: #34
- When Your New Number Doesn't Live up to the Hype
  - o   Nicklas Bendtner: #52—The Fortune-Teller's Advice
  - o   Deion Sanders: #21—The Owner's Prank
  - o   John Davidson: #00—Looking for Shutouts
- Before They Became Legends
  - o   Hank Aaron: #5 Before He Was #44
  - o   Reggie White: #91 Before He Was #92
  - o   Roberto Clemente: #13 Before He Was #21
  - o   Walter Payton: #21 Before He Was #34
  - o   Mickey Mantle: #6 Before He Was #7

Chapter 19: Quirky Numbers

- The Pun Masters
  - o   Heinz 57: A Saucy Selection
  - o   Andrei Kirilenko: #47—"AK-47"
  - o   Natasha Cloud: #9—"Cloud 9"
  - o   Chad Johnson: #85—Ochocinco
- The Name Games
  - o   Jim Otto: #00—"Aught-O"
  - o   Adam Ottavino: #0—"O" for Ottavino
- When Your Name IS the Number
  - o   Deron Quint: #5
  - o   Scott Lachance: #7
  - o   Neil Sheehy: #0—Adding the Missing "O" in O'Sheehy
  - o   Jordin Tootoo: #22—Just Like It Sounds
  - o   What Could Have Been—Missed Opportunities
- Size Matters
  - o   Derek Jeter: #2—The Smallest Jersey
  - o   Brett Butler: #22—Too Small to Matter
  - o   Shawn Bradley: #76—Perfect Alignment
  - o   Dellin Betances: #68—Standing Tall on the Mound
  - o   Bixente Lizarazu: #69—Using the Metric System
- Mathematical Minds
  - o   Iván Zamorano: #18—$1 + 8 = 9$
  - o   Aron Baynes: #46—A Family Equation
  - o   Dennis Rodman: #91 & #73—The Ten Man
  - o   Kenyon Martin: #6—Unconfirmed, but the Math Works
- The Double-Digit Workarounds
  - o   Phil Esposito & Ken Hodge: #77 and #88
- The Superstitious Minded
  - o   Turk Wendell: #99—Not Just a Jersey Number, but a Way of Life
- The Bold Statements

Chapter 20: A Brand in a Number

Chapter 21: Forever Numbers

NOTES AND SOURCES

[1] Shane Garry Acedera, "The Real Explanation on Why Michael Jordan Wore 23 Since High School," *Basketball Network*, February 23, 2022, accessed November 25, 2025, https://basketballnetwork.net/off-the-court/the-real-explanation-on-why-michael-jordan-wore-23-since-high-school

[2] Anuj Tazhatuveetil, "Tom Brady Never Wanted His Iconic No. 12 Jersey After Getting Drafted in the NFL," *Essentially Sports*, March 14, 2023, accessed November 25, 2025, https://www.essentiallysports.com/nfl-news-tom-brady-never-wanted-his-iconic-no-12-jersey-after-getting-drafted-in-the-nfl-despite-generating-20-million-annually-under-tb12-trademark/

[3] Chris Landers, "This Day in Baseball History: The Yankees Become the First MLB Team to Put Numbers on Uniforms," *MLB.com*, January 22, 2018, accessed November 25, 2025, https://www.mlb.com/cut4/this-day-in-baseball-history-the-yankees-become-the-first-mlb-team-to-put-number

[4] "1973," Pro Football Hall of Fame, accessed January 19, 2026, https://www.profootballhof.com/football-history/football-history/1960-1979/1973/

[5] SCD Newswire, "William 'Refrigerator' Perry's Super Bowl Jersey Goes to Auction," Sports Collectors Digest, August 6, 2020, accessed November 25, 2025, https://sportscollectorsdigest.com/auctions/william-refrigerator-perry-jersey-heritage-auction

[6] Kevin Seifert, "Behind the Wide Receivers' Numbers Shift: Why the NFL's Best Are Donning Nos. 10–19," *ESPN*, December 5, 2019, accessed November 25, 2025, https://www.espn.com/nfl/story/_/id/28224466/behind-wide-receivers-numbers-shift-why-nfl-best-donning-nos-10-19

[7] Kevin Patra, "NFL Owners Pass Rule Expanding Eligible Jersey Numbers for Certain Positions," *NFL.com*, April 21, 2021, accessed November 25, 2025, https://www.nfl.com/news/nfl-passes-rule-expanding-eligible-jersey-numbers

[8] Ryan Huffman, "What Basketball Numbers Are Allowed: Decoding Jersey Number Rules," *Huff Sports*, accessed November 25, 2025, https://huffsports.com/sports/what-basketball-numbers-are-allowed/

[9] Max Molski, "Here's Why NBA and WNBA Stars Wear Different Jersey Numbers for Team USA," *NBC Boston*, July 9, 2024, accessed November 25, 2025, https://www.nbcboston.com/paris-2024-summer-olympics/usa-basketball-jersey-number-rules-olympics/3421796/

[10] Tal Pinchevsky, "Why Goalies Are Increasingly Ditching Traditional No. 1," *ESPN*, November 30, 2016, accessed November 25, 2025, https://www.espn.com/nhl/story/_/id/18268822/nhl-goalies-increasingly-ditching-traditional-no-1-other-numbers-their-sweaters

11 Benjamin Kenyon, "The Mystique of Numbers: Why Are Hockey Goalies Number 1 or 30?" *The Bruins Blog*, April 21, 2024, accessed November 25, 2025, https://thebruinsblog.net/nhl-goalie-numbers

12 Ben Clayfield, "The Number 10 in Soccer – Why It's So Significant," *Your Soccer Home*, accessed November 25, 2025, https://yoursoccerhome.com/the-number-10-in-soccer-why-its-so-significant/

13 Barnaby Lane, "The Best No. 10s in Soccer History—Past and Present," *Sports Illustrated*, September 4, 2025, accessed November 25, 2025, https://si.com/soccer/best-no10s-soccer-history-past-present

14 April Weiner, "Heinze 57, Commodore 64 and the 25 Most Meaningful Jersey Numbers in NHL History," *Bleacher Report*, June 4, 2018, https://bleacherreport.com/articles/796087-heinze-57-commodore-64-and-the-25-most-meaningful-jersey-numbers-in-nhl-history

15 "The Numerology of Ron Artest," YouTube video, 2:08, posted by NBA, September 2, 2010, accessed November 25, 2025, https://www.youtube.com/watch?v=qCxgtxo0fXY

16 Jordan Giorgio, "NBA Jersey Number Expert Ish Smith Explains His Process to Wizards PGL Crew," *NBC Sports Washington*, March 2, 2021, accessed November 25, 2025, https://www.nbcwashington.com/news/sports/nbcsports/nba-jersey-number-expert-ish-smith-explains-his-process-to-wizards-pgl-crew/2592560/

17 Tyler Kepner, "13 Teams Over 16 Seasons, but He Is More Than a Journeyman," *New York Times*, July 14, 2018, accessed November 25, 2025, https://www.nytimes.com/2018/07/14/sports/baseball/oakland-as-home-run-derby.html#:~:text=Dan%20Evans%2C%20the%20former%20Dodgers,wherever%20the%20game%20takes%20him; Baseball-Reference, "Edwin Jackson Stats," accessed November 25, 2025, https://www.baseball-reference.com/players/j/jacksed01.shtml

18 Maria Pasquini, "Why Kobe Bryant Changed Numbers and the Special Meaning Behind No. 24 and No. 8," *People*, February 1, 2020, accessed November 13, 2025, https://people.com/sports/why-kobe-bryant-changed-jersey-numbers/

19 Craig Muder, "Fisk Changed Sox in 1981," *Baseball Hall of Fame*, accessed November 13, 2025, https://baseballhall.org/discover/inside-pitch/fisk-changed-sox-by-heading-to-chicago

20 Nick Khairi, "Why Does Messi Wear No. 30 at PSG?" *Goal.com*, March 17, 2022, accessed November 13, 2025, https://goal.com/en-us/news/why-does-messi-wear-no-30-psg/blta5407755655341bf

21 Nina Mandell, "Russell Westbrook Explains the Origin of His 'Why Not' Slogan," *USA Today: For The Win*, December 12, 2017, https://ftw.usatoday.com/story/sports/nba/2017/12/12/russell-westbrook-whynot-meaning/81833787007/

[22] Chris, "New Swansea Striker Bony Chooses Number 2 Instead Of 9 – Here Is Why," *Footy Headlines*, September 2, 2017, https://www.footyheadlines.com/2017/09/new-swansea-city-striker-bony-chooses-number-2-instead-of-9.html

[23] "2011 NFL Draft Listing," *Pro-Football-Reference.com*, accessed November 13, 2025, https://www.pro-football-reference.com/years/2011/draft.htm

[24] "NBA Draft Listings," *Basketball Reference*, accessed November 13, 2025, https://www.basketball-reference.com/draft/

[25] Kalan Hooks, "Cam Newton Explains Why He Wore No. 1 for Carolina Panthers," *ESPN*, November 9, 2023, https://espn.com/nfl/story/_/id/38851266/cam-newton-jimmy-clausen-carolina-panthers-jersey

[26] "D. Rose Explains Why He Wears No. 1," *NBC Chicago*, July 15, 2013, accessed November 25, 2025, https://nbcchicago.com/news/local/chicago-bulls-derrick-rose-9/1958777/

[27] James Foglio, "Anthony Edwards to Wear No. 5 Jersey to Honor Mother, Grandmother," *Basketball Insiders*, August 1, 2023, accessed November 25, 2025, https://www.basketballinsiders.org/news/timberwolves-anthony-edwards-to-wear-no-5-jersey-to-honor-mother-grandmother/

[28] "Rapid Fire with Andre Iguodala," YouTube video, 2:15, posted by Golden State Warriors, October 9, 2013, accessed November 25, 2025, https://www.youtube.com/watch?v=dMk20DF05Zo

[29] Orlando Silva, "Klay Thompson Explains Why He Wears #11: 'I Was A Draftee Of The 2011 Draft Class, I Was The 11th Pick. It Took Me 11 Dribbles to Get To 60 Points'," *Fadeaway World*, August 2, 2020, accessed November 25, 2025, https://fadeawayworld.net/klay-thompson-explains-why-he-wears-11-i-was-a-draftee-of-the-2011-draft-class-i-was-the-11th-pick-it-took-me-11-dribbles-to-get-to-60-points

[30] NFL Nation, "What's Behind the Number? 15 Rookies Explain Why They Chose Their NFL Uniform Number," *ESPN*, August 5, 2022, https://www.espn.com/nfl/story/_/id/34125083/number-15-rookies-explain-why-chose-their-nfl-uniform-number

[31] Ben Rohrbach, "NBA Countdown: Which Player Wore No. 27 Best in League History?" *Yahoo Sports*, September 25, 2019, https://sports.yahoo.com/nba-countdown-which-player-wore-no-27-best-in-league-history-141158060.html

[32] Bill Ladson, "Downing, Pitcher for 715, Reflects on Aaron," *MLB.com*, January 22, 2021, https://www.mlb.com/news/al-downing-remembers-hank-aaron-hr-715

[33] "Willie McCovey," *National Baseball Hall of Fame*, accessed November 13, 2025, https://baseballhall.org/hall-of-famers/mccovey-willie

[34] Kevin Keman, "Advisor Reggie Passing on Lessons, Legacy," *New York Post*, April 25, 2009, https://nypost.com/2009/04/25/advisor-reggie-passing-on-lessons-legacy/

[35] Editorial Staff, "No. 44 Will Always Belong to Reggie," *Yanks Go Yard*, December 22, 2011, https://yanksgoyard.com/2011/12/22/no-44-will-always-belong-to-reggie-jackson/

[36] C. Trent Rosecrans, "No. 44 on No. 44: Reds Legend Eric Davis Watches Prospect Elly De La Cruz," *The Athletic*, February 28, 2023, https://www.nytimes.com/athletic/4258375/2023/02/28/eric-davis-elly-de-la-cruz-reds/

[37] Jason Beck, "Partly Named After Aaron, Malloy Now Wears His Uniform Number," *MLB.com*, June 14, 2024, https://www.mlb.com/news/justyn-henry-malloy-gets-no-44-uniform-from-tigers-coach

[38] Chris Creamer, "All Players to Wear #3 and #44 in Home Run Derby," *SportsLogos.net*, July 3, 2025, https://news.sportslogos.net/2025/07/03/all-players-to-wear-3-and-44-in-home-run-derby-to-honour-ruth-and-aaron/baseball/

[39] Mike Cameron, quoted in "Mike Cameron Responds to Julio Choosing to Wear 44," Reddit post, r/Mariners, November 22, 2021, https://www.reddit.com/r/Mariners/comments/qzequy/mike_cameron_responds_to_julio_choosing_to_wear/

[40] "Stephen Curry on Why He Picked #30," YouTube video, 0:15, posted by "Basketball Action," November 14, 2021, accessed November 25, 2025, https://www.youtube.com/watch?v=iq7UR6urOa0

[41] Joaquin Ruiz, "Why Seth Curry Hilariously Couldn't Take Steph's No. 30 Warriors Jersey from Him," *NBC Sports Bay Area*, October 2, 2025, accessed November 25, 2025, https://www.nbcsportsbayarea.com/nba/golden-state-warriors/steph-curry-jersey-seth/1878801

[42] Randy Mills, "As if by Magic: The Story of Young Larry Bird's Explosion onto the Indiana High School Basketball Scene," *Randy & Roxanne Mills Blog*, July 10, 2021, accessed November 25, 2025, https://randrmillsauthors.com/2021/07/as-if-by-magic-the-story-of-young-larry-birds-explosion-onto-the-indiana-high-school-basketball-scene/

[43] Julian Eschenbach, "'A Lot of People Think I Wear It Because of Hakeem' – Giannis Antetokounmpo Once Revealed a True Reason Why He Wears Number 34 on His Jersey," *Basketball Network*, March 4, 2025, accessed November 25, 2025, https://basketballnetwork.net/off-the-court/giannis-explained-that-he-doesnt-wear-34-because-of-hakeem

[44] "How a Hurricane Helped Get Tim Duncan to Wake Forest and into Basketball History," *FOX Sports*, May 13, 2016, accessed November 25, 2025, https://www.foxsports.com/stories/nba/how-a-hurricane-helped-get-tim-duncan-to-wake-forest-and-into-basketball-history; Josh Paredes, "Spurs: Tim Duncan's Hall of Fame Career,

from 21-1," *Air Alamo*, May 15, 2021, accessed November 25, 2025, https://airalamo.com/posts/san-antonio-spurs-tim-duncan-by-numbers-21-1

[45] Bob Garcia, "Why Peyton Manning Chose to Wear No. 18," *Sportscasting*, accessed November 25, 2025, https://www.sportscasting.com/news/why-peyton-manning-chose-to-wear-no-18

[46] Nima Murugan, "Why Does Angel Reese Wear Jersey Number 10?," *EssentiallySports*, December 5, 2023, accessed November 25, 2025, https://www.essentiallysports.com/ncaa-college-basketball-news-why-does-angel-reese-wear-jersey-number-ten/

[47] TMZ Staff, "Angel Reese Gets New Jersey No. 5, Kamilla Cardoso Keeps No. 10," *TMZ*, April 17, 2024, accessed November 25, 2025, https://www.tmz.com/2024/04/17/angel-reese-new-jersey-number-kamilla-cardoso-10-chicago-sky-wnba-ncaa/

[48] Julian Eschenbach, "When Shaquille O'Neal Honored His Stepdad with His Lakers Jersey Number: 'This One's for You, Sarge'," *Basketball Network*, December 25, 2024, accessed November 25, 2025, https://www.basketballnetwork.net/off-the-court/when-shaquille-oneal-honored-his-stepdad-with-his-lakers-jersey-number

[49] "About Us," *PS43 Foundation*, accessed November 25, 2025, https://www.ps43foundation.com/about-us/; Pratik Sharma, "Who Are Pascal Siakam's Parents? All About the Pacers Star's Family and Personal Life," *Pro Football Network*, May 12, 2025, accessed November 25, 2025, https://www.profootballnetwork.com/nba/who-are-pascal-siakams-parents

[50] "Domantas Sabonis to Wear No. 11 for the Sacramento Kings," *NBA.com*, June 14, 2024, accessed November 25, 2025, https://www.nba.com/kings/news/domantas-sabonis-to-wear-no-11-for-the-sacramento-kings

[51] Madeline Kenney, "The Inside Story of How Every Liberty Player Picked Her Number," *New York Post*, May 30, 2025, accessed November 25, 2025, https://nypost.com/2025/05/30/sports/inside-story-of-how-every-liberty-player-picked-her-number

[52] Mikey Partington, "Why Le Tissier Wears No. 4 for United," *Manchester United*, January 17, 2024, accessed November 25, 2025, https://www.manutd.com/en/news/detail/maya-le-tissier-explains-why-she-wears-man-utd-women-number-four-shirt-in-teamviewer-diaries-episode

[53] Natasha Dye, "Denver Nuggets' Aaron Gordon Changes Jersey Number to Honor Late Brother Drew After Car Accident," *People*, August 26, 2024, accessed November 25, 2025, https://people.com/aaron-gordon-change-jersey-number-honor-late-brother-8701415

[54] Ben Rohrbach, "NBA Countdown: Which Player Wore No. 36 Best in League History?," *Yahoo Sports*, September 16, 2019, accessed November 25, 2025, https://sports.yahoo.com/nba-countdown-which-player-wore-no-36-best-in-league-history-171909747.html; Jeff Hawkins, "NBA AM: Same Team, New Number," *Basketball Insiders*,

October 15, 2021, accessed November 25, 2025,
https://www.basketballinsiders.com/news/nba-am-same-team-new-number

55 Conor Roche, "The Touching Reason Why New Celtics Player Mike Muscala Wears 57 as His Jersey Number," *Boston.com*, February 12, 2023, accessed November 25, 2025, https://www.boston.com/sports/boston-celtics/2023/02/12/why-mike-muscala-wears-jersey-number-57-mom-celtics; Mike Thomas, "Boston Celtics Newcomer Mike Muscala Has a Personal Reason for Wearing No. 57," *Sportscasting*, February 12, 2023, accessed November 25, 2025, https://www.sportscasting.com/news/boston-celtics-newcomer-mike-muscala-has-a-personal-reason-for-wearing-no-57

56 John Chick, "DeAndre Bembry to Honor Late Brother with Number," *The Score*, July 15, 2016, accessed November 25, 2025, https://www.thescore.com/news/1059950; Dick Jerardi, "Brother of Hawks' Bembry Shot and Killed in North Carolina," *The Philadelphia Inquirer*, June 12, 2016, accessed November 25, 2025, https://www.inquirer.com/philly/sports/colleges/st_josephs/20160613_Brother_of_Hawks__Bembry_shot_and_killed_in_North_Carolina.html

57 Jesse Reed, "DeAndre Hopkins Reveals Powerful Reason He Wears No. 10 Jersey," *Sportsnaut*, June 4, 2020, accessed November 25, 2025, https://sportsnaut.com/deandre-hopkins-reveals-powerful-reason-he-wears-no-10-jersey

58 Ed Hochuli, email to Rob Lorton, December 2020

59 Tim Booth (Associated Press), "Hall of Fame Done, Ken Griffey Jr. Preps for Number Retirement," *Spokesman Review*, August 5, 2016, accessed November 25, 2025, https://www.spokesman.com/stories/2016/aug/05/hall-of-fame-done-ken-griffey-jr-preps-for-number-/

60 Kevin McCormick, "Why Does Kyrie Irving Wear 11 on His Jersey? All You Need to Know," *Sportskeeda*, January 2, 2023, accessed November 25, 2025, https://www.sportskeeda.com/basketball/why-kyrie-irving-wear-11-jersey-all-need-know

61 Arjun Julka, "'I Was Always a Huge Fan of Allen Iverson': Chris Paul Reveals the Reason Behind Choosing Number 3 for His Jersey and How It Meshed with His Initials," *The SportsRush*, December 25, 2021, accessed November 25, 2025, https://thesportsrush.com/nba-news-i-was-always-a-huge-fan-of-allen-iverson-chris-paul-reveals-the-reason-behind-choosing-number-3-for-his-jersey-and-how-it-meshed-with-his-initials

62 Glen R. Goodhand, "The Rise and Fall of Sweater Number 9," *Society for International Hockey Research*, January 23, 2019, accessed November 25, 2025, https://sihrhockey.org/2020/columns/article.cfm?aid=554

63 Marshall Garvey, "Random Dodger of the Week: Joe Beimel," *Dodgers Nation*, January 12, 2019, accessed November 25, 2025, https://dodgersnation.com/random-dodger-of-the-week-joe-beimel/2019/01/12

[64] Nicole Ganglani, "'Why I Wear Number Six, There Are Multiple Reasons' – LeBron James Details What Fascinates Him About the Jersey Number 6," *Basketball Network*, May 18, 2023, accessed November 25, 2025, https://www.basketballnetwork.net/latest-news/lebron-james-details-what-fascinates-him-about-the-jersey-number-6

[65] Ian Begley, "Why Carmelo Chose to Wear No. 7," *ESPN*, February 24, 2011, accessed November 25, 2025, https://www.espn.com/blog/new-york/knicks/post/_/id/2889/why-carmelo-chose-to-wear-no-7

[66] Hockey Feed, "Jaromir Jagr Explains Why He Wears 68," October 21, 2015, accessed November 25, 2025, https://www.hockeyfeed.com/nhl-news/jaromir-jagr-explains-why-he-wears-68

[67] RevUp Sports, "What Number Does Sidney Crosby Wear and Why?" March 9, 2023, accessed November 25, 2025, https://revupsports.com/athletes/hockey/sidney-crosby/discover/what-number-does-sidney-crosby-wear-and-why

[68] Paul Taylor, "Connor McDavid to Have Number 97 Jersey Retired," *Oil On Whyte*, October 6, 2024, accessed November 25, 2025, https://oilonwhyte.com/posts/connor-mcdavid-to-have-number-97-jersey-retired

[69] Sal Barry, "The End of Birth Year Numbers' is Here," *Puck Junk*, October 24, 2017, accessed November 25, 2025, https://puckjunk.com/2017/10/24/end-birth-year-numbers/#:~:text=..and%20for%20that%20I%20am,Kaner%E2%80%9D%20or%20%E2%80%9CSharpie.%E2%80%9D

[70] Hockey Reference, player pages for Patrick Kane, Sam Gagner, Marcus Johansson, Vladimir Tarasenko, Gabriel Landeskog, and Ryan Nugent Hopkins, accessed November 25, 2025, https://www.hockey-reference.com

[71] "AC Milan Squad 2008/2009," *Transfermarkt*, accessed November 25, 2025, https://www.transfermarkt.us/ac-milan/kader/verein/5/saison_id/2008

[72] Martina Alcheva, "From PSG to Manchester City, Gianluigi Donnarumma Breaks Premier League Tradition with Rare Kit Number," *World Soccer Talk*, September 2, 2025, accessed November 25, 2025, https://worldsoccertalk.com/news/from-psg-to-manchester-city-gianluigi-donnarumma-breaks-premier-league-tradition-with-rare-kit-number

[73] Dan Mount, "Behind the Sweater Number: No. 92," *Last Word On Sports*, July 10, 2023, accessed November 25, 2025, https://lastwordonsports.com/hockey/2023/07/10/behind-the-sweater-number-92/

[74] Kyle Irving, "Caitlin Clark Jersey Number: The Reason Why Fever Star Wears No. 22 in the WNBA," *Sporting News*, September 22, 2024, accessed November 25, 2025, https://sportingnews.com/us/wnba/news/caitlin-clark-jersey-number-22-fever-wnba/e4bcad397faa95667b29dea2

[75] Daniel Connolly, "UConn Women's Basketball Players Explain Why They Picked Their Jersey Numbers," *The UConn Blog*, December 16, 2019, accessed November 25, 2025,

https://www.theuconnblog.com/2019/12/16/20961557/behind-the-number-uconn-huskies-womens-basketball-players-the-significance-of-their-jersey-numbers

[76] Rich Hofmann, "Initial Thoughts on How Matisse Thybulle Fits with the Sixers," *The Athletic*, June 21, 2019, accessed November 25, 2025, https://www.nytimes.com/athletic/1040969/2019/06/21/initial-thoughts-on-the-matisse-thybulles-fit-with-the-sixers

[77] Colby Giacubeno, "Dwight Howard Explains Why He Chose No. 8," *Soaring Down South*, July 16, 2016, accessed November 25, 2025, https://soaringdownsouth.com/2016/07/16/dwight-howard-explains-why-he-chose-no-8/

[78] T.R. Sullivan, "Donning No. 84, Prince Unveiled by Texas," *MLB.com*, November 25, 2013, accessed November 25, 2025, https://www.mlb.com/news/slugger-prince-fielder-introduced-by-rangers/c-64203954

[79] Mike Lowe and Kevin Doellman, "'May Day': Former White Sox All-Star Only Player in MLB History to Wear His Birthday on His Back," *WGN-TV*, May 17, 2022, accessed November 25, 2025, https://wgntv.com/news/cover-story/may-day-former-white-sox-all-star-only-player-in-mlb-history-to-wear-his-birthday-on-his-back/

[80] Clyde Drexler, *Basketball Reference*, accessed November 25, 2025, https://www.basketball-reference.com/players/d/drexlcl01.html

[81] Joel Bartilotta (Rotowire.com), "NBA Birthdays: Players Born on March 6," *NBA.com*, June 7, 2025, accessed November 25, 2025, https://www.nba.com/news/nba-birthdays-players-born-on-march-6

[82] "NBA Player Pages," *Basketball Reference*, accessed November 25, 2025, https://www.basketball-reference.com/
Player pages consulted for jersey numbers and birth dates include Semih Erden, Danilo Gallinari, Nicolas Batum, Brodric Thomas, Eugene Omoruyi, and Tyrese Haliburton.

[83] WGRZ, "Unknown Story of WNY: The Defection of Alexander Mogilny," July 25, 2014, accessed November 25, 2025, https://www.wgrz.com/article/news/unknown-story-of-wny-the-defection-of-alexander-mogilny/71-272900317

[84] Dan Mount, "Behind the Sweater Number: No. 89," *Last Word on Sports*, July 13, 2023, accessed November 25, 2025, https://lastwordonsports.com/hockey/2023/07/13/behind-the-sweater-number-89/

[85] Dan Holmes, "The Defection of Petr Klima Was Like a Bad Spy Novel, but Red Wings Got Their Man," *Vintage Detroit*, January 31, 2016, accessed November 25, 2025, https://vintagedetroit.com/the-defection-of-petr-klima-was-like-a-bad-spy-novel-but-red-wings-got-their-man

[86] Dave Mount, "Behind the Sweater Number: No. 96," *Last Word on Sports*, July 6, 2023, accessed November 25, 2025, https://lastwordonsports.com/hockey/2023/07/06/behind-the-sweater-number-96/

[87] Nicole Ganglani, "'My Two Favorite Players Were Dominique Wilkins and Malik Sealy' – Kevin Garnett on Why He Chose to Wear Jersey Number 21," *Basketball Network*, September 28, 2023, https://www.basketballnetwork.net/off-the-court/kevin-garnett-on-why-he-chose-to-wear-jersey-number-21

[88] Martin Maranga, "Why Does Kevin Durant Wear No. 35 Jersey? All You Need to Know," *Sportskeeda*, September 19, 2023, https://www.sportskeeda.com/basketball/why-kevin-durant-wear-no-35-jersey-all-need-know

[89] Bill Meltzer, "88 Facts to Know About Eric Lindros," *NHL.com* (Philadelphia Flyers), January 17, 2018, https://www.nhl.com/flyers/news/88-facts-to-know-about-eric-lindros-philadelphia-flyers-295020934

[90] Greg Wyshynski, "Pat Tillman Tribute Featured on Jason LaBarbera's Stunning Mask," *Yahoo Sports*, October 4, 2011, https://sports.yahoo.com/blogs/nhl-puck-daddy/pat-tillman-tribute-featured-jason-labarbera-stunning-mask-113016612.html

[91] Hiram Martinez, "Clemente and the Magic of 21," *ESPN*, December 31, 2012, https://www.espn.com/mlb/story/_/id/8795834/roberto-clemente-magic-no-21-mlb

[92] Alan Saunders, "Lorenzen, Reds Celebrate Clemente's Legacy," *MLB.com*, September 15, 2021, https://www.mlb.com/news/michael-lorenzen-reds-honor-roberto-clemente

[93] Chris Creamer, "All MLB Teams Wearing #21 Patches Today," *SportsLogos.Net*, September 15, 2025, https://news.sportslogos.net/2025/09/15/all-mlb-teams-wearing-21-patches-today/baseball/

[94] Anthony DiComo, "Lindor Homers Idol with Record HR on Clemente Day," *MLB.com*, September 16, 2022, https://www.mlb.com/marlins/news/francisco-lindor-homers-on-roberto-clemente-day

[95] Kareem Abdul-Jabbar, *Becoming Kareem: Growing Up On and Off the Court* (Little, Brown Books for Young Readers, 2017)

[96] George Vecsey, *Ewing* (New York: Simon & Schuster, 1995)

[97] Bill Walton, *Back from the Dead: Searching for the Sound, Shining the Light and Throwing It Down* (New York: Simon & Schuster, 2016)

[98] Chris Landers, "These Legends Once Wore Other Numbers," *MLB.com*, April 21, 2020, https://mlb.com/news/mlb-stars-with-different-uniform-numbers

[99] Jeph Duarte, "Spurs 50 for 50, Number 2- David Robinson," *Pounding The Rock*, September 28, 2022, https://www.poundingtherock.com/2022/9/28/23373241/nba-san-antonio-spurs-50-number-2-david-robinson-tim-duncan-nba-rookie-of-the-year-chanpionship-pop

100 Ken Reed, "Walt Weiss," Society for American Baseball Research, accessed November 25, 2025, https://sabr.org/bioproj/person/walt-weiss/

101 "Why Does Luka Dončić Wear The Number 77?" *RevUp Sports*, December 31, 2022, accessed November 25, 2025, https://revupsports.com/athletes/basketball/luka-doncic/discover/why-does-luka-doncic-wear-77/

102 R. Nikhil Parshy, "Derek Jeter's Exemplary Behavior Inspired Padres Star Xander Bogaerts Who Wears Number 2 in His Honor," Sportskeeda, February 10, 2023, accessed November 25, 2025, https://sportskeeda.com/baseball/derek-jeter-s-exemplary-behavior-inspired-padres-star-xander-bogaerts-wears-number-2-honor

103 NBA.com Staff, "Legends profile: Chris Mullin," September 13, 2022, https://www.nba.com/news/history-nba-legend-chris-mullin

104 Bob Pockrass, "Brad Daugherty calls team's Daytona 500 win 'pinnacle of my sports career,'" Fox Sports, February 22, 2023, https://www.foxsports.com/stories/nascar/brad-daugherty-calls-daytona-500-win-pinnacle-of-my-sports-career; Deb Williams, "5-Time NBA All-Star Brad Daugherty Schooled Michael Jordan ... on NASCAR," Autoweek, February 23, 2023, https://www.autoweek.com/racing/nascar/a43052033/nba-daugherty-schooled-michael-jordan-nascar/

105 "Behind the Numbers: Stories of How MLB Players Picked Their Uniforms," ESPN.com, August 16, 2017, https://www.espn.com/mlb/story/_/id/20276096/behind-numbers-stories-how-mlb-players-picked-their-uniform

106 Julian Ojeda, "Tracy McGrady Says Meeting Magic's Penny Hardaway 'Opened the Door' for His Career," *Clutch Points*, September 12, 2025, accessed November 25, 2025, https://clutchpoints.com/nba/orlando-magic/magic-news-tracy-mcgrady-says-penny-hardaway-opened-the-door-for-career

107 Tim Kurkjian, "Tim Kurkjian's Baseball Fix: Why Players Wear the Numbers They Wear," *ESPN*, May 17, 2020, accessed November 25, 2025, https://www.espn.com/mlb/story/_/id/29143411/tim-kurkjian-baseball-fix-why-players-wear-numbers-wear

108 Wheat Hotchkiss, "Granger's Peak as Great as Any Player in Pacers History," *NBA.com*, March 9, 2017, https://www.nba.com/pacers/news/grangers-peak-great-any-player-pacers-history

109 "Be Like Mike Gatorade Commercial (ORIGINAL)," YouTube video, 1:00, posted by bigwayne84, October 24, 2006, accessed November 25, 2025, https://www.youtube.com/watch?v=b0AGiq9j_Ak

110 Jose Martinez, "The Story Behind Your Favorite NBA Player's Jersey Number," *Complex*, January 7, 2025, https://complex.com/sports/a/jose-martinez/reason-behind-your-favorite-current-nba-players-jersey-number

[111] Edvinas Kuzas, "Why LeBron Wears 23 and Changed Numbers 4 Times," *BasketNews*, June 18, 2025, https://basketnews.com/news-225696-why-does-lebron-wear-23.html

[112] SLAM Staff, "Ron Artest Changing His Name and Jersey Number," August 26, 2011, https://slamonline.com/archives/ron-artest-changing-his-name-and-jersey-number

[113] Srashti Sharma, "Michael Jordan & Co. Send a Heartfelt Gift to Maya Moore at Lynx Jersey Retirement 13 Years After Statement Deal," *Essentially Sports*, August 24, 2024, https://essentiallysports.com/wnba-basketball-news-michael-jordan-co-send-a-heartfelt-gift-to-maya-moore-at-lynx-jersey-retirement-thirteen-years-after-statement-deal

[114] Julian Eschenbach, "'It Was a No Brainer' – How Michael Jordan Influenced David Beckham's Real Madrid Jersey Number," *Basketball Network*, December 30, 2023, https://www.basketballnetwork.net/off-the-court/how-michael-jordan-influenced-david-beckhams-real-madrid-jersey-number

[115] Natasha Dye, "Jayson Tatum to Wear Kobe Bryant's No. 10 Team USA Jersey at Olympics: 'Nothing Short of An Honor'," *People*, July 9, 2024, https://people.com/jayson-tatum-wear-kobe-bryant-number-at-olympics-8675304

[116] Mike Chiari, "Paul George Reveals 76ers' No. 8 Jersey in Photos, Video; Honors 'Idol' Kobe Bryant," *Bleacher Report*, July 7, 2024, https://bleacherreport.com/articles/10127462-paul-george-reveals-76ers-no-8-jersey-in-photos-video-honors-idol-kobe-bryant

[117] "NBA, NBPA and Nike to Honor Kobe and Gianna Bryant on NBA All-Star Uniforms," *NBA.com*, January 31, 2020, https://www.nba.com/news/2020-all-star-uniforms-honor-kobe-and-gianna-bryant

[118] Brian Jones, "Dodgers Players Wear Kobe Bryant Jerseys to Celebrate 42nd Birthday," *Pop Culture* August 25, 2020, https://popculture.com/sports/news/dodgers-players-wear-kobe-bryant-jerseys-celebrate-42nd-birthday/

[119] Nick Villano, "Why Did Wayne Gretzky Choose 99?" *FanSided*, January 2, 2024, https://fansided.com/posts/wayne-gretzky-choose-99

[120] Dave Mount, "Behind the Sweater Number: No. 66," *Last Word On Sports*, August 5, 2023, https://lastwordonsports.com/hockey/2023/08/05/behind-the-sweater-number-66

[121] Bruno Feliks, "Dirk Nowitzki Revealed Why He Wore Jersey Number 41," *Basketball Sphere*, May 5, 2024, https://basketballsphere.com/en/dirk-nowitzki-revealed-why-he-wore-jersey-number-41

[122] Scott Gleeson, "The Reason Bryce Harper Will Wear No. 3 with Philadelphia Phillies," *USA Today*, March 2, 2019, https://usatoday.com/story/sports/mlb/phillies/2019/03/02/bryce-harper-why-superstar-wear-no-3-philadelphia-phillies/3040707002

[123] Reese Patanjo, "Given How Close Their Families Are, Magic Johnson's AIDS Reveal Urged Charles Barkley To Beg His Teammate For His No 32 Jersey," *The SportsRush*, June 3,

2025, https://thesportsrush.com/nba-news-given-how-close-their-families-are-magic-johnsons-aids-reveal-urged-charles-barkley-to-beg-his-teammate-for-his-no-32-jersey

[124] Nicole Ganglani, "'I Was Happy For Him to Try and Get That Goal' - Magic Johnson Revealed Why He Offered His Retired Jersey Number to Karl Malone When He Joined the Lakers," *Basketball Network*, January 11, 2025, https://basketballnetwork.net/old-school/magic-johnson-revealed-why-he-offered-his-retired-jersey-number-to-karl-malone-when-he-joined-the-lakers

[125] Fitted Hawaii, "Homegrown: El Sid," accessed November 25, 2025, https://fittedhawaii.com/blogs/updates/homegrown-el-sid

[126] Anthony DiComo, "Mets' Hurlin' Hawaiian Takes Pride in Roots," *MLB.com*, February 21, 2021, https://www.mlb.com/news/jordan-yamamoto-on-hawaiian-pride-jersey-number

[127] Benjamin Klein, "Grading Team USA's Shane Victorino at the 2013 World Baseball Classic," *Bleacher Report*, June 1, 2018, https://bleacherreport.com/articles/1563085-grading-team-usas-shane-victorino-at-the-2013-world-baseball-classic

[128] Saul Wisnia, "Bill Voiselle," SABR Baseball Biography Project, Society for American Baseball Research, accessed November 25, 2025, https://sabr.org/bioproj/person/bill-voiselle/

[129] Jason Ounpraseuth, "Red Sox's Kenley Jansen Has Touching Reason He Wears No. 74," *NESN*, April 12, 2023, https://nesn.com/2023/04/red-soxs-kenley-jansen-has-touching-reason-he-wears-no-74/

[130] "NBA – Evan Fournier's Unique Distinction in History," *Parlons Basket*, April 1, 2021, https://www.parlons-basket.com/2021/04/01/nba-la-particularite-unique-devan-fournier-dans-lhistoire/

[131] Chris Wright, "Why Has Mesut Ozil Selected Fenerbahce Squad No. 67," ESPN, January 28, 2021, https://www.espn.com/soccer/story/_/id/37613362/why-ozil-selected-fenerbahce-squad-no-67

[132] RevUp Sports, "Why Does Damian Lillard Wear The Number 0?" December 9, 2022, https://revupsports.com/athletes/basketball/damian-lillard/discover/why-does-damian-lillard-wear-the-number-0

[133] Dan Mount, "Behind the Sweater Number: No. 17," *Last Word on Sports*, September 23, 2023, https://lastwordonsports.com/hockey/2023/09/23/behind-the-sweater-number-17/

[134] Tom Garry, "Katie Startup: Charlton Goalkeeper Wears Number 40 Shirt to Raise Suicide Awareness," *BBC Sport*, October 10, 2019, https://bbc.com/sport/football/50005164

[135] Ben Golliver, "Nets' Jason Collins Presents Matthew Shepard's Family with No. 98 Jersey," *Sports Illustrated*, February 28, 2014, https://www.si.com/nba/2014/02/28/jason-collins-matthew-shepard-brooklyn-nets-jersey; Halimah Abdullah, "Jason Collins: How No.

98 Became a Symbol," *CNN*, February 28, 2014,
https://www.cnn.com/2014/02/28/us/jason-collins-interview

[136] Manny Randhawa, "'No Bigger Honor': Rox Retire Walker's No. 33," *MLB.com*,
September 25, 2021, accessed November 25, 2025, https://www.mlb.com/news/larry-
walker-s-number-retired-by-rockies

[137] Jeff Owens, "'Chicken Man' Wade Boggs and Baseball's Greatest Superstitions," *Sports
Collectors Digest*, March 27, 2024, https://sportscollectorsdigest.com/news/chicken-man-
wade-boggs-and-baseballs-greatest-superstitions-
*Boggs never publicly stated why he wore #26, but the number remained consistent throughout his time with
the Red Sox and has since been retired by the team in his honor.*

[138] DeAntae Price, "Jason Terry's Superstitions Stretch to Wearing Opponent's Shorts the
Night Before Games," *Sporting News*, October 27, 2021, accessed November 25, 2025,
https://www.sportingnews.com/us/nba/news/jason-terry-nets-mavs-hawks-arizona-
superstitions-opponents-shorts-shoe-change-headband-high-
socks/85p4hqdmk0r116rkuf98cwts1

[139] Josh Benjamin, "MLB Power Rankings: Roger Clemens and MLB's 10 Most
Superstitious Players Ever," *Bleacher Report*, June 15, 2011,
https://bleacherreport.com/articles/735759-mlb-power-rankings-roger-clemens-and-mlbs-
10-most-superstitious-players-ever

[140] Justin Hokanson, "Jason Giambi Wears Magic Gold Thong for Sake of New York
Yankees," *Bleacher Report*, May 19, 2008, https://bleacherreport.com/articles/24203-jason-
giambi-wears-magic-gold-thong-for-sake-of-new-york-yankees

[141] "After Lou Lamoriello's Exit, It Appears Many of His Quirks Will Leave with Him," *All
About The Jersey*, August 5, 2015, accessed November 25, 2025,
https://www.allaboutthejersey.com/2015/8/5/9094865/as-lou-lamoriello-departs-so-do-
many-of-his-quirks

[142] Scott Pitoniak, "Unlucky Number 13 Gets a Bad Rap in Sports and Life," *Rochester
Business Journal*, May 13, 2016, https://rbj.net/2016/05/13/unlucky-number-13-gets-a-bad-
rap-in-sports-and-
life/#:~:text=Wilt%20Chamberlain%20was%20a%20towering,the%20rest%20of%20his%2
0career

[143] Krishna Prasad, "Why Is Number 13 So Special to Alex Morgan?" *Essentially Sports*,
September 8, 2024, https://essentiallysports.com/soccer-football-news-why-is-number-so-
special-for-alex-morgan-understanding-the-importance/

[144] "Lucky Numbers and Unlucky Numbers in China," *China Highlights*, accessed November
25, 2025, https://chinahighlights.com/travelguide/culture/lucky-number-8.htm

145 Ryan, "You Won't Believe How Numbers Hold the Secret Power Behind Sports Superstitions," *Deep Symbol*, July 24, 2025, accessed November 25, 2025, https://deepsymbol.com/the-role-of-numbers-in-sports-superstitions

146 Ryan, "Unlock the Secrets of the Lucky Number 8 in Chinese Superstitions That Could Change Your Life," *Deep Symbol*, July 10, 2025, accessed November 25, 2025, https://deepsymbol.com/the-lucky-number-8-in-chinese-superstitions

147 Kevin Moore, "Why Does Mookie Betts Wear No. 50?" *Sportscasting*, accessed November 25, 2025, https://sportscasting.com/news/why-does-dodgers-star-mookie-betts-wear-no-50/

148 Jeet Pukhrambam, "Dwyane Wade Has Unyielding Faith in God and It Helped Him Give Away $20 Million," *The SportsRush*, November 12, 2022, accessed November 25, 2025, https://thesportsrush.com/nba-news-dwyane-wade-has-unyielding-faith-in-god-and-it-helped-him-give-away-20-million/

149 Russell Wilson (@DangeRussWilson), Twitter post, May 27, 2012, 12:01 p.m., "@Tobybear my old number was 16… So now John 3:16 is fitting. Also 3= the Trinity. Father, the Son, and the Holy Spirit. 3 is Godly #," accessed November 25, 2025, https://twitter.com/DangeRussWilson

150 Mike Thomas, "Why Does Russell Wilson Wear No. 3?" *Sportscasting*, May 15, 2023, accessed November 25, 2025, https://sportscasting.com/news/why-russell-wilson-wears-no-3/

151 Paul Batura, "Kevin Durant: 'God's Love for Me, the Sacrificial Death of Jesus for My Sins … Saves Me'," *Focus on the Family Daily Citizen*, February 27, 2024, accessed November 25, 2025, https://dailycitizen.focusonthefamily.com/kevin-durant-gods-love-for-me-the-sacrificial-death-of-jesus-for-my-sins-saves-me/; Advait Jajodia, "'No. 7 Stands for Completion in the Bible': Kevin Durant Explains Switching Jersey Numbers from #35 to #7 for the Brooklyn Nets," *The SportsRush*, October 21, 2022, accessed November 25, 2025, https://thesportsrush.com/no-7-stands-for-completion-in-the-bible-kevin-durant-explains-switching-jersey-numbers-from-35-to-7-for-the-brooklyn-nets/

152 "Biblical Verse Nudged Curtis Martin Toward 28," *NBC Sports*, June 18, 2014, accessed November 25, 2025, https://nbcsports.com/nfl/profootballtalk/rumor-mill/news/bible-nudged-curtis-martin-toward-28

153 Jesse T. Jackson, "This NBA Player Wears #23 Because of a Bible Verse; Monty Williams' Faith Influences Coaching," *ChurchLeaders*, October 4, 2021, accessed November 25, 2025, https://churchleaders.com/news/406675-this-nba-player-wears-23-because-of-a-bible-verse-monty-williams-faith-influences-coaching.html

154 Tyler Horka, "'LLTY': How Remembering Ty Jordan Impels Notre Dame Defensive End Nana Osafo-Mensah," *On3*, October 27, 2023, accessed November 25, 2025, https://www.on3.com/teams/notre-dame-fighting-irish/news/notre-dame-football-nana-osafo-mensah-ty-jordan-utah-llty-long-live-fighting-irish/

155 "Kirk Cousins Shares His Draft Day Experience, Reaction to Being Drafted by the Commanders & More!, YouTube video, 3:47, posted by *Pure Athlete*, May 30, 2024, accessed November 25, 2025, https://www.youtube.com/watch?v=uf8AbEqOz_M

156 Sports Spectrum, "SS Podcast: NFL Wide Receiver Robbie Chosen on Changing His Name, Growing in His Faith," *Sports Spectrum Podcast*, August 15, 2025, accessed November 25, 2025, https://sportsspectrum.com/podcast/2025/08/15/podcast-robbie-chosen-changing-name-growing-faith/

157 Scott Jenkins, "Kurt Warner's Rams Jersey Was No. 13 Because He Was 'Never Dictated by Superstitions'," *Sportscasting*, July 11, 2023, accessed November 25, 2025, https://www.sportscasting.com/news/kurt-warner-rams-jersey-number-13-never-dictated-superstitions/

158 CBS News/AP, "MLB Player Sandy León Changed His Uniform Number to Remember the Worst Day of His Life: It's So Special For Me'," May 5, 2023, accessed November 25, 2025, https://www.cbsnews.com/news/sandy-leon-mlb-uniform-number-12-special-meaning-daughter

159 Atlwbryant, "Atlanta Hawks to Retire 'Pistol' Pete Maravich's Iconic No. 44," *NBA.com*, January 13, 2017, accessed November 25, 2025, https://www.nba.com/hawks/news/atlanta-hawks-retire-pistol-pete-maravichs-iconic-no-44

160 Larry Schwartz, "Ghost of Illinois," *ESPN SportsCentury*, October 2005, https://espn.com/sportscentury/features/00014216.html

161 Sarah Langs, Andrew Simon, and Thomas Harrigan, "8 Amazing Facts About Ripken's Streak: The Numbers Behind the Iron Man's Famous Record," *MLB.com*, September 6, 2020, accessed November 25, 2025, https://www.mlb.com/news/amazing-facts-about-cal-ripken-jr-s-games-played-streak

162 Jelani Scott, "Aaron Rodgers Explains Why He Won't Wear No. 12 with Jets," *Sports Illustrated*, April 26, 2023, accessed November 25, 2025, https://si.com/nfl/2023/04/26/aaron-rodgers-classy-answer-why-he-wont-wear-ro-12-with-jets-joe-namath

163 Utathya Nag, "Cristiano Ronaldo – Football's Eternal No. 7," *Olympics.com*, October 5, 2024, accessed November 25, 2025, https://olympics.com/en/news/cristiano-ronaldo-number-jersey-squad-football

164 Efe Özenc, "All You Want to Know About Pau Gasol," *ABC Spor*, September 18, 2015, accessed November 25, 2025, https://abespor.com/all-you-want-to-know-about-pau-gasol/

165 Mike O'Hara, "No. 20 a Symbol of Excellence in Lions' History," *Detroit Lions*, November 4, 2020, accessed November 25, 2025, https://detroitlions.com/news/o-hara-no-20-a-symbol-of-excellence-in-lions-history-sanders-sims-barney

166 RJ Ochoa, "Cowboys CTK: The Legend of 22, From Bob Hayes to Emmitt Smith," *Inside the Star*, November 13, 2023, accessed November 25, 2025, https://archives.insidethestar.com/cowboys-ctk-the-legend-of-22-from-bob-hayes-to-emmitt-smith

167 Frank Urbina, "The Best NBA Player to Wear Each Jersey Number," *USA Today/HoopsHype*, October 10, 2025, accessed November 25, 2025, https://www.usatoday.com/story/sports/nba/2025/10/10/the-best-nba-player-to-wear-each-jersey-number/85293201007/

168 Luke Norris, "James Worthy Wore No. 52 at North Carolina," *Sportscasting*, accessed November 25, 2025, https://www.sportscasting.com/news/how-james-worthys-dad-convinced-him-to-wear-no-42-for-the-lakers/

169 Michael Scotto, "Stackhouse's Path to Brooklyn, Iconic No. 42," *Real GM*, May 2, 2012, accessed November 25, 2025, https://basketball.realgm.com/analysis/227282/Stackhouses-Path-To-Brooklyn-Iconic-No-42

170 Luke Norris, "Why Did Jackie Robinson Wear No. 42?" *Sportscasting*, July 26, 2024, accessed November 25, 2025, https://sportscasting.com/news/why-did-jackie-robinson-wear-no-42/

171 Rick Cleveland, "Favre and No. 4: Accidental History," *Mississippi Today*, August 5, 2016, accessed November 25, 2025, https://mississippitoday.org/2016/08/05/favre-and-no-4-accidental-history/

172 Matt Young, "Here's How Nolan Ryan, Earl Campbell, Hakeem Olajuwon Became No. 34," *Houston Chronicle*, updated February 10, 2021, accessed November 25, 2025, https://www.chron.com/sports/article/Nolan-Ryan-Earl-Campbell-Hakeem-Olajuwon-became-34-12563783.php

173 Oscar Robertson, *The Big O: My Life, My Times, My Game* (Emmaus, PA: Rodale Books, 2003)

174 Ben Clayfield, "Pelé Jersey Number: Why He Wore the Number 10," *Your Soccer Home*, July 2022, accessed November 25, 2025, https://yoursoccerhome.com/pele-jersey-number-why-he-wore-the-number-10/

175 "Why Does Mike Trout Wear #27?" *Trout.LA*, May 27, 2014, accessed November 25, 2025, https://www.trout.la/why-does-mike-trout-wear-27/

176 Mark Feinsand, "Mariano 'Blessed' to be Last with Jackie's 42," *MLB.com*, April 14, 2021, accessed November 25, 2025, https://mlb.com/news/mariano-rivera-linked-to-jackie-robinson-for-no-42

177 Michael Hurley, "Patriots Rookie Jersey Numbers Still Not a Priority in Foxboro," *CBS News Boston*, July 31, 2023, accessed November 25, 2025, https://www.cbsnews.com/boston/news/patriots-rookie-jersey-numbers/

178 Creg Stephenson, "Titans QB Charlie Whitehurst Admits He Lied About Losing Jersey Number in Arm-Wrestling Match," *The Tennessean*, June 4, 2014, quoted in *AL.com*, accessed November 25, 2025, https://al.com/sports/2014/06/titans_qb_charlie_whitehurst_a_1.html

179 Stefan Bondy, "Jalen Brunson's No. 11 Wasn't His First Choice — But He Wouldn't Trade It for Anything Now," *New York Daily News* via *MSN*, accessed November 25, 2025, https://www.msn.com/en-us/sports/nba/jalen-brunson-s-no-11-wasn-t-his-first-choice-but-he-wouldn-t-trade-it-for-anything-now/ar-AA1Emj5l.

180 Patrik Walker, "DeMarvion Overshown Assigned No. 0, Makes History as First Cowboys' Player to Wear It," *DallasCowboys.com*, April 9, 2025, accessed November 25, 2025, https://dallascowboys.com/news/demarvion-overshown-assigned-no-0-makes-history-as-first-cowboys-player-to-wear-it

181 Scott Rafferty, "Anthony Edwards Jersey Number: Why Timberwolves Star Changed from No. 1 to No. 5," *Sporting News*, October 23, 2023, accessed November 25, 2025, https://sportingnews.com/us/nba/news/anthony-edwards-changed-jersey-number-5-timberwolves/d0e3a41f1e6a87c5a04262d3

182 Samuel Waihenya, "Why Did Ronaldo Wear Number 9," *Soccer Whizz*, May 9, 2024, accessed November 25, 2025, https://soccerwhizz.com/why-ronaldo-wore-number-9-jersey/

183 Laura Arriero, "Kylian Mbappé's Numbers," *Fútbol Emotion*, July 5, 2024, accessed November 25, 2025, https://futbolemotion.com/en/blogs/straight-from-the-oven/kylian-mbappes-numbers

184 Matt Maiocco, "Pearsall Changes 49ers Jersey Number Ahead of 2025 NFL Season," *NBC Sports Bay Area*, May 13, 2025, accessed November 25, 2025, https://nbcsportsbayarea.com/nfl/san-francisco-49ers/ricky-pearsall-jersey-number-change/1849902/

185 "Washington Bullets – Champion Jersey," *Champion Blogger*, September 14, 2015, accessed November 25, 2025, http://championblogger.com/blog/?p=1493

186 Eric Chesterton, "Want My Uni Number? Send My Kid to College: The Best Trades in Baseball," *MLB.com*, March 27, 2020, accessed November 25, 2025, https://mlb.com/news/history-of-uniform-number-compensations

187 "Flannery Still a Favorite Among Fans," *San Diego Union Tribune*, July 4, 2014, accessed November 25, 2025, https://www.sandiegouniontribune.com/2014/07/04/flannery-still-a-favorite-among-fans/

188 Ian Hunter, "Flashback Friday: Turner Ward Sells His Number 24 to Rickey Henderson," August 14, 2015, accessed November 25, 2025, https://bluejayhunter.com/2015/08/flashback-friday-turner-ward-sells-his-number-to-rickey-henderson.html

Multiple conflicting versions of the Henderson/Hassey transaction exist, including accounts involving stereo equipment, an autograph session, or no payment at all. The golf clubs and suit story remains the most widely reported version.

[189] "Kluwe to McNabb No. 5," YouTube video, 1:22, posted by *Parody*, July 30, 2011, accessed November 25, 2025, https://www.youtube.com/watch?v=57gSm6zRilY

[190] Jenifer Langosch, "Lackey Gives Neshek Ruth-Signed Ball for No. 41," *MLB.com*, August 20, 2014, accessed November 25, 2025, https://www.mlb.com/news/lackey-gives-neshek-ruth-signed-ball-for-no-41/c-90596938

[191] Steve DelVecchio, "A.J. Burnett Giving Daniel McCutchen's Daughter a College Fund in Exchange for Jersey Number," *Larry Brown Sports*, February 27, 2012, accessed November 25, 2025, https://larrybrownsports.com/baseball/aj-burnett-daniel-mccutchen-jersey-exchange/119651

[192] Nick Dimengo, "Athletes Who Have Paid for Jersey Numbers," *Bleacher Report*, April 10, 2014, accessed November 25, 2025, https://bleacherreport.com/articles/2023251-athletes-who-have-paid-for-jersey-numbers

[193] Steve Gilbert, "MadBum 'Sets a Presence' in D-backs Camp: Lefty Negotiating with Chafin for Jersey No. 40 Compensation," *MLB.com*, February 12, 2020, accessed November 25, 2025, https://mlb.com/dbacks/news/madison-bumgarner-keeps-no-40-with-d-backs

[194] Craig Calcaterra, "Alexi Casilla Got a Rolex," *NBC Sports*, March 2, 2010, accessed November 25, 2025, https://nbcsports.com/mlb/news/alexi-casilla-got-a-rolex

[195] TMZ Staff, "Mets' Jeff McNeil I Got a Rolex From Starling Marte!!!...In Exchange for Jersey Number," April 19, 2022, accessed November 25, 2025, https://www.tmz.com/2022/04/19/mets-jeff-mcneil-starling-marte-gifted-him-rolex-for-jersey-number/

[196] Martín Gallegos, "Sevy Gifts Spence a Rolex for Jersey No. 40," *MLB.com*, February 21, 2025, accessed November 25, 2025, https://www.mlb.com/news/luis-severino-gifts-mitch-spence-rolex-for-jersey-number

[197] Pat Pickens, "Bobrovsky Acquires No. 72 from Vatrano for Watch, Season's Worth of Meals," *NHL.com*, July 1, 2019, accessed November 25, 2025, https://www.nhl.com/news/florida-panthers-frank-vatrano-trades-jersey-number-72-to-new-teammate-308152356

[198] "Brett Kulak Got a Rolex for Giving Number 17 to Ilya Kovalchuk," *Sportsnet*, January 5, 2020, accessed November 25, 2025, https://www.sportsnet.ca/hockey/nhl/brett-kulak-got-rolex-giving-number-17-ilya-kovalchuk/

[199] Joseph McBride, "NHL Star Traded Away After Gifting Teammate Rolex for His Jersey Number," *Daily Express US*, Mar 10, 2025, accessed November 25, 2025, https://the-express.com/sport/ice-hockey/165953/Mikko-Rantanen-Jack-Roslovic-Hurricanes-Stars-Avalanche

200 Kristie Rieken, "LA Clippers Trade Chris Paul to Houston Rockets: The All-Star Guard is Headed to Houston After Opting-In to His Contract," *NBA.com*, June 28, 2017, accessed November 25, 2025, https://www.nba.com/news/chris-paul-trade-houston-rockets-la-clippers-opt
While the trade and number swap can be confirmed, there is an unverified anecdote about luxury watches and a charitable donation in exchange for jersey No. 3 circulating in Reddit fan forums (e.g., r/nba).

201 "Emmanual Sanders Stats", *Pro Football Reference*, accessed November 25, 2025, https://www.pro-football-reference.com/players/S/SandEm00.htm

202 *Mitch Richmond is rumored to have offered Derek Fisher a Rolex to obtain a preferred jersey number. (Unverified anecdote, cited in note only).*

203 Jeff Pearlman, "'Neon Deion' Helped, and Hindered, the 'Boys," *ESPN Page 2*, September 19, 2008, accessed November 25, 2025, https://www.espn.com/espn/page2/story?page=pearlman/080919&sportCat=nfl

204 "Sanders Possibility Intrigues McAlister," *Baltimore Sun*, August 18, 2004, accessed November 25, 2025, https://www.baltimoresun.com/2004/08/18/sanders-possibility-intrigues-mcalister/

205 "Sanders Chooses to Flaunt His Age," *ESPN.com*, September 7, 2004, accessed November 25, 2025, https://www.espn.com/nfl/news/story?id=1876190

206 Zachary Roberts, "Shohei Ohtani Once Light-Heartedly Expressed His Desire to Sport Mike Trout's #27 Jersey Ahead of His MLB Debut," *Sportskeeda*, September 9, 2023, accessed November 25, 2025, https://www.sportskeeda.com/baseball/news-shohei-ohtani-light-heartedly-expressed-desire-sport-mike-trout-s-27-jersey-ahead-mlb-debut

207 Scott Chiusano, "Ohtani Gives Teammate Amazing Gift in Exchange for No. 17," *MLB.com*, December 24, 2023, accessed November 25, 2025, https://mlb.com/news/shohei-ohtani-gifts-joe-kelly-porsche-for-no-17

208 Paul Gutierrez, "Gutierrez: The Story Behind the Daniel Carlson–Ashton Jeanty No. 2 Jersey Negotiations," *Raiders.com*, May 29, 2025, accessed November 25, 2025, https://raiders.com/news/the-story-behind-the-daniel-carlson-ashton-jeanty-no-2-jersey-nfl-2025

209 Kalan Hooks, "Mets' Juan Soto Swaps SUV with Brett Baty for Jersey Number," *ESPN*, February 20, 2025, accessed November 25, 2025, https://espn.com/mlb/story/_/id/43938112/new-york-mets-juan-soto-brett-baty-22-suv-gift

210 Peter Dewey, "Mario Chalmers Reveals Players Sometimes Pay Up to $10K for a Teammate's Jersey Number," *Ahn Fire Digital*, March 10, 2025, accessed November 25, 2025, https://ahnfiredigital.com/nba/mario-chalmers-reveals-players-sometimes-pay-up-to-10k-for-a-teammates-jersey-number/

211 Associated Press, "Winslow Buys No. 80 Off Teammate," *ESPN*, September 8, 2004, archived May 24, 2024, Wayback Machine, accessed November 25, 2025, https://web.archive.org/web/20240524042714/https://www.espn.com/nfl/news/story?id=1877576

212 Ryan Wilson, "Report: Eric Decker Pays Jeff Cumberland $25K for No. 87 Jersey," *CBS Sports*, April 1, 2014, accessed November 25, 2025, https://cbssports.com/nfl/news/report-eric-decker-pays-jeff-cumberland-25k-for-no-87-jersey/

213 ESPN.com News Services, "Darrelle Revis Paid $50K for No. 24," June 19, 2013, accessed November 25, 2025, https://espn.com/nfl/story/_/id/9403863/darrelle-revis-paid-50k-get-24-tampa-bay-buccaneers-source

214 John Breech, "Three-Time Pro Bowler Had to Pay Thousands to Buy Number From New Lions Teammate After Being Traded to Detroit," *CBS Sports*, November 10, 2024, accessed November 25, 2025, https://www.cbssports.com/nfl/news/three-time-pro-bowler-had-to-pay-thousands-to-buy-number-from-new-lions-teammate-after-bring-traded-to-detroit/

215 DJ Bien-Aime, "Texans' New WR Stefon Diggs Pays Jimmie Ward for No. 1 Jersey," *ESPN*, April 5, 2024, accessed November 25, 2025, https://espn.com/nfl/story/_/id/39882168/houston-texans-stefon-diggs-pays-jimmie-ward-wide-receiver-jersey-number

216 Mike Kaye, "Former All-Pro Gerald McCoy Paid a Ridiculous Amount of Cash to Get No. 93 Jersey with Carolina Panthers," *Pro Football Network*, June 15, 2022, accessed November 25, 2025, https://profootballnetwork.com/former-all-pro-gerald-mccoy-paid-a-ridiculous-amount-of-cash-to-get-no-93-jersey-with-carolina-panthers/

217 Anthony McCarron, "Mets to Retire Mike Piazza's No. 31 Jersey This Season," *New York Daily News*, January 25, 2016, accessed November 25, 2025, https://www.nydailynews.com/2016/01/25/mets-to-retire-mike-piazzas-no-31-jersey-this-season/

218 Dan Cichalski, "May 23, 1998: Mike Piazza Makes His Mets Debut," *Society for American Baseball Research*, accessed November 25, 2025, https://sabr.org/gamesproj/game/may-23-1998-mike-piazza-makes-his-mets-debut/

219 Clint Buckley, "Chris Godwin Reveals Why He Gave Up No. 12 to Tom Brady," *247Sports*, June 25, 2020, accessed November 25, 2025, https://247sports.com/Article/Chris-Godwin-reveals-why-he-gave-up-No-12-jersey-to-Tom-Brady-Tampa-Bay-Buccaneers-Penn-State-Michigan-Football-148537975/

220 Aakash Nair, "Mario Chalmers Clears the Air on LeBron James 'Stealing' #6 Jersey From Him in Miami," *The SportsRush*, September 12, 2024, accessed November 25, 2025, https://thesportsrush.com/nba-news-mario-chalmers-clears-the-air-on-lebron-james-stealing-jersey-no-6-from-him-in-miami/

[221] "Vick to Donate $10K to Charity for No. 1 with Jets," *NBC Sports Philadelphia*, May 5, 2014, accessed November 25, 2025, https://nbcsportsphiladelphia.com/nfl/vick-to-donate-10k-to-charity-for-no-1-with-jets/359996/

[222] Associated Press, "Bryant Gives Owens No. 81," *Worcester Telegram*, July 30, 2010, accessed November 25, 2025, https://telegram.com/story/news/local/north/2010/07/30/bryant-gives-owens-no-81/51522739007/

[223] Zak Gilbert, "Here's What Davante Adams Gave Up to Get No. 17 From Puka Nacua," *Sports Illustrated*, March 14, 2025, accessed November 25, 2025, https://si.com/nfl/rams/onsi/news/here-s-what-davante-adams-gave-up-to-get-no-17-from-puka-nacua

[224] "Russell Wilson to Wear No. 3; Deonte Banks Changes to No. 2," *Giants.com*, April 3, 2025, accessed November 25, 2025, https://giants.com/news/russell-wilson-to-wear-no-3-deonte-banks-changes-to-no-2-jersey-uniform-number-swap-2025

[225] Ari Mayer, "Steelers Player Gave Aaron Rodgers New Jersey Number," *Sports Illustrated*, June 13, 2025, accessed November 25, 2025, https://www.si.com/nfl/steelers/onsi/news/pittsburgh-steelers-corliss-waitman-gave-aaron-rodgers-new-jersey-number

[226] Dan Wetzel, "Aaron Hernandez's Lawyer: Ex-Patriot Sold His Jersey Number to Finance Drug Deal," *Yahoo Sports*, August 22, 2018, accessed November 25, 2025, https://sports.yahoo.com/aaron-hernandezs-lawyer-ex-patriot-sold-jersey-number-chad-ochocinco-used-money-finance-drug-dealer-203130437.html

[227] "Aaron Hernandez Found Dead After Hanging in Prison Cell," *ESPN*, April 19, 2017, accessed November 25, 2025, https://www.espn.com/nfl/story/_/id/19191248/former-new-england-patriots-te-aaron-hernandez-found-dead-hanging-prison-cell

[228] fugaziozbourne, "Joe Montana Called Len Dawson and Told Him That the 16 Jersey Belonged to Him and That He'd Wear 19," *Reddit*, r/KansasCityChiefs, 2022, accessed November 25, 2025, https://www.reddit.com/r/KansasCityChiefs/comments/wz3f90/joe_montana_called_len_dawson_and_told_him_that/
Includes scanned UPI memo, dated April 23, 1993, supporting the anecdote; source remains unverifiable by traditional standards. (Unverified anecdote, cited in note only).

[229] Nico Martinez, "LeBron James Offered No. 23 Jersey to Anthony Davis – the Former Lakers Star Declined," *Fadeaway World*, March 8, 2025, accessed November 25, 2025, https://fadeawayworld.net/nba/los-angeles-lakers/lebron-james-offered-no-23-jersey-to-anthony-davis-the-former-lakers-star-declined

[230] "Why AD Wears Number 3 For the Lakers," YouTube video, 0:34, posted by *ClutchPoints*, July 7, 2022, accessed November 25, 2025, https://www.youtube.com/shorts/4Htk51dceRY

[231] Adel Ahmad, "'If 'Nique Decides to Stay, I'm Not Gonna Take 21' – Dominique Wilkins Says Tim Duncan Would've Never Worn His Jersey Number Out of Respect," *Basketball Network*, May 4, 2025, accessed November 25, 2025, https://basketballnetwork.net/off-the-court/dominique-wilkins-says-tim-duncan-wouldve-never-worn-his-jersey-number-out-of-respect

[232] Tom Rock, "Eli Manning, Jeff Feagles and the Story of the Giants' No. 10 Jersey," *Newsday*, September 24, 2021, accessed November 25, 2025, https://www.newsday.com/sports/football/giants/eli-manning-10-jersey-retirement-jeff-feagles-r88487

[233] "Former Giants Punter Says Plaxico Owes Him a Kitchen for Number: Report," *New York Post*, August 25, 2010, accessed November 25, 2025, https://nypost.com/2010/08/25/former-giants-punter-says-plaxico-owes-him-a-kitchen-for-number-report/

[234] Darren Urban, "Number Nothing to Jay Feely," *Arizona Cardinals*, April 4, 2013, accessed November 25, 2025, https://www.azcardinals.com/news/number-nothing-to-jay-feely-9834884

[235] Ben Weinrib, "Rams Cornerback Troy Hill Could Make a Small Fortune Because of His Coveted Uniform Number," *Yahoo Sports*, October 20, 2019, accessed November 25, 2025, https://sports.yahoo.com/troy-hill-made-a-small-fortune-coveted-uniform-number-163129133.html

[236] Joseph White (Associated Press), "Portis Pays $18,000 to Settle Jersey Dispute with Former Redskins Teammate," *The Seattle Medium*, June 9, 2005, accessed November 25, 2025, https://seattlemedium.com/portis-pays-18000-to-settle-jersey-dispute-with-former-redskins-teammate/

[237] Timothy Rapp, "Jalen Ramsey Switches Jersey to No. 5 from No. 20; Rams Tweet Photo of Uniform," *Bleacher Report*, June 13, 2021, accessed November 25, 2025, https://bleacherreport.com/articles/10005608-jalen-ramsey-switches-jersey-to-no-5-from-no-20-rams-tweet-photo-of-uniform

[238] Todd Archer, "Dallas Cowboys LB Jaylon Smith Changing to No. 9, Will Pay Six-Figure Sum for Switch, Sources Say," *ESPN*, May 25, 2021, accessed November 25, 2025, https://espn.com/nfl/story/_/id/31509551/dallas-cowboys-lb-jaylon-smith-changing-no-9-pay-six-figure-sum-switch-sources-say

[239] Andrew Lind, "A Look at Which NFL Players Have Changed Their Uniform Numbers This Offseason," *SportsLogos.net*, May 25, 2021, accessed November 25, 2025, https://news.sportslogos.net/2021/05/25/a-look-at-which-nfl-players-have-changed-their-uniform-numbers-this-offseason/football/

[240] "Given the Cost of Buying Unsold Jerseys, Dalvin Cook Will Stick with No. 33," *NBC Sports – Pro Football Talk*, April 23, 2021, accessed November 25, 2025,

https://nbcsports.com/nfl/profootballtalk/rumor-mill/news/given-the-cost-of-buying-unsold-jerseys-dalvin-cook-will-stick-with-no-33

[241] Kevin Flaherty, "Los Angeles Rams' Cam Akers to Switch Jersey Number," *247Sports*, April 27, 2022, accessed November 25, 2025, https://247sports.com/Article/Los-Angeles-Rams-Cam-Akers-to-switch-jersey-number-186849855/

[242] Charles Curtis, "A Running List of NFL Players Who Have Changed Their Jersey Numbers in the 2022 Offseason," *USA Today*, July 26, 2022, accessed November 25, 2025, https://ftw.usatoday.com/story/sports/nfl/2022/07/26/nfl-number-changes-jersey-list-2022/81338945007/

[243] Sean Leahy (Yahoo! Sports), "MLB CBA Rule Meant Joe Ryan Giving Carlos Santana No. 41 Would Cost $225K," *AOL.com*, March 2, 2024, accessed November 25, 2025, https://aol.com/sports/mlb-cba-rule-meant-joe-163822545.html

[244] Christian Arnold, "Juan Soto May Have to Clear Expensive CBA Hurdle to Wear No. 22 as a Met," *New York Post*, December 10, 2024, accessed November 25, 2025, https://nypost.com/2024/12/10/sports/juan-soto-may-have-to-clear-expensive-cba-hurdle-to-wear-no-22-with-mets/

[245] Teddy Ricketson, "Juan Soto Jersey Number: Why Mets Star Got to Keep No. 22 From Brett Baty as Part of Historic Contract," *Sporting News*, December 12, 2024, accessed November 25, 2025, https://www.sportingnews.com/us/mlb/new-york-mets/news/juan-soto-jersey-number-mets-brett-baty/b0866b0302db774c4b7417b0

[246] Sean Keeley, "Anthony Rendon Hates His #6, Doesn't Want to Pay $40,000 to Change It," *The Comeback*, August 16, 2017, accessed November 25, 2025, https://thecomeback.com/mlb/anthony-rendon-hates-6-doesnt-want-pay-40000-change.html

[247] Advait Jajodia, "'You Need to Shut Your A** Up': No 45 Michael Jordan Getting Heckled by Nick Anderson Didn't Go Over Well with Brian Shaw and the Magic," *The SportsRush*, February 20, 2024, accessed November 25, 2025, https://thesportsrush.com/nba-news-you-need-to-shut-your-a-up-no-45-michael-jordan-getting-heckled-by-nick-anderson-didnt-go-over-well-with-brian-shaw-and-the-magic/

[248] John Jefferson Tan, "Tim Hardaway Reveals Manute Bol Asked for $500K Before Letting Go of Warriors Jersey #10: 'Give Me Your Whole Contract'," *Basketball Network*, June 26, 2022, accessed November 25, 2025, https://www.basketballnetwork.net/old-school/tim-hardaway-reveals-manute-bol-asked-for-500k-before-letting-go-of-warriors-jersey-10-give-me-your-whole-contract

[249] Baseball Almanac, "Dwight Gooden Quotes," quoted in *The Sporting News*, August 7, 1989, accessed November 25, 2025, https://baseball-almanac.com/quotes/quogood.shtml

[250] Patricia Traina, "Giants Rookie QB Jaxson Dart Unsuccessful in Obtaining Jersey No. 2 from Teammate," *Sports Illustrated*, May 26, 2025, accessed November 25, 2025,

https://si.com/nfl/giants/onsi/news/giants-rookie-qb-jaxson-dart-unsuccessful-in-obtaining-jersey-no-2-from-teammate-01jw78gzhe8b

251 Do-Hyoung Park, "No. 1? No. 4? Correa's New Number the Talk of Twins Clubhouse," *MLB.com*, March 22, 2022, accessed November 25, 2025, https://mlb.com/news/twins-react-to-carlos-correa-new-jersey-number

252 Tim Capurso, "Davante Adams Tells Wild Story of Jets Receiver's Expensive Demand for Jersey No. 17," *Sports Illustrated*, September 4, 2025, accessed November 25, 2025, https://si.com/nfl/davante-adams-story-jets-malachi-corley-demand-jersey-no-17

253 "Bills Announce That Owens Gets 81, Hardy Gets 84," *NBC Sports – ProFootballTalk*, March 12, 2009, accessed November 25, 2025, https://nbcsports.com/nfl/profootballtalk/rumor-mill/news/bills-announce-that-owens-gets-81-hardy-gets-84

254 Pete Caldera, "Todd Frazier Won't Request O'Neill's No. 21 After All," *Asbury Park Press*, July 20, 2017, accessed November 25, 2025, https://app.com/story/sports/mlb/yankees/2017/07/20/todd-frazier-request-oneills/103879342/

255 Maggie Vanoni, "From Role Models to Celebrity Crushes, Why UConn Women's Players Choose Their Jersey Numbers," *CT Insider*, April 5, 2024, accessed November 25, 2025, https://www.ctinsider.com/sports/uconn-womens-basketball/article/huskies-players-numbers-final-four-iowa-19381866.php

256 "Orlando Magic Make Major Jersey Number Change for Desmond Bane After Blockbuster Trade with Memphis Grizzlies," *Times of India*, June 16, 2025, accessed November 25, 2025, https://timesofindia.indiatimes.com/sports/nba/top-stories/orlando-magic-make-major-jersey-number-change-for-desmond-bane-after-blockbuster-trade-with-memphis-grizzlies/articleshow/121872571.cms

257 Ryan Morik, "Giants Rookie Abdul Carter Settles on Jersey Number After Lawrence Taylor, Phil Simms Fiasco," *Fox News*, May 9, 2025, accessed November 25, 2025, https://foxnews.com/sports/giants-rookie-abdul-carter-settles-jersey-number-after-lawrence-taylor-phil-simms-fiasco

258 Shane Garry Acedera, "David Stern Vetoed Dennis Rodman's Request to Wear No. 69 for the Mavericks," *Basketball Network*, July 14, 2023, accessed November 25, 2025, https://basketballnetwork.net/old-school/david-stern-vetoed-dennis-rodmans-request-to-wear-no-69-for-the-dallas-mavericks

259 Tribune News Services, "NFL Won't Bend Rules, So Bush Won't Wear 5," *Chicago Tribune*, May 24, 2006, accessed November 25, 2025, https://chicagotribune.com/2006/05/24/nfl-wont-bend-rules-so-bush-wont-wear-5/

260 "Back in the News: Should Linebackers Be Allowed to Wear Numbers in the 40s?," *Seattle Seahawks*, March 18, 2015, accessed November 25, 2025,

https://www.seahawks.com/news/back-in-the-news-should-linebackers-be-allowed-to-wear-numbers-in-the-40s-120931

261 Curtis Crabtree, "NFL Passes 'Brian Bosworth Rule,' Linebackers Can Now Wear Jerseys Numbered 40–49," *NBC Sports – ProFootballTalk*, March 25, 2015, accessed November 25, 2025, https://nbcsports.com/nfl/profootballtalk/rumor-mill/news/nfl-passes-brian-bosworth-rule-linebackers-can-now-wear-jerseys-numbered-40-49

262 Nathaniel Horton, "Jackson Returns to Oakland to End Career," *National Baseball Hall of Fame and Museum, Inside Pitch*, accessed November 25, 2025, https://baseballhall.org/discover/inside-pitch/jackson-returns-to-oakland#:~:text=Written%20by%20Nathaniel%20Horton,he%20went%20to%20New%20York.%20

263 John Jeansonne, "New (NFL) Math," *Medium*, April 30, 2021, accessed November 25, 2025, https://johnfjeansonne.medium.com/new-nfl-math-1e975bfa6528

264 Bill Coats, "Smoker Loses Battle of Wills with Martz," *St. Louis Post-Dispatch*, June 6, 2005. Available via *St. Louis Post-Dispatch Archives* (NewsBank), accessed November 25, 2025, https://stltoday.newsbank.com
Subscription required.

265 Cameron DaSilva, "Eric Dickerson Tells Hilarious Story of How He Chose No. 29 with Rams," *USA Today – The Rams Wire*, August 12, 2019, accessed November 25, 2025, https://theramswire.usatoday.com/story/sports/nfl/rams/2019/08/12/nfl-rams-eric-dickerson-jersey-number-story/80841737007/

266 Leon T. Shams et al., "Big Number, Big Body: Jersey Numbers Alter Body Size Perception," *PLOS ONE*, September 7, 2023, accessed November 25, 2025, https://journals.plos.org/plosone/article?id=10.1371/journal.pone.0287474

267 Ada McVean M.Sc., "Dressing to Look a Certain Way: Athletes and Jersey Numbers," *McGill Office for Science and Society*, September 12, 2023, accessed November 25, 2025, https://mcgill.ca/oss/article/did-you-know/dressing-look-certain-way-athletes-and-jersey-numbers

268 Will Starjacki, "Allen Iverson Explains How Changing His Jersey Number with the Detroit Pistons Affected Him: 'S**t Didn't Feel Right'," *Basketball Network*, March 22, 2022, accessed November 25, 2025, https://www.basketballnetwork.net/latest-news/allen-iverson-explains-how-changing-his-jersey-number-with-the-detroit-pistons-affected-him-s-t-didnt-feel-right

269 Larry Brown, "Derek Fisher Chose Jersey No. 37 with Thunder to Show Lakers He's Proud of His Age," *Larry Brown Sports*, March 22, 2012, accessed November 25, 2025, https://larrybrownsports.com/basketball/derek-fisher-jersey-37-thunder-lakers-age/125182

270 Eva Geitheim, "Amon-Ra St. Brown's Girlfriend Accidentally Led Him to Pick Wrong Jersey Number," *Sports Illustrated*, July 12, 2025, accessed November 25, 2025,

https://si.com/nfl/amonra-st-brown-girlfriend-accidentally-led-him-pick-wrong-jersey-number

271 Shane Garry Acedera, "Orlando Magic Equipment Manager Explained How Michael Jordan's Jersey Was Stolen: 'The Security Member Tried to Come Through the Ceiling'," *Basketball Network*, November 10, 2024, accessed November 25, 2025, https://basketballnetwork.net/off-the-court/magic-equipment-manager-explained-how-jordans-jersey-was-stolen

272 "Kareem Abdul-Jabbar Stats," *Basketball Reference*, accessed November 25, 2025, https://www.basketball-reference.com/players/a/abdulka01.html

273 Shane Garry Acedera, "Why Isiah Thomas Wore Jersey No. 42 Versus the Celtics in the 1985 Playoffs: 'The Leprechaun Took My #11 Jersey That Night in Boston'," *Basketball Network*, September 3, 2024, accessed November 25, 2025, https://www.basketballnetwork.net/latest-news/why-isiah-thomas-wore-jersey-no-42-versus-the-celtics-in-the-1985-playoffs

274 "Elgin Baylor Stats," *Basketball Reference*, accessed November 25, 2025, https://www.basketball-reference.com/players/b/bayloel01.html

275 "Nicklas Bendtner Switched from No 26 to No 52 at Arsenal Due to Advice from Fortune Teller," *Inside World Soccer*, September 5, 2025, accessed November 25, 2025, https://www.insideworldsoccer.com/2020/10/nicklas-bendtner-switched-no-26-no-52-arsenal-advice-fortune-teller.html

276 Rick Snider, "Ol' Ricky's Redskins Tales — Deion Sanders," *Sports Illustrated*, May 13, 2020, accessed November 25, 2025, https://si.com/nfl/commanders/news/ol-rickys-redskins-tales-deion-sanders

277 "How John Davidson Became the First to Wear 00 — What's in a Number?" *Sportsnet* video, 0:59, March 28, 2020, accessed November 25, 2025, https://www.sportsnet.ca/hockey/nhl/john-davidson-became-first-wear-00-whats-number/

278 "Reggie White," *Wikipedia*, last modified November 5, 2025, accessed November 25, 2025, https://en.wikipedia.org/wiki/Reggie_White; "Philadelphia Eagles Uniform Numbers," *Pro-Football-Reference.com*, accessed November 25, 2025, https://www.pro-football-reference.com/players/uniform.cgi?team=phi&number=91

279 Larry Mayer, "Top 10: Bears Who Switched Jersey Numbers," *Chicago Bears*, accessed November 25, 2025, https://www.chicagobears.com/photos/top-10-bears-who-switched-jersey-numbers#a230de40-ee0b-4d02-9c09-f5b3fa569fb0

280 "Walter Payton," *Pro Football Hall of Fame*, accessed November 25, 2025, https://www.profootballhof.com/players/walter-payton/

281 Dan Mount, "Behind the Sweater Number: No. 57," *Last Word on Sports*, August 14, 2023, accessed November 25, 2025, https://lastwordonsports.com/hockey/2023/08/14/behind-the-sweater-number-57

282 "Steve Heinze," *Hockey-Reference.com*, accessed November 25, 2025, https://www.hockey-reference.com/players/h/heinzst01.html

283 Julian Eschenbach, "'The Most Famous Machine Gun. You Have to Pick 47' - Andrei Kirilenko on the Origin of His Memorable 'AK-47' Nickname," *Basketball Network*, October 11, 2024, accessed November 25, 2025, https://basketballnetwork.net/old-school/andrei-kirilenko-on-the-origin-of-his-memorable-ak-47-nickname

284 Jared Ebanks, "Back on Cloud 9: New York Liberty Star Natasha Cloud Covers SLAM 256," *SLAM*, May 27, 2025, accessed November 25, 2025, https://www.slamonline.com/the-magazine/slam-256/natasha-cloud-256/

285 Jacob Camenker, "Why Chad Johnson Changed His Name Back, Explained: 'Ochocinco is Still in Me'," *Sporting News*, September 18, 2021, accessed November 25, 2025, https://sportingnews.com/us/nfl/news/chad-johnson-ochocinco-name-change-explained/1s60yh73fr01e154hmvot53mg0

286 Associated Press, "Jim Otto, 'Mr. Raider' and Pro Football Hall of Famer, Dies at 86," *NPR*, May 20, 2024, accessed November 25, 2025, https://www.npr.org/2024/05/20/1252613087/jim-otto-dies-mr-raider-hall-of-famer-oakland

287 Dakota Gardner, "Rockies Reliever Adam Ottavino Wears No. 0 – Which Other MLBers Donned the Digit?," *MLB.com*, August 9, 2013, accessed November 25, 2025, https://mlb.com/cut4/adam-ottavino-and-players-who-wore-number-zero/c-56044476

288 Josh Wilson, "Derek Jeter Finally Reveals the Real Reason Behind No. 2 Jersey Number," *FanSided*, November 10, 2022, accessed November 25, 2025, https://fansided.com/2022/11/10/derek-jeter-finally-reveals-real-reason-given-no-2-yankees/

289 Mike O'Halloran, "Why Pro Players Chose Their Jersey Numbers," *Sports Feel Good Stories*, December 12, 2023, accessed November 25, 2025, https://sportsfeelgoodstories.com/why-pro-players-chose-their-jersey-numbers/

290 Chris Wright, "What Inspires Soccer Players' Strange Squad Numbers? Clairvoyants, Michael Jordan, Basic Arithmetic," *ESPN*, February 5, 2021, accessed November 25, 2025, https://www.espn.com/soccer/story/_/id/37613741/what-inspires-soccer-players-strange-squad-numbers-clairvoyants-michael-jordan-basic-arithmetic

291 "Zamorano explains story behind famous 1+8 shirt at Inter," *Football-Italia*, July 30, 2022, accessed November 25, 2025, https://football-italia.net/zamorano-explains-story-behind-famous-18-shirt-at-inter/

292 Keith Pearson, "Aron Baynes Ready to Add Some Heft to Celtics," *Boston Herald*, July 20, 2017, accessed November 25, 2025, https://www.bostonherald.com/2017/07/20/aron-baynes-ready-to-add-some-heft-to-celtics/; "Why Aron Baynes Chose to Wear No. 46 While Playing for Celtics," *Sportsnet* video, 0:53, January 4, 2021, accessed November 25, 2025, https://www.sportsnet.ca/nba/video/significance-behind-baynes-choosing-46-boston-sticking/

293 "The Stories Behind Dennis Rodman Uniform Numbers," YouTube video, 1:20, posted by Dunkman827, February 17, 2022, accessed November 25, 2025, https://www.youtube.com/watch?v=XkhdXcVwxCQ

294 John Jefferson Tan, "'What Are The First Two Numbers You Dial in an Emergency?' - Dennis Rodman on Why He Wore No. 91 Jersey in Chicago," *Basketball Network*, March 21, 2025, accessed November 25, 2025, https://basketballnetwork.net/old-school/dennis-rodman-on-why-he-wore-no-91-jersey-in-chicago

295 ESPN, "Kenyon Martin Biography," *ESPN.com*, accessed November 25, 2025, https://www.espn.com/nba/player/bio/_/id/515/kenyon-martin
Perhaps the math rationale for wearing #6 has some truth to it or maybe the story was initiated on social media and fan blogs, but the facts remain: his birthday is 12/30, and if you add up all the digits it comes out to 6. (Unverified anecdote, cited in note only).

296 "All for Nought," *Puckstruck*, February 27, 2025, accessed November 25, 2025, https://puckstruck.com/2025/02/27/all-for-nought/#:~:text=%E2%80%9CThat%20was%20a%20Phil%20Esposito,the%20'75%2D76%20campaign

297 Matt Monagan, "Let Us Recall the Day That Turk Wendell Signed a $9,999,999.99 Contract," *MLB.com*, December 1, 2015, accessed November 25, 2025, https://mlb.com/cut4/happy-anniversary-to-turk-wendell-signing-a-999999999-contract/c-158523450

298 Shane Garry Acedera, "'That's How Many Minutes They Said I Would Play' – Gilbert Arenas on Why He Wore Number 0," *Basketball Network*, March 4, 2023, accessed November 25, 2025, https://basketballnetwork.net/latest-news/gilbert-arenas-explains-why-he-wore-number-zero

299 "After Much Thought, Manny Wearing 99," *RealGM Wiretap*, June 21, 2014, accessed November 25, 2025, https://baseball.realgm.com/wiretap/11018/After-Much-Thought-Manny-Wearing-99

300 Blake Harris, "Dodgers: How Mannywood Came to Be Ten Years Ago," *Dodgers Nation*, July 31, 2018, accessed November 25, 2025, https://dodgersnation.com/dodgers-how-mannywood-came-to-be-ten-years-ago-bh0796/2018/07/31/

301 "Rogério Ceni," *Wikipedia*, last modified November 2025, accessed November 25, 2025, https://en.wikipedia.org/wiki/Rog%C3%A9rio_Ceni

302 Brian McKenna, "Eddie Gaedel," *Society for American Baseball Research*, accessed November 25, 2025, https://sabr.org/bioproj/person/eddie-gaedel/

303 Jacob Mountz, "This Day in Braves History: Beloved Atlanta Braves Owner Becomes Manager," *House That Hank Built*, May 11, 2024, accessed November 25, 2025, https://housethathankbuilt.com/posts/this-day-in-braves-history-beloved-atlanta-braves-owner-becomes-manager-01hxg3rbn0hs

304 Mark Craig, "How the Vikings' Jared Allen, the Only Hall of Famer to ever wear No. 69, Ended Up with That Number," *The Minnesota Star Tribune*, March 4, 2025, accessed November 25, 2025, https://startribune.com/jared-allen-pro-football-hall-of-fame-minnesota-vikings-story-behind-no-69/601230824

305 Adam C. Better, "The History of the Air Jordan 23," *Shoe Palace Blog*, February 23, 2023, accessed November 25, 2025, https://www.shoepalace.com/blogs/all/the-history-of-the-air-jordan-23

306 Tarik Arslan, "The Jordan Brand History: From Rookie Phenom to Global Icon," *OldSkoolBBall*, accessed November 25, 2025, https://oldskoolbball.com/jordan-brand-history-evolution-global-icon/

307 Wayne D. Gretzky, "99 GRETZKY Trademark Information," *TrademarkElite.com*, accessed November 25, 2025, https://trademarkelite.com/trademark/trademark-detail/77945302/99-GRETZKY

308 Suyash Deep Sinha, "Which Number Was Worn by the Most Super Bowl-Winning Quarterback? The Most Iconic Jersey Number in NFL History," Sportskeeda, February 16, 2023, accessed November 25, 2025, https://www.sportskeeda.com/nfl/which-number-worn-super-bowl-winning-quarterback
Number 12 has been worn by more Super Bowl-winning quarterbacks than any other number. Nine consecutive Super Bowls (VI–XIV) were won by quarterbacks wearing #12 (Bradshaw, Staubach, Stabler). Brady added seven more to that legacy.

309 John Lonsdale, "Tom Brady's Health and Wellness Brand Scoring with Fans as Super Bowl Approaches," *Rolling Stone*, February 3, 2021, accessed November 25, 2025, https://www.rollingstone.com/product-recommendations/lifestyle/tom-brady-tb12-gear-1123199/

310 "Explained: Why Cristiano Ronaldo Is Called CR7," *Goal.com*, October 9, 2021, accessed November 25, 2025, https://goal.com/en-za/news/explained-why-cristiano-ronaldo-is-called-cr7/3mdex5ukjjtv1c8uqo4c3ixlx

311 Brendon Schunck, "The Evolution of Chris Paul's Signature Sneaker Line," *Sneaker Reporter*, October 16, 2019, accessed November 25, 2025, https://sneakerreporter.com/the-evolution-of-chris-pauls-signature-sneaker-line/

312 Dave Elbert, "Caitlin Clark in the Wall Street Journal," *Business Record*, June 14, 2024, accessed November 25, 2025, https://www.businessrecord.com/caitlin-clark-in-the-wall-street-journal/

313 Joel Harris (Sports Illustrated), "Behind the Design: Inside the Making of Paul George's Signature Shoe," *Fox Sports*, March 4, 2020, accessed November 25, 2025, https://foxsports.com/stories/nba/behind-the-design-inside-the-making-of-paul-georges-signature-shoe

314 Nice Kicks, "A Brief History of the Nike KD Signature Line," April 9, 2023, accessed November 25, 2025, https://nicekicks.com/nike-kd-line/

315 Jahmal Cornell Williams, "The Fall of RG3 and the Rise of Robert Griffin III," *The Sports Fan Journal*, accessed November 25, 2025, https://thesportsfanjournal.com/columns/the-fam/fall-rg3-rise-robert-griffin-iii-washington-redskins-cleveland-browns/

316 Jamison Hensley, "Lamar Jackson-Dale Earnhardt Jr. Trademark Dispute Resolved," *ESPN*, April 4, 2025, accessed November 25, 2025, https://www.espn.com/nfl/story/_/id/44533662/lamar-jackson-trademark-dispute-dale-earnhardt-jr

317 Greg Atoms, "This New Orleans Pelicans Rookie Could Have One of the Greatest Jerseys in NBA History," *710 KEEL*, June 27, 2025, accessed November 25, 2025, https://710keel.com/pelicans-zero-fears-jersey/

318 Darian Kelly, "Texas Quarterback Arch Manning Signs with Red Bull," *Business of College Sports*, February 10, 2025, accessed November 25, 2025, https://businessofcollegesports.com/name-image-likeness/texas-quarterback-arch-manning-signs-with-red-bull/

319 Pete Nakos, "Shedeur Sanders Releases New Merchandise, Building NIL Brand with SS2LEGENDARY," *On3*, September 22, 2023, accessed November 25, 2025, https://www.on3.com/nil/news/shedeur-sanders-colorado-buffaloes-football-deion-prime-nil-brand-ss2legendary/

320 Jasmine Browley, "Shedeur Sanders and Bronny James are Highest Paid NCAA Athletes for NIL Deals," *Essence*, October 23, 2023, accessed November 25, 2025, https://www.essence.com/news/money-career/shedeur-sanders-bronny-james-nil/

321 Meghan Durham Wright, "New NIL, Health and Academic Benefits Take Effect for NCAA Student-Athletes Thursday," *NCAA Newsroom*, August 1, 2024, accessed November 25, 2025, https://www.ncaa.org/news/2024/8/1/media-center-new-nil-health-and-academic-benefits-take-effect-for-ncaa-student-athletes-aug-1

322 John Erardi, "History of Retired Numbers Dates Back to Lou Gehrig Day," *Baseball Hall of Fame*, accessed November 25, 2025, https://baseballhall.org/discover/retired-numbers-date-back-to-lou-gehrig-day

323 Craig Muder, "April 15, 1997: Jackie Robinson's Number Retired," *Baseball Hall of Fame*, accessed November 25, 2025, https://baseballhall.org/discover-more/stories/inside-pitch/jackie-robinson-number-retired-throughout-baseball

324 Dan Rosen and Tom Gulitti, "'NHL's Who Wore It Best?': Nos. 99–81," *NHL.com*, May 15, 2020, accessed November 25, 2025, https://www.nhl.com/news/nhl-s-who-wore-it-best-jersey-numbers-99-81-316921746

325 NBA Communications, "Bill Russell's No. 6 Jersey to be Retired Throughout NBA," *NBA.com*, August 11, 2022, accessed November 25, 2025, https://www.nba.com/news/bill-russells-no-6-jersey-to-be-retired-throughout-nba

326 "Every Team's Retired Numbers," *MLB.com*, February 1, 2025, accessed November 25, 2025, https://mlb.com/news/every-mlb-team-s-retired-numbers-c300753386

327 Mike Gavin, "How Many NBA Players Have Numbers Retired by Multiple Teams? Is Pau Gasol Next?" *NBC Bay Area*, March 28, 2023, accessed November 25, 2025, https://nbcbayarea.com/news/sports/how-many-nba-players-have-numbers-retired-by-multiple-teams-is-pau-gasol-next/3174926

328 "List of National Hockey League Retired Numbers," *Wikipedia*, last modified October 2025, accessed November 25, 2025, https://en.wikipedia.org/wiki/List_of_National_Hockey_League_retired_numbers

329 "List of NFL Retired Numbers," *Wikipedia*, last modified October 2024, accessed November 25, 2025, https://en.wikipedia.org/wiki/List_of_NFL_retired_numbers

330 Billy Heyen (The Sporting News), "Why Tony Dorsett's No. 33 Isn't Retired by Dallas Cowboys and is Instead the Jersey Number for New RB," *Yahoo Sports Canada*, September 4, 2025, accessed November 25, 2025, https://ca.sports.yahoo.com/news/why-tony-dorsett-no-33-024751298.html

331 Matt Young, "Why Texans are One of Five NFL Teams Who Won't Retire Jersey Numbers," *Houston Chronicle*, June 15, 2023, accessed November 25, 2025, https://www.houstonchronicle.com/texas-sports-nation/texans/article/houston-texans-retired-jersey-numbers-nfl-watt-18154558.php

332 Nick Raguz, "'You Know How Many Numbers Are Retired in Boston?' - Blake Griffin on Wearing Dennis Rodman's Jersey Number with the Celtics," *MSN.com*, accessed November 25, 2025, https://www.msn.com/en-us/sports/nba/you-know-how-many-numbers-are-retired-in-boston-blake-griffin-on-wearing-dennis-rodman-s-jersey-number-with-the-celtics/ar-AA1xdLxl

333 Ian O'Connor, "Jackie's Widow: Mo Worthy of No. 42," *ESPN.com.au*, March 6, 2013, accessed November 25, 2025, https://www.espn.com.au/mlb/story/_/id/9028898/jackie-robinson-widow-rachel-proud-new-york-yankees-mariano-rivera

334 Josh Kirshenbaum, "'51mply the Best': Mariners Retire Ichiro's Number; Next Up: A Statue," *MLB.com*, August 10, 2025, accessed November 25, 2025,

https://www.mlb.com/mariners/news/ichiro-suzuki-mariners-number-retirement-ceremony

335 JavaMan, "#10: 1998 – Sue Bird, 2016 – Molly Bent," *The Boneyard Forum*, June 30, 2016, accessed November 25, 2025, https://the-boneyard.com/threads/10-1998-sue-bird-2016-molly-bent.94050/

336 "The Incredible Moment When Bourque 'Surrendered' #7 to Esposito at Espo's Retirement," *HockeyFeed*, May 18, 2020, accessed November 25, 2025, https://hockeyfeed.com/nhl-news/the-incredible-moment-when-bourque-surrendered-7-to-esposito-at-espo-s-retirement

337 "The Incredible Moment When Bourque 'Surrendered' #7 to Esposito at Espo's Retirement," *HockeyFeed*, May 18, 2020, accessed November 25, 2025, https://hockeyfeed.com/nhl-news/the-incredible-moment-when-bourque-surrendered-7-to-esposito-at-espo-s-retirement

338 "The Legend of #44," *Syracuse University Athletics*, accessed November 25, 2025, https://cuse.com/sports/2006/1/18/fb44bios

339 "Sonny Styles is Ohio State's Sixth Block 'O' Recipient," *Ohio State Buckeyes*, August 16, 2025, accessed November 25, 2025, https://ohiostatebuckeyes.com/news/2025/8/16/football-sonny-styles-is-ohio-states-sixth-block-o-recipient

340 "Chucky Mullins Courage Award," *Ole Miss Athletics*, accessed November 25, 2025, https://olemisssports.com/sports/2018/7/20/trads-mullins-courage-html

341 Austin Curtright, "LSU's Garrett Nussmeier Earns No. 18 Jersey, Becomes First Tiger Since 2003 with Honor," *USA Today*, August 24, 2025, accessed November 25, 2025, https://www.usatoday.com/story/sports/ncaaf/2025/08/24/garrett-nussmeier-lsu-football-18-jersey-matt-mauck/85809068007/

342 Yuri Karasawa, "Number 18: The Ace Tradition in Japanese Baseball," *JapanBall*, April 28, 2024, accessed November 25, 2025, https://japanball.com/japanese-baseball-introduction/number-18-the-ace-tradition-in-japanese-baseball

343 Travis Sawchik, "'Your 18': Why the Number Is Significant to Japanese Pitchers," *theScore*, accessed November 25, 2025, https://www.thescore.com/mlb/news/3071953

344 Scott Thompson, *"Giants Make Unprecedented Move to Unretire Number for Rookie Malik Nabers," Fox News*, August 29, 2024, accessed November 25, 2025, https://www.foxnews.com/sports/giants-make-unprecedented-move-unretire-number-rookie-malik-nabers

345 Laurie Lattimore-Volkmann, "Tripucka Had Just One Request for Manning to Wear No. 18 — a Super Bowl Win," *Mile High Report*, March 7, 2016, accessed November 25, 2025,

https://www.milehighreport.com/2016/3/7/11171742/peyton-manning-frank-tripucka-denver-broncos-No-18

346 "Ex-Bronco Tripucka Fine with Manning Taking Jersey No. 18," *NFL.com*, March 14, 2012, accessed November 25, 2025, https://nfl.com/news/ex-bronco-tripucka-fine-with-manning-taking-jersey-no-18-09000d5d8279e14d

347 "White Sox to Unretire Aparicio's No. 11 for Vizquel," *FOX Sports*, February 8, 2010, accessed November 25, 2025, https://www.foxsports.com/stories/mlb/white-sox-to-unretire-aparicios-no-11-for-vizquel

348 Julian Eschenbach, "When Grant Hill Got the Green Light from a Suns Legend to Wear No. 33: 'There Aren't Many NBA Players I Can Say I'd Be Happier to See Playing with That Number'," *Basketball Network*, October 25, 2024, accessed November 25, 2025, https://www.basketballnetwork.net/old-school/when-grant-hill-got-the-green-light-from-a-suns-legend-to-wear-no-33

349 Associated Press, "Coyotes to 'Un-Retire' Bobby Hull's No. 9 for Son," *ESPN*, September 30, 2005, accessed November 25, 2025, https://www.espn.co.uk/nhl/news/story?id=2177217

350 Ankit Kumar, "When Mark Messier Was Adamant about Wearing No. 11 Canucks Jersey Despite Team Retiring It to Honor Player Who Died of Brain Cancer," *Sportskeeda*, July 16, 2023, accessed November 25, 2025, https://sportskeeda.com/us/nhl/news-when-mark-messier-adamant-wearing-no-11-canucks-jersey-despite-team-retiring-honor-player-died-brain-cancer

351 "Guy Lapointe: A Boston Bruins Legend Jersey #?" *HFBoards*, May 3, 2025, accessed November 25, 2025, https://forums.hfboards.com/threads/guy-lapointe-a-boston-bruins-legend-jersey.3012562/
Documentation comes from historical reporting and fan forums containing clippings from The Leader Post (October 21, 1983) and The Daily Item (November 22, 1983).

352 George Sullivan, *Any Number Can Play: The Numbers Athletes Wear* (Brookfield, CT: Millbrook Press, 2000), 58. ISBN 0761315578; *"List of Los Angeles Chargers Retired Numbers,"* Wikipedia, accessed November 25, 2025, https://en.wikipedia.org/wiki/List_of_Los_Angeles_Chargers_retired_numbers

353 Charles F. Faber, "Willard Hershberger," SABR BioProject, accessed December 27, 2024, https://sabr.org/bioproj/person/willard-hershberger/

354 Bruce R., "Indy Disses Unitas by Still Using #19 Jersey," *Baltimore Beatdown*, October 8, 2011, accessed November 25, 2025, https://www.baltimorebeatdown.com/2011/10/8/2475250/indy-disses-unitas-by-still-using-19-jersey
Fan blog; anecdotal commentary rather than institutional reporting.

355 Jamal Collier, "Nats' and Expos' All-Time Retired Numbers," *MLB.com*, December 1, 2021, accessed November 25, 2025, https://mlb.com/news/nationals-and-expos-retired-numbers-c300042640

356 Shane Garry Acedera, "'F—k Oklahoma City Because I Ain't Never Been There' - Gary Payton Refuses to Get His Jersey Retired by the Thunder," *Basketball Network*, July 5, 2025, accessed November 25, 2025, https://www.basketballnetwork.net/latest-news/gary-payton-refuses-to-get-his-jersey-retired-by-the-okc-thunder

357 Adam Reisinger, "Inside the Numbers on Retired Numbers Around the NBA," *ESPN*, September 7, 2017, accessed November 25, 2025, https://www.espn.com/nba/story/_/id/20624645/nba-numbers-nba-retired-numbers

358 "Thunder Set to Retire Nick Collison's No. 4," *NBA.com*, January 12, 2019, accessed November 25, 2025, https://www.nba.com/news/release-thunder-collison-jersey-retirement

359 David Suggs, "Why Did the Browns Move to Baltimore? Revisiting Art Modell's 1995 Relocation Controversy That Created Ravens," *Sporting News*, September 14, 2025, accessed November 25, 2025, https://www.sportingnews.com/us/nfl/news/why-browns-move-baltimore-art-modell-relocation-ravens/a829b97dd42665a5af2e77d4#Did%20the%20Browns%20become%20the%20Ravens

360 Sam Jarden, "Why Is Jordan Hicks Wearing No. 12 for Blue Jays? How Roberto Alomar's Former Number Was Unretired," *Sporting News*, July 31, 2023, accessed November 25, 2025, https://sportingnews.com/ca/mlb/news/jordan-hicks-number-12-blue-jays-roberto-alomar-unretired/uwmzbqac8liwroyhy5tazvkp

361 Pete Thamel, "Reggie Bush Gets Heisman Trophy Back 14 Years after Forfeiting," *ESPN*, April 24, 2024, accessed November 25, 2025, https://espn.com/college-football/story/_/id/40014492/reggie-bush-heisman-trophy-returned

362 "Dale Jr. Gets Daytona Win in No. 3 Car," *FOX Sports*, July 2, 2010, accessed November 25, 2025, https://foxsports.com/stories/nascar/dale-jr-gets-daytona-win-in-no-3-car

363 Joe Posnanski, "Retired Numbers and the Yankees," *NBC Sports*, December 11, 2013, accessed November 25, 2025, https://nbcsports.com/mlb/news/retired-numbers-and-the-yankees

364 "Cubs' All-Time Retired Numbers," *MLB.com*, December 1, 2021, accessed November 25, 2025, https://mlb.com/news/cubs-retired-numbers-c300070560

365 Joey Ramirez, "Lakers Retire Kobe Bryant's Jersey Numbers," NBA.com *Los Angeles Lakers*, December 18, 2017, accessed November 25, 2025, https://nba.com/lakers/news/171218-kobe-bryant-jersey-retirement

366 "Utah Jazz: Jerry Sloan's Banner Gets a Significant Number," *Deseret News*, January 27, 2014, accessed November 25, 2025, https://www.deseret.com/2014/1/27/20533827/utah-jazz-jerry-sloan-s-banner-gets-a-significant-number/

367 "If a Star Doesn't Reach the Hall of Fame, Maybe Their Number Will Be Retired, and That Could Be Just as Good," *Jugs Sports*, August 30, 2024, accessed November 25, 2025, https://jugssports.com/blog/mlb-retired-jersey-numbers

368 NBA.com Staff, "Retired Numbers for the Boston Celtics," October 21, 2024, accessed November 25, 2025, https://www.nba.com/news/boston-celtics-retired-numbers

369 Jay Winkler, "Ford on the Field," *Bentley Historical Library*, accessed November 25, 2025, https://bentley.umich.edu/news-events/magazine/ford-on-the-field/

370 José Miguel Romero, "No. 80 Unretired for Rice," *The Seattle Times*, October 20, 2004, accessed November 25, 2025, https://archive.seattletimes.com/archive/?date=20041020&slug=hawk20

371 Florencia Godoy, "When Legends Transcend: NBA Teams That Retired the Numbers of Players Who Never Wore Their Jersey," *Mundo Deportivo US*, September 24, 2025, accessed November 25, 2025, https://www.mundodeportivo.com/us/en/20250924/731135/when-legends-transcend-nba-teams-that-retired-the-numbers-of-players-who-never-wore-their-jersey.html

372 Tommy McArdle, "Every Retired Number for the Celtics and Who Wore It," *Boston.com*, February 21, 2019, accessed November 25, 2025, https://boston.com/sports/boston-celtics/2019/02/21/celtics-retired-numbers-nba/

373 "Baseball," *RobertMerrill.org*, accessed November 25, 2025, https://robertmerrill.org/baseball

374 "Golden Voices: Eight NBA Announcers with Retired Microphones," *Basketball, Listed*, November 11, 2024, accessed November 25, 2025, https://basketballlisted.com/2024/11/11/golden-voices-eight-nba-announcers-with-retired-microphones/

375 Ari Horton, "The History of the 12s," *Seattle Seahawks*, December 12, 2024, accessed November 25, 2025, https://seahawks.com/news/the-history-of-the-12s

376 James Herbert, "NBA Retires Bill Russell's Number: Who Will Be the Last Player to Wear No. 6?" *CBS Sports*, August 14, 2022, accessed November 25, 2025, https://cbssports.com/nba/news/nba-retires-bill-russells-number-who-will-be-the-last-player-to-wear-no-6/

377 Maria Guardado, "Angels' All-Time Retired Numbers," *MLB.com*, December 1, 2021, accessed November 25, 2025, https://mlb.com/news/angels-retired-numbers-c300081390

378 "Atlanta, Number 17 Is for You," *ATLUTD.com*, February 10, 2017, accessed November 25, 2025, https://www.atlutd.com/news/atlanta-number-17-you

379 Dan O'Leary, "Kraken Retire No. 32 Before Home Opener to Honor Fans," *NHL.com*, October 24, 2021, accessed November 25, 2025, https://www.nhl.com/news/seattle-kraken-retire-number-32-before-home-opener-327186108

380 "Progressive Field", *Ballparks of Baseball*, accessed November 25, 2025, https://ballparksofbaseball.com/ballparks/progressive-field/

381 Associated Press, "Golden Knights Retire No. 58 to Honor Las Vegas Shooting Victims," *ESPN*, April 1, 2018, accessed November 25, 2025, https://espn.com/nhl/story/_/id/22991812/vegas-golden-knights-retire-no-58-honor-shooting-victims

382 Jack Bogaczyk, "BOGACZYK: Retire a Very Special Marshall Number - 75," *HerdZone.com*, November 11, 2013, accessed November 25, 2025, https://herdzone.com/news/2013/11/11/BOGACZYK_Retire_a_Very_Special_Marshall_Number_75